D1547955

The Cross of War

STUDIES IN AMERICAN THOUGHT AND CULTURE

Series Editor

Paul S. Boyer

Advisory Board

Charles M. Capper

Mary Kupiec Cayton

Lizabeth Cohen

Nan Enstad

James B. Gilbert

Karen Halttunen

Michael Kammen

James T. Kloppenberg

Colleen McDannell

Joan S. Rubin

P. Sterling Stuckey

Robert B. Westbrook

The Cross of War

*Christian Nationalism and U.S. Expansion
in the Spanish-American War*

Matthew McCullough

THE UNIVERSITY OF WISCONSIN PRESS

The University of Wisconsin Press
1930 Monroe Street, 3rd Floor
Madison, Wisconsin 53711-2059
uwpress.wisc.edu

3 Henrietta Street, Covent Garden
London WC2E 8LU, United Kingdom
eurospanbookstore.com

Copyright © 2014
The Board of Regents of the University of Wisconsin System
All rights reserved. Except in the case of brief quotations embedded in critical articles and reviews, no part of this publication may be reproduced, stored in a retrieval system, transmitted in any format or by any means—digital, electronic, mechanical, photocopying, recording, or otherwise—or conveyed via the Internet or a website without written permission of the University of Wisconsin Press. Rights inquiries should be directed to rights@uwpress.wisc.edu.

Printed in the United States of America

Library of Congress Cataloging-in-Publication Data

McCullough, Matthew, author.
The cross of war: Christian nationalism and U.S. expansion
in the Spanish-American War / Matthew McCullough.
pages   cm—(Studies in American thought and culture)
ISBN 978-0-299-30034-0 (pbk.: alk. paper)
ISBN 978-0-299-30033-3 (e-book)
1. Spanish-American War, 1898—Religious aspects—Christianity.
2. Intervention (International law)—Moral and ethical aspects.
3. Civil religion—United States—History—19th century.
4. Religion and international relations.
5. United States—Foreign relations—19th century.
6. Spanish-American War, 1898—Influence.
I. Title.   II. Series: Studies in American thought and culture.
E725.5.C5M33 2014
973.8′9—dc23
2013042701

A portion of chapter 1 appeared as "Biblical Metaphors for Interventionism in the Spanish-American War" in *The Blackwell Companion to Religion and Violence*, edited by Andrew R. Murphy (Malden, MA: Blackwell, 2011), and is reprinted with the permission of John Wiley & Sons.

JKM Library
1100 East 55th Street
Chicago, IL 60615

in an era when men were symbol
this book is published with a grant from
Figure Foundation

For Lindsey

Contents

Acknowledgments

It was my adviser, James Byrd, who first showed me the importance of America's wars—and the Spanish-American War in particular—for exploring my questions about the history of American Christianity. I am grateful to him for that nudge, and for his steady guidance as a mentor and friend throughout my graduate career. I am also thankful to the others who served on my dissertation committee—Dennis Dickerson, Kathleen Flake, Gary Gerstle, and James Hudnut-Beumler—who through years of coursework and many patient and engaging conversations helped lay the foundation for this work. On conference panels, through the review process, or through sheer kindness, several colleagues offered invaluable feedback on earlier drafts of the manuscript. I am especially grateful to Jonathan Ebel, Ken Minkema, Andrew Murphy, Mark Noll, and Harry Stout. This final product is much stronger because of their insights; it would have been even stronger had I been more able to implement their suggestions.

My research was made possible in part by the generous funding and helpful staffs of the Presbyterian Historical Society, the Southern Baptist Historical Library and Archives, and the Congregational Library.

The wonderful staff at the University of Wisconsin Press has been a pleasure to work with at every stage of the process. I'm especially grateful to the late Paul Boyer, who first took interest in my work, and to Gwen Walker, who was my faithful guide along the path from dissertation to book.

The preparation of this book has been an intellectual and emotional marathon made possible by the deep personal investment of many friends and family members. For specific times of encouragement along the way, I am grateful to Bill Heerman, Dave Hunt, Jonathan Leeman, Mike and Debbie Leys, Jamie Mosley, Scott Patty, Drew Raines, and Andrew Smith. Special thanks are due to my mother, Amy—my first and best teacher—and to my father,

Mark—who passed to me his own love for learning, his love for the study of history, and especially his love for the church.

My two sons, Walter and Sam, are sources of incredible joy, mostly welcome distraction, and much-needed perspective on the relative significance of my scholarship. Most of all, I am grateful to my wife, Lindsey, my truest love and best friend. From beginning to end, she shared with me the burden of this work. She never doubted that the pain was a worthy price for the end result. This was our work, and it is dedicated to her.

Chronology of Events

February 25, 1895	Cuban insurrection begins.
February 1896	General Valeriano Weyler initiates reconcentration policy.
January 15, 1898	USS *Maine* arrives in Havana.
February 15, 1898	USS *Maine* destroyed by mysterious explosion.
March 17, 1898	Senator Redfield Proctor reports to Congress on brutal conditions in Cuba.
March 28, 1898	Board of inquiry reports external cause of *Maine* explosion.
April 11, 1898	President McKinley issues war message to Congress.
April 19, 1898	Congress passes joint resolution in favor of intervention in Cuba.
May 1, 1898	Admiral George Dewey commands decisive victory over Spanish fleet in Manila.
July 1, 1898	U.S. ground troops win battles near Santiago at El Caney and the San Juan Heights.
July 3, 1898	U.S. squadron destroys Spanish fleet outside Santiago.
July 26, 1898	U.S. troops invade Puerto Rico.
August 12, 1898	United States and Spain agree to ceasefire.
October 1898	President McKinley takes speaking tour through the Midwest focusing on U.S. expansion.
December 10, 1898	Treaty of Paris formally concludes war with Spain and cedes authority over Cuba, Puerto Rico, the Philippines, and Guam to the United States.
February 4, 1899	First shots fired in the Philippine-American War.
February 6, 1899	Treaty of Paris ratified by U.S. Senate.

The Cross of War

Introduction

When Abraham Lincoln delivered the words of the Gettysburg Address, as many as fifty-one thousand men had just fallen in one of the many catastrophic battles of an indisputably catastrophic war. To locate meaning in these events—meaning worthy of such sacrifice—was the president's unenviable task. This war, in Lincoln's formulation, was to test whether a nation such as America, "conceived in liberty" and dedicated to the equality of humankind, "can long endure." The only fitting tribute to the sacrifice of the dead, he argued, was for the living to resolve that "this nation under God shall have a new birth of freedom, and that government of the people, by the people, and for the people shall not perish from the earth."[1] America, Lincoln had written to Congress a year earlier, was the world's "last best hope."[2] Not sixty years later another American president, standing on the precipice of another catastrophic war, sent another rousing message to Congress. Woodrow Wilson, in what became known as his "War Message," called the nation to arms on battlefields thousands of miles away in a war that could make the world "safe for democracy."[3] Both presidents believed that America, in the providence of God, existed for the sake of the world and that their respective wars factored directly into the success or failure of America's global purpose. But Lincoln's war was a war of preservation, to protect the purity of the nation's luminous example and to ensure that this example would survive intact. Wilson's war, by contrast, was not primarily for the survival of America but for the survival of democracy abroad, America's gift to the world. What had emerged during those intervening decades was a notion I shall call messianic interventionism. The burden of this book is to show that its emergence had a great deal to do with an often forgotten little war with Spain in 1898.

To study this sense of national purpose is to study American nationalism. My understanding of nationalism leans upon the work of Liah Greenfeld, who describes nationalism as a style of thought or self-perception that "locates the source of individual identity within a 'people,' which is seen as the bearer of sovereignty, the central object of loyalty, and the basis of collective solidarity."[4] The content of a given nationalism takes shape over time and by negotiation, so that nationalism varies from place to place. But nationalism always consists of those traits by which individuals define themselves as a people marked off from the peoples of the world. Near the heart of nationalism lies ideology, by which I mean the set of beliefs and values that give meaning to a society and its experiences.[5] And in American nationalism ideology has played an especially visible role. Lacking the relatively static tribal, geographical, or ecclesial ties of more venerable nations, American nationality has always relied upon the force of ideas for any sense of coherent and cohesive identity.[6]

Among its several ideological streams, American nationalism has often been infused with the generically Christian conviction that God—the same God incarnate in Christ and working history toward his purposes through the church—has a distinct, world-redemptive purpose for America. Far from a mere ploy of policymakers like Lincoln or Wilson, such conviction has been widely held and most carefully developed by Christian ministers. Indeed, the religious meaning and significance of the nation have remained a perennial preoccupation of American Christianity. Mine is primarily a book about Christian nationalism—an understanding of American identity and significance held by Christians wherein the nation is a central actor in the world-historical purposes of the Christian God.[7]

Times of war have consistently encouraged the strongest expressions of Christian nationalism. There has been no generation of Americans that has not known war or military action of some kind, nor has there ever been an American war about which American Christians have had little to say.[8] War always involves more than battlefields, bullets, and body-bags. War also inspires a conflict of meaning—the cause, the stakes, the identity of the combatants. War, Jill Lepore reminds us, is always a "contest of injuries and interpretation."[9] War is about taking life and giving life, sacred acts that always require sacred justifications. In every war through American history, religious folk have crafted ideologies in which those acts would make sense. The Spanish-American War was no exception.

But, for a variety of reasons, this was a war that called for new variations on familiar themes. This war came barely three decades after the cataclysmic division of the Civil War and Reconstruction eras; it offered the first dramatic opportunity for Americans North and South to affirm a common understanding of the nation's identity and purpose. Before the Civil War, expressions of nationalism were limited by a pervasive localism that privileged town, state, or regional loyalties over any sense of national identity.[10] The Christian nationalism on display during the war with Spain confirms that Americans self-consciously united across regional lines in celebration of the nation's identity and mission. But, even more important, rhetoric prominent throughout the war shows a significant reorientation in the conception of national purpose that now offered a basis for common identity.

Wherever Christian nationalism has appeared throughout American history, in however nascent a form, it has included some sense of messianic purpose, some vision for how America should benefit the nations of the world. The only question has been how America would play the role of "redeemer nation," to borrow Ernest Tuveson's classic phrase.[11] Scholars have noted two primary conceptions. First, from the colonial era through the end of the nineteenth century, the dominant understanding of the nation's vocation had been as an example of the blessings of God-honoring liberty, winning the world by force of attraction. In this model, Americans were responsible only for their faithfulness to the ideal before the eyes of the world. This theme, reflected in what one historian has called the "exemplarist" model of foreign policy, undergirds some of the most famous statements of American purpose, from John Winthrop's "city on a hill" to Abraham Lincoln's "last best hope of earth."[12] And this posture has encouraged an isolationist tendency to emphasize the problems within American society rather than those in the world at large, with the cultivation of a pure, Edenic society as the primary task at hand. This model—world redemption through example—has never disappeared from discourse on American identity and purpose.

As defined by Conrad Cherry, the second conception of national purpose views America as "a chosen people with an obligation actively to win others to American principles and to safeguard those principles around the world."[13] This ideology is perhaps most closely associated with the vivid rhetoric of the World War I era, with Woodrow Wilson's pledge to make the world safe for democracy. But I argue that this particular strand of American nationalism— this messianic interventionism—was embraced in the Spanish-American War as both Christian duty and providential destiny, first for liberation and then for subjugation.

More specifically, though this interventionist vision existed prior to 1898 and enjoyed its greatest prominence in the decades to follow, I argue that its emergence and codification was inextricable from the distinctive features of the Spanish-American War context. This war marked America's dramatic arrival as an active world power, setting the stage for the foreign policy of the next one hundred years. It began for America in the midst of widespread humanitarian outrage over the abuses of the Spanish imperial government. When it ended, America stood in possession of its own de facto empire, sole ruler of a network of far-flung islands and millions of unfamiliar people. Along the way, Christian ministers sought to explain the meaning of events that caught almost everyone by surprise, to trace the hand of God in a victory more painless and complete than anyone could have imagined, and to justify the new departure in American foreign policy as a divine calling. Responding to the distinctive features of the war with Spain, America's Christian leadership endorsed—even insisted upon— an active, interventionist foreign policy as God-ordained national destiny. America, by these leaders' reckoning, held a responsibility under God to extend American freedoms to those unable to free themselves and to do this by force if necessary. To be a Christian nation, in this formulation, meant more than the cultivation of domestic virtue and ordered liberty; a Christian nation was also a nation that shared Christ's disposition toward the world, a disposition of self-sacrifice on behalf of the weak. With remarkable sameness across regional and denominational lines, their rhetoric exposed an ideology that justified this new sense of national purpose in three ways. It explained why America *should* take up the cross on behalf of the weak and the oppressed. It explained why America *could* interfere in the affairs of other nations without incurring the guilt of self-interest condemned in the record of Europe's colonial powers. And, invoking evidence of providential favor, it explained why American efforts *would* inevitably succeed.[14]

The structure of my argument generally follows the course of the war, seeking to highlight the way this ideology developed in response to unfolding events. The story begins in earnest with the mysterious demise of the USS *Maine*, which sparked an immediate and nationwide clamoring for war. Chapter 1 describes the events of February–April 1898 and the religious justification for a "disinterested" war that emerged in the national debate. Isolating vengeance, blood lust, territorial acquisition, and even self-defense from the humanitarian issues at stake, a wide swath of Christian leaders applied an ethic of neighbor-love and Christlike sacrifice to national policy. In effect, they offered a full-fledged argument for why America should fight for the world's oppressed even where national interests were not concerned; they defined a national duty of self-sacrifice for the weak. The concept of messianic interventionism was defined here. And when the fighting began, many hailed the event as a new kind of war, for America and for the world.

Chapter 2 then explains the basis for the widespread confidence that America could avoid the greed and selfishness that marked other powers' interaction with the weak. This confidence, I argue, was inseparable from the self-definition made possible via contrast with the Spanish enemy. Here I investigate the categories used to compare America and Spain, categories that reinforced a conviction that America possessed the precise character qualities necessary for their new messianic obligation. The only major question in this conversation was where Spain's Catholicism fit into the picture. I argue that even though some Protestants and Catholics bitterly disagreed over whether Catholicism caused Spain's fall and Protestantism America's rise, the claims of both sides converged on the conviction that America's essentially Christian principles gave the nation an exceptional quality that prepared it to set aside selfish interests for the sake of others.

If the first two chapters establish the justification for an interventionist foreign policy and the confidence of national fitness to carry out such a policy, chapters 3 and 4 explain how ministers interpreted the events of the war as providential guarantors of the holiness of their newfound purpose and their certainty of success. Chapter 3 describes the dominant response to the remarkable and unblemished record of the American military in the war's several major battles. Invoking the categories of historical providentialism now reinforced by the immanentism prevalent at century's end, Christian leaders saw these events as unmistakable signs of the divine hand and cast all of American history as a providentially guided ascent to this climactic moment. Chapter 4 then takes up another major theme in the providentialism inspired by the war, namely the conviction that the ambitions of Anglo-Saxonism were irreversibly thrust forward. In this chapter, I argue that another significant source of confirmation for an interventionist destiny was the Anglo-Saxonism through which many viewed the events of 1898. Seen through the lens best represented by Josiah Strong, the Spanish-American War and the unity it inspired within America and across the Atlantic promised the imminent realization of long-held, race-based hopes for world renovation.

Chapter 5 shows how these themes converged to shape the dominant Christian perspective on American expansion. I argue that, though most were not rabid imperialists, church leaders cast ongoing control of the former Spanish territories as an extension of the newfound interventionist policy embraced at the onset of the war. Their justification of ongoing American control of the islands rested precisely on the convictions about American identity and purpose shaped over the course of the war: guided by humanitarian principles and divine providence, America would uplift these peoples and not oppress them. America would succeed where others had failed.

The ideology of messianic interventionism proved to be a powerful force. Measured by its own ideals in the light of history, it was also deeply misguided.

Those Christians most responsible for shaping and promoting this ideology seem to me more sincere than sinister in their motives. But their confidence in American exceptionalism was quickly belied by the course of events, events sketched in my concluding chapter. To readers living on this side of wars in Vietnam, Iraq, and Afghanistan, the abuses of the American military in the Philippines will appear more inevitable than surprising. The most natural reaction to the ideas that enabled such abuse is surely disgust for an optimism at best naïve, at worst malevolent, and at any rate dangerous. My goal in this study is to push beyond condemnation into understanding—an understanding of how messianic interventionism took shape and why it was so compelling to those who embraced it. To stop short of understanding—to rest content with condemnation—would make us guilty of our own form of self-righteous exceptionalism.

❖

The nature of Christian nationalism as subject, particularly its ideological dimension, shapes my selection of source material in several important ways. First and foremost, wherever this aspect of Christian nationalism appears, it appears as a feature of public rhetoric. This should come as no surprise given Clifford Geertz's important account of ideology as a cultural phenomenon. Ideology, according to Geertz, gives public expression to what would otherwise remain private and disconnected emotions. Ideology enters the public square as an attempt to persuade people to think and act in certain ways, offering a roadmap for navigating difficult or unfamiliar terrain.[15] So, looking for the ideological content of Christian nationalism among America's church leadership means searching those places where they were most likely to address their public. It means searching all the sources in which such leaders were most likely to discuss the meaning of America and the nature of its role in the world in light of current events. In 1898, those outlets were sermons and the religious press.

First, sermons on the war provide the most extensive analyses of key themes. I have drawn from private manuscript collections, newspapers, and published pamphlets to compile a group of these sermons across denominational lines. Second, I rely heavily on editorials and contributed articles in the burgeoning religious periodical press, from small denominational state papers like the *Alabama Baptist* to large nondenominational weeklies with national circulation, like the *Outlook* and the *Independent*.[16] In many significant ways, sermons and periodicals overlap; the ideas and to some extent the individuals voicing them remain consistent across both genres. The editors of religious periodicals were often ministers themselves, and at the very least these weeklies included regular articles or printed sermons from prominent local or denominational pastors. The primary difference, and what makes these two types of sources nicely complementary, is that they often approach the issues from variant angles and attention to detail. Editorials, for example, were typically brief and highly specific but more responsive to the twists and turns of events as they unfolded. Indeed, given the sort of material included in a typical weekly edition, often combining denominational information with editorial content and entire pages of "current news," editors seemed to assume they provided readers their primary source of information of any kind.[17] Sermons, by contrast, provided more extensive treatment of themes. The sermon in this period did not serve the same function or carry the same weight that it had in Puritan New England. It was not the primary source of news or entertainment; it was not the organizing event in the town each week; and it was far less likely to be published. But the sermon remained a major vehicle of communication throughout the country, not just because people continued to sit under preaching but also because sermons found their way into print even in prominent secular newspapers like the *New York Times*. Even more important, ministers still viewed their sermons as an opportunity to interpret the world for their hearers, to locate the meaning of events through spiritual eyes and with a view to the workings of providence. Both sermons and the religious press reveal a profound and pervasive interest in the events of 1898 among America's religious leadership. Taken together, given their number, their geographical distribution, and their denominational diversity, these sources represent the broadest base of material for any study of Christian nationalism and the Spanish-American War to date.

In 1900, more than four-fifths of the country's estimated twenty-six million church members were affiliated with the Methodists, Baptists, Presbyterians, Lutherans, Disciples of Christ, Episcopalians, Congregationalists, or Roman Catholics. According to the relevant census data, no other group had even a half-million members.[18] Therefore, this study relies on the sermons and major denominational periodicals of these eight dominant religious bodies. The most nationalistic of America's denominations, these groups displayed a remarkable level of unity in their support for the war and in their central assessment of its significance.

Given the interests of the twenty-first-century academy and given the undeniable ethnic and religious diversity of late nineteenth-century America, readers may wonder whether my study unjustly flattens a variety of nationalisms, even a variety of Christian nationalisms. It is true that I do not give extensive attention to voices that opposed the war or offered alternative perspectives on America's global purpose.[19] But my aim is not to catalog everything Christians said about the war. My aim is to explain messianic interventionism and why Christian leaders came to support it so passionately. I am describing the view of American character and purpose used to justify war and empire on altruistic grounds, giving greatest attention to those who did hold such a view.

Finally, I must offer three clarifications regarding the scope of my project and the corresponding evidence. Mine is primarily a study of the content of an ideology, first of all, and not the effects of that ideology on the lives of individuals. Therefore, mine is primarily a study of the ideas propagated by elite shapers of public opinion. Second, in the late nineteenth century most of those elites with access to the public ear were white Protestants, and their ideas reflect this perspective.[20] That said, though never fully successful in its attempts at unity, Christian nationalism has consistently represented an aspect of consensus in American religious history.[21] In response to the events of 1898, church leaders otherwise divided by polity and theology and ethnicity sounded remarkably similar in their commentary on the nation, its identity and purpose. And this consensus also existed beyond the bounds of Euro-American Protestantism. The war with Spain, like wars before and since, offered an opportunity for some historically outside America's religious mainstream to appropriate something of the dominant vision of the nation's religious significance.[22] As the following chapters seek to illustrate, perspectives from black Protestants and some American Catholics show, in fact, that Christian nationalism, if predominantly a white Protestant phenomenon, was never exclusively so.

Third, and finally, I have chosen to focus on those employed in Christian ministry not because Christian nationalism was limited to the churches but because it is here that the ideological groundwork for messianic interventionism appears most clearly. Historians have noted the pervasive presence of Christian nationalism (or civil religion) in the rhetoric of America's public officials through the course of 1898.[23] And the prominence of religion in political discourse should come as no surprise to those familiar with American public culture of the 1890s. These years mark the apogee of what Robert Handy has best described as the Protestant Establishment, an era in which Protestant leaders held a powerful influence over American public life through a web of personal friendships with the nation's political and cultural elite.[24] Catholics, too, had reached a new level of political relevance by this time, in part through the well-placed friendships of leaders like Archbishop John Ireland and in part because of Catholic dominance within the powerful Irish-American voting bloc.[25] But my interest is less in the influence of Christian nationalism on policy decisions than in the content of Christian nationalism itself. It was the clergy, according to Winthrop Hudson, who "were more apt to give a full exposition of specific concepts, whereas in other writings the concepts were often introduced incidentally as axiomatic assumptions."[26] In short, placing Christian nationalism in historical context and tracing the impact of the events of 1898 require a close look at the rhetoric of the church leaders who served as custodians of this ideology.

Thus far, historians have given less attention than one might expect to the discourse of Christian leaders on American identity during the war with Spain. Some important spadework has certainly been done, but the existing literature has significant limitations. Some accounts are more anecdotal, considering a small sample of Christian voices as one subset of a larger tapestry of public opinion.[27] Others focus narrowly on specific denominations.[28] Still others draw from a wide swath of Christian opinion on the war but rely on sources confined to the northeast quadrant of the United States, leaving questions about the perspectives of those in the South or the Far West.[29] What remains to be done, and what I attempt to do here, is to compare commentary from every major Christian denomination and from every region of the United States. Built upon the most comprehensive base of sources to date, my study offers a glimpse into what was, in many important respects, a fully national Christian nationalism with explicitly international aspirations.

1

"My Brother's Keeper"

Justifying a New Kind of Sacrifice, Defining a New Kind of War

On the night of February 15, 1898, the U.S. battleship *Maine* mysteriously exploded and sank to the bottom of Cuba's Havana Bay, carrying with it 266 navy sailors. The cause of the explosion was never determined. But, given that the ship was there to monitor the war between Cuban insurgents and the Spanish military, it is hardly surprising that so many suspected foul play. Just two months later America would be at war with Spain.[1] The sinking of the *Maine* has passed into American memory as one of two or three defining events of the "splendid little war" of 1898. Survivors of the disaster—especially Captain Charles Sigsbee—were hailed as national heroes. The battle cry—"Remember the Maine"—inspired more willing volunteers than the U.S. Army was prepared to handle. And monuments to the ship and its dead went up all over the country in places as far removed as New York's Columbus Circle and the State House at Columbia, South Carolina.[2] With this crucial event, the spark of interest in American responsibility toward the Cuban-Spanish War blew into an all-consuming popular blaze.

Yet, for a vocal group of American church leaders, the issues at the heart of America's dispute with Spain went so far beyond the *Maine* explosion that the event appeared to them very nearly irrelevant. From February through late April, as the American public engaged in a heated debate over whether and why to go to war with Spain, Christian ministers worked hard to sort through arguments for and against intervention in Cuba. Amid the swirl of possible casus belli, Christian arguments across denominational lines isolated humanitarian duty from any concern for vengeance, conquest, or even self-defense.

12

War for such a cause, they argued, was unqualified altruism and nothing short of unprecedented. Church leaders rode the tide of war fever directly into a new definition of America's international responsibility. They defined war in Cuba as necessary because Christian principles demanded it. The goal of this chapter is to introduce the basic shape of messianic interventionism as it emerged in response to the crisis in Cuba and the outbreak of war with Spain.

My argument unfolds in two sections, one chronological and the other thematic. The first half of the chapter traces the path from sympathy with the Cubans among church leaders restrained by traditional isolationism and generic pacifism to outright and widespread support for war as a sacred calling. Placing in context the events and the rhetoric of spring 1898, this section shows simply that a shift occurred and that the key was the ability to isolate "humanity" as the efficient cause of intervention. The second part of the argument probes more deeply into the justification for war upon which this widespread support came to rest. Here I illustrate the rationale for a more expansive Christian nationalism by focusing on two prominent biblical models used to establish humanitarian intervention as a sacred duty for a Christian nation: the parable and principle of the Good Samaritan and the sacrificial death of Christ.

The Battle to Define the War

On one hand, when church leaders embraced America's intervention in Cuba as a "sacred crusade," as most came to do, their support represented the dramatic escalation of a growing interest among American Christians in international affairs. On the other hand, this support marked a departure from past policy preferences that was just shy of radical. Some awareness of this context, of the perspectives on American policy foreign and domestic in the late nineteenth century, is necessary to grasp the full significance of the Spanish-American War for the development of Christian nationalism.

The Background to Messianic Interventionism

The final quarter of the nineteenth century brought an increased attention among American Christians to goings on in the rest of the world, and nothing did more to spark this interest than Protestant foreign missions. Missionary work, of course, had long been central to the activism of American Protestants. Hopes for spreading the gospel and, with it, the building blocks of Christian civilization had fired both the initial European colonization of North America and the steady march of westward expansion. But, by the final decades of the nineteenth century, through the work of groups like the American Board of Commissioners for Foreign Missions, the international missions movement had come into its own. "By 1900," William Hutchison estimates, "the sixteen American missionary societies of the 1860s had swelled to about ninety," marking what he calls the "heyday" of a movement then "involving tens of thousands of Americans abroad and millions at home."[3]

This new global presence brought with it a heightened awareness of world events, so it is hardly surprising that protests against cases of humanitarian abuse became more regular, especially where American missionary interests were concerned. There was no more striking example than the response to the mass killing of Armenians in the Ottoman Empire in the mid-1890s, a brutal foretaste of the genocide to come twenty years later. Roughly three hundred thousand Armenians were slaughtered between 1894 and 1896. As members of a racial, cultural, and Christian minority population, these Armenians fell victim to a devastating cocktail of ethnic hatred, militant Islam, and the political calculations of an empire struggling to ward off European encroachment. Because of the Christian identity of the Armenians and because of long-standing missionary efforts among that population, American Protestants and Catholics alike were immediately sympathetic. Many passed resolutions or wrote editorials or made impassioned speeches condemning the Ottoman government and calling for U.S. action.[4] A few, including the Social Gospeler Josiah Strong, even lobbied for an American military intervention.[5]

Understandably, then, rumors of genocide in Cuba during these same years, on an island so close to American shores, caused no insignificant stir. For the American public, interest in the "pearl of the Antilles" dated back decades before the *Maine* exploded. Strategically located as the gateway to the Gulf of Mexico, the island held great promise for American naval defense. In the days before the Civil War, because of their slave-based economy, Southerners viewed Cuba as an attractive acquisition in the race for control of Congress. And in the postbellum decades American business interests grounded a growing concern over the instability of the island government. But humanitarian concerns—the concerns most often voiced by America's church leaders—began to emerge with the onset of outright war between the Spanish government and Cuban insurgents.

Violence reigned on the island for the better part of three decades, from the late 1860s through the end of the century, beginning with the Ten Years War of 1868–1878. On October 10, 1868, a group of Cuban planters and professionals frustrated by failed reforms in the Spanish government, not to mention a host of new taxes, declared independence from Spain. The ten years of guerrilla warfare that followed took a heavy toll on the island in lives and goods, with very little of lasting value in return. Maximo Gomez and Antonio Maceo led a ragtag army cobbled together of farmers and former slaves, and they held on long enough to gain promises of reform and some measure of autonomy in exchange for peace. But the Spanish forces were too strong for them to win outright independence, and the autonomy arrangement ultimately could not hold.[6]

Christian commentary on the Ten Years War was sporadic at best, but seeds of future arguments were planted—a severe assessment of Spanish rule, a deep sympathy for the plight of the Cubans, a sense that principle and proximity might require American action. These seeds came to flower when the fragile peace came crashing down in 1895. The level of brutality escalated dramatically in this final conflict. This was true on both sides, but the figure who came to define this phase of the Spanish-Cuban struggle was the Spanish general Valeriano Weyler. Concerned with the support insurgents received from the civilian population, Weyler instituted a policy of "reconcentration," shuffling rural dwellers by the hundreds of thousands into closely controlled urban centers, hoping to isolate and starve out the insurgent army. Ultimately it was the captive civilians who starved, by the tens of thousands. These *reconcentrados*, as they came to be called, struggled to live without suitable housing, food, or medical care, so that, as John Offner summarizes, "by 1897 the concentration camps had become death camps, with tens of thousands dying and thousands more living under the threat."[7] Though contemporary reports of as many as four hundred thousand slaughtered Cubans were embellished, approximately one hundred thousand had died by early 1898.[8]

Many prominent Christian periodicals regularly condemned the reconcentration policy and Spanish rule on the whole as a barbaric relic of the Middle Ages. From 1895 to 1898, in fact, there was almost universal sympathy for the Cuban insurgents, who were often cast as revolutionaries on the model of America's founding generation.[9] But, still, this dominant sympathy for the Cuban cause remained merely that—sympathy. Even as ministers, editors, and denominational resolutions called for an end to Spanish rule on the island, they also continued to insist on American neutrality in the conflict. Where support for some form of intervention did appear during these years, it was typically for a peaceful arbitration process rather than a full-blown military offensive.[10]

In fact, though Christian interest in international affairs was growing through the century's final decades, the predominant focus of public comment on American identity or national policy remained centered on the ills of American society. And, given the dramatic challenges of the postwar years, this preoccupation was understandable. Waves of immigrants had created logistical problems for a fast-growing population and sparked fear among the native born that their society might be diluted with these undesirables. Domestic migration patterns added stress to the nation's social infrastructure, as thousands upon thousands flocked to cities in search of greater opportunities. In many ways, both these demographic trends—immigration and urbanization—were encouraged by a broader shift from an agricultural to an industrial economy. New and high-profile clashes between business and labor interests also marked the path toward industrialization, the birth pangs of a lasting economic realignment.[11] Given long-standing hopes for a Christian America, it is hardly surprising that the challenges of urbanization, immigration, and industrialization would rivet the rhetoric and activism of church leaders on the problems threatening the home front. In their view, after all, a stable and prosperous and holy America was still the last and best hope of earth. Christian activists would, as Robert Handy has summarized, "save America for the world's sake."[12] With this domestic vision firmly entrenched, sporadic appeals for intervention abroad—whether in the Cuban-Spanish War or as with Strong and the Armenia crisis—continued to fall flat. Some more dramatic turn of events would be necessary before American Christians would articulate a new foreign policy mandate as the nation's divine calling.

In the days following the disaster on the *Maine*, it was far from clear that this latest crisis in Cuba would be the catalyst for an adjusted sense of national purpose. During the weeks immediately following the explosion, church leaders mostly stood with business leaders and with the more conservative of the national weeklies against the popular outcry for war. Those dailies known to history as the "yellow press" drew the special ire of religious editors, who cast themselves as voices of reason over against "sensationalists" like Joseph Pulitzer, publisher of the *New York World*, and William Randolph Hearst, publisher of the *New York Journal*.[13] Alongside this universal condemnation of the "sensationalist" journalism, William McKinley came off especially well in religious press and pulpit alike. With almost formulaic consistency, church leaders praised the president as the single force holding back the tide of popular enthusiasm and a warmongering Congress.[14]

Immediately following the sinking of the *Maine*, President McKinley appointed a board of inquiry to investigate the cause of the explosion; pending the results of the investigation, he was willing to consider the incident a tragic accident. Though historians have debated McKinley's posture on the crisis in Cuba, labeling him everything from an eager imperialist to a spineless poll-watcher, his wait-and-see approach was fully consistent with his attitude since taking office. For well over a year he had resisted pressure to act from elements of the press and Congress, seeking to give Spain every opportunity to cancel the reconcentration policy and put an end to the war. His motives are notoriously hard to read, but in his diplomacy McKinley consistently sought to preserve as many options as possible. At least through the end of March, it seems, he believed a peaceful solution would emerge.[15] Whatever his objectives, church leaders viewed the president as no less than heroic.

Take, for example, the sermon preached by McKinley's own pastor just two weeks after the *Maine* disaster. On February 27, the Reverend Hugh Johnston of the Metropolitan Methodist Episcopal Church in Washington, DC, preached to a congregation that included the president, a devout Methodist. Johnston lamented that "restlessness without God clamors for blood, blood, blood—the regime of savagery and barbarism—as the ultimatum of the Maine disaster," but "in the interest of humanity, civilization, and Christianity, we can afford to wait until we know the truth and the whole truth." Even if Spain was found to be at fault, he maintained, the nation would "be better served by a calm self control [*sic*] in calling another nation to strict account than by a frantic and unreasoning rush into the unspeakable horrors of war." Reserving some of his strongest language for support of the president's policy and leadership, Johnston concluded, "Our duty as citizens, as patriots, as Christians, is to stand by the President, who stands at the helm of the ship of State, cool-headed, clear of eye, strong handed, and warm-hearted; to stand by our Government rather than by any intemperate speech or action to stir up the worst passions of our people."[16]

In a sermon preached that same day, Charles Parkhurst of the Madison Square Presbyterian Church combined support for McKinley with a strong condemnation of New York's sensationalist dailies. His sermon, entitled "The State of the Country," took for its text Isaiah 30:15: "In quietness and in confidence shall be your strength." The quiet strength so necessary in times of national stress and that had characterized the president's leadership, he argued, had been thoroughly undermined by certain elements of the press. Parkhurst insisted that "it is to the Press in its debased, its unconscienced, its de-virilized [*sic*] membership more than to any other one cause that the strain and the nervousness and nation-wide exasperation of the past two weeks has been due." Noting that he had in mind one particular unnamed journal, one with an unfortunately large circulation, he spoke for many—and more eloquently than most—in his scathing assessment of its effects:

It is the journalistic nutriment of hundreds of thousands through this city and on up through New England, hundreds of thousands of inconsiderate ones who are not necessarily without conscience, but who are childishly fascinated by its flamboyancy and who become in time so debilitated, intellectually and morally debilitated, by its stimulating piquancy as to come in time really to love a lie well seasoned, better than the truth. And that is boring into the brain and into the moral marrow of the vast population that morning by morning gloats over its pungent mendacities. For the past fourteen days it has been lying—lying deliberately, systematically, laboriously![17]

None other than the *Nation*, a prominent secular periodical highly critical of rampant jingoism, confirmed that the tone set by Johnston and Parkhurst was typical of the ministerial response nationwide. Writing for the March 3 issue, the editor claimed that while in the past the clergy have been prominent forces in bringing on wars, in this case it could not be said "that the clergy as a whole are now adding anything to the war fury, except as their words are distorted by lying newspapers. Nearly all the references from the pulpit to the *Maine* disaster are moderate and calming in tone."[18]

Throughout March, as the *Maine* board of inquiry quietly went about its work, the religious press with overwhelming unity continued to condemn the sensationalist press and to express support for McKinley. In Cincinnati, the *Christian Standard*, a prominent Disciples of Christ periodical, called for resistance to the "spirit of war" growing throughout the nation, stoked by "vain talkers," and instead urged patience as evidence was gathered.[19] In New York, Lyman Abbott's *Outlook* offered an even more positive assessment of the president's leadership in resisting those who would plunge the nation into an unjust conflict. In bold language typical of the broader religious press, one March 12 editorial argued that "war declared in the feverish excitement of a moment, caused by the disaster to the Maine, would have impeached the honor as well as imperiled the prosperity of the nation." More than anyone, according to the *Outlook*, McKinley deserved credit for preserving the nation from such a fate:

That we have been carried safely by this peril, that the Nation has maintained sobriety and steadiness, that it is waiting the result of an investigation, and that when that result is made known it will not then proceed to war (whatever the result of the investigation may be) until every resource is exhausted in the endeavor to maintain honorable peace, is due primarily to the steadiness, to the sobriety, and the strength of purpose of the President, who has had no little pressure to resist, and who has resisted it with a calmness and an equipoise which deserve all praise.[20]

The Great Reversal

At least through late March, the predominant mood in American civil religious dialogue was one of restraint and even pious scorn for any trace of warmongering. And, given the traditional posture of Christian nationalism in America, a posture that favored isolationism as a safeguard for national purity, this aversion to intervention or military retaliation is unsurprising. What is surprising is that barely one month later, when McKinley and Congress finally declared war on Spain, they acted with nearly universal approval from the same group of Christian leaders. In fact, the clergy widely hailed the war as the most holy war in history, an altogether new kind of war fought not for self-interest or vengeance or conquest but only in the interests of humanity. And with this celebration of the war came a new definition of national purpose, a mandate to extend the blessings of liberty and Christian civilization wherever possible by whatever means necessary.[21]

Whatever the underlying motives or broader context for Christian support for American action in Cuba, the galvanizing moment came with a speech delivered to Congress by Senator Redfield Proctor of Vermont. On March 17, the day of the speech, Proctor had just returned from a trip to Cuba, where he had conducted a survey of civilian living conditions on the island, and he gave a report to Congress on what he had seen. On one hand, according to Gerald Linderman, there was nothing about the content of the speech or the man who delivered it that could explain its incredible power. The speech communicated no new facts, and there was nothing about Proctor's reputation in the Senate prior to the speech that made him more or less effective than anyone else.[22] Yet contemporaries across the country latched onto two features in particular. First, many believed Proctor had traveled to the island openly skeptical of the way the popular press had described conditions in the concentration camps, but he returned convinced that things were actually far worse than he had read. And, second, reporters noted that Proctor read his speech describing the starvation of tens of thousands without any trace of dramatic flourish. The calm, deliberate manner in which he offered his testimony to Congress made for a striking contrast with the sensational claims of the "yellow" journalists.[23] In short, when this man described what he had seen in this way, conditions of mass starvation and widespread Spanish brutality, people believed him. So decisive was this event that the *Advance*, writing more than a month later, could claim that "perhaps in all the history of the country no speech ever delivered at the nation's capital so profoundly affected the nation. From that hour the die was cast."[24] In the religious press, in the wake of this report, focus shifted from resistance to jingoes over possible retaliation for the *Maine* to wholehearted support for intervention to relieve the suffering in Cuba. This support, if not immediate in all quarters, grew swiftly. What began as advocacy of diplomatic, peaceful intervention grew from late March through mid-April into widespread endorsement of military action. But wherever there was support for intervention—and whatever kind of intervention was being supported—the constant remained a disavowal of any cause other than concern for "humanity." So, Proctor's report laid the foundation for the central contribution of the religious argument for an unprecedented American foreign policy: intervention was justifiable not for national self-defense, revenge, or conquest but only in the interests of the oppressed.[25]

Some ministers came down strong and early for war, and then there were others who just as strongly insisted on peaceful solutions.[26] From late March into early April, most religious commentary fell somewhere in between these poles, hoping for a peaceful, diplomatic solution but decisive about the nation's duty to act immediately. In these weeks following the Proctor report, religious periodicals including the Baptist *Watchman*; the Disciples of Christ *Christian Evangelist*; the Congregationalist *Herald of Gospel Liberty*, *Advance*, *Pacific*, and *Congregationalist*; the Presbyterian *Evangelist* and *New York Observer*; and the nondenominational *Outlook* and *Independent*, among others, regarded some form of intervention as a foregone conclusion. No less common was the hope that, as the *Congregationalist* prayed, God would "accomplish through us as a nation thine own blessed purposes for the whole human race through Jesus Christ our Lord."[27]

There was similar agreement about the justification for intervention, peaceful or otherwise. America would act not out of vengeance for the *Maine*, not out of lust for more territory, not out of self-defense, but solely out of concern for oppressed humanity. The report of the *Maine* board of inquiry created barely a stir when released just two weeks after Proctor's speech. The report failed to attribute conclusive blame for the explosion, though it did confirm, in contrast to the findings of the Spanish inquiry, that the explosion was due to an external cause rather than internal weapons magazines.[28] It had already been decided, as the New York *Christian Advocate* of March 31 commented, that the "chief question . . . is not the destruction of the Maine, but the civil war in Cuba, and our duty toward it."[29] At this point, according to the *Herald of Gospel Liberty*, the *Maine* issue was simply a distraction, and, as the *Outlook* had argued on March 26, it was irrelevant to the settlement of "The Cuban Question": "We are inclined, in light of this report of Senator Proctor, to regard the disaster to the Maine as an incident on which the future relations of this country and Spain will not hinge. . . . But the condition of a people almost upon our borders struggling to be free, and struggling against a power whose methods in the past have been so barbaric, presents a very different question."[30] This was a question that American religious leaders agreed had a clear answer: the war in Cuba must end, and the United States had a duty to end it by force if necessary.

President McKinley's government had been preparing in earnest since early March for the possible war he hoped to avoid. On March 7, he had introduced legislation that Congress quickly passed, putting $50 million at his disposal for national defense preparations. In the meantime, through the end of March, his agents continued searching for acceptable diplomatic solutions that seemed always just out of reach. Given that the report of the *Maine* investigation was insufficiently conclusive, the president continued negotiating with Spain in an effort to bring the war to a close. He settled upon several demands: an end to the reconcentration policy, an armistice to begin immediately, and, fatefully, Spain's agreement to grant Cuban independence if McKinley should deem that the necessary solution. By April 9, Spain had conceded the first two demands, putting an end to concentration camps and agreeing to negotiate a temporary ceasefire with the Cuban insurgents. Independence, however, was something Spain was unwilling to grant. According to the historian David Trask, no "American leader of 1898 fully comprehended the extent to which the loss of Cuba represented a repudiation of Spain's most pervasive and emotional national myth—the conviction that Cuba and the rest of the great overseas empire had been a gift from God as reward for the *reconquista*, the reconquest of Spain from the Muslims."[31] Just as Spain was concluding that independence was unacceptable, McKinley was pressed by Congress and by a swelling tide of public opinion to regard independence as absolutely essential.[32]

On April 11, the president finally sent a message to Congress requesting authority to intervene in Cuba. The message recounted the bleak history of insurgency and war in the island over the previous several years, including the horrible effects of the reconcentration policy, concluding that the "war in Cuba is of such a nature that, short of subjugation or extermination, a final military victory for either side seems impracticable." McKinley then gave four grounds for American intervention. First, and worth quoting in full, "In the cause of humanity and to put an end to the barbarities, bloodshed, starvation, and horrible miseries now existing there, and which the parties to the conflict are either unable or unwilling to stop or mitigate. It is no answer to say this is all in another country, belonging to another nation, and is therefore none of our business. It is specially our duty, for it is right at our door." The remaining grounds focused on the national interests at stake: protection of life and property for U.S. citizens in Cuba; serious injury to American commercial interests; and the "constant menace" to national peace created by the poor state of affairs on the island. Only in regard to this last argument did the *Maine* issue arise, treated as "impressive proof of a state of things in Cuba that is intolerable" even if blame could not be fixed.[33] Over the next two weeks it fell to Congress to act on the president's recommendations, and, after much wrangling over the details, mostly regarding official recognition of the insurgent Cuban government, both houses agreed on the following resolutions of April 20:

> *Resolved by the Senate and House of Representatives of the United States of America in Congress assembled,* First. That the people of the island of Cuba are and of right ought to be free and independent.
>
> Second. That it is the duty of the United States to demand, and the Government of the United States does hereby demand, that the Government of Spain at once relinquish its authority and government in the island of Cuba and withdraw its land and naval forces from Cuba and Cuban waters.
>
> Third. That the President of the United States be, and he hereby is, directed and empowered to use the entire land and naval forces of the United States and to call into the actual service of the United States the militia of the several States to such extent as may be necessary to carry these resolutions into effect.
>
> Fourth. That the United States hereby disclaims any disposition or intention to exercise sovereignty, jurisdiction, or control over said island except for the pacification thereof, and asserts its determination, when that is accomplished, to leave the government and control of the island to its people.[34]

These resolutions, though not precisely a declaration of war, rendered any peaceful solution virtually impossible. Within a week, the United States would be at war.

Widespread Support for a "Humanitarian" War

The response among church leaders to the actions of the president and Congress was immediate and consistent with the themes that had been dominant to that point. Support for armed intervention had been growing in the religious press through early April; all that remained was to interpret its significance once begun.[35] In defining an America that would go to war for a weak and downtrodden neighbor, the operative motive was humanitarian concern; the operative attribute was unselfishness. To establish this understanding of the nation and its actions, church leaders provided a selective appropriation of the messages by McKinley and Congress. Specifically, they focused on the humanitarian ground of McKinley's case for intervention, to the explicit exclusion of revenge or even the national interests the president had enumerated. Similarly, they celebrated the resolution of Congress absolutely denying any American desire to claim Cuba for itself. The portrait of America that emerged from the pulpits and the religious press, then, was of a nation willing to act without regard to its own welfare, solely for the good of another.

In an April 21 editorial titled "Worthy and Unworthy Motives," the *Watchman* assessed the variety of arguments made in support of war with Spain. Some politicians in Congress believed their parties would benefit from it; others argued it would be good for business; the "sensational newspapers" were convinced war would sell more papers; and then there were all too many "moved by the passion of vengeance and revenge upon Spain" for its role in the destruction of the *Maine*, whatever that role might have been. "If such considerations influence our action, a war with Spain is unholy and cursed." But, according to this column, these "base motives" cannot on their own "account for the great ground swell of public feeling against the rule of Spain in the West Indies that has surged and rolled through the nation during the past three weeks." Most Americans believe the "issue is higher and larger than these dark and self-seeking schemes," and it is rather "hatred of oppression and injustice that has aroused the hearts of the people." The duty of ministers in this climate, the column concluded, is to work hard to "keep the public temper responsive to the true and worthy motives that should inspire our action."[36] The *Congregationalist* reflected a nearly identical perspective in its lead column for April 28. In particular, the column condemned the popular slogan "Remember the Maine" as a relic of the dark ages. Though this watchword and the sentiment behind it "may be the only word that can spur on men of limited mental capacity and low moral ideals," it had no place in the psyche of a nation acting selflessly to relieve a suffering neighbor. "For a great, intelligent, dignified nation, rising in the closing years of this Christian nineteenth century to put down oppression, such a watchword is simply barbarous." For the *Congregationalist*, as for many others, the "only possible justification for this war on our part is that it is a holy war."[37]

What sanctified this war in the minds of those who believed it to be holy was the conviction that it would be waged for humanity.[38] For R. S. MacArthur of Calvary Baptist Church in New York City, this war's cause was even higher than a war for self-defense. Rather than revenge or military glory, America would fight for peace and justice in Cuba. This cause, he claimed, established the war as nothing less than "a crusade."[39] And for the *Western Christian Advocate*, this war at the dawn of the twentieth century proved that "the cause of humanity" is "the only cause great enough to justify the resort to arms." America's action "mocks the selfish cry of human greed. It puts martial glory in bonds to human advancement. It subordinates revenge to the holiest purposes of charity."[40] All agreed, of course, that wars were to be avoided if possible, but agreement was just as strong that, in the words of the *Christian Standard*, war whenever declared "should be in behalf of the weak against the strong, to secure liberty for the down-trodden of the earth."[41]

In addition to this emphasis on the humanitarian motive driving the war, ministers and editors heralded Congress's promise not to annex Cuba as clear evidence of national unselfishness. W. H. P. Faunce, another Baptist minister, celebrated the American declaration to the "civilized world" that they have "no wish to conquer territory and enrich" national treasure as something "inconceivable 2,000 years ago." Far from adding to national wealth, another minister insisted, "this war is a colossal exhibition of self-sacrifice and disinterested effort" that will surely "cost us hundreds of millions of dollars, and possibly thousands of precious lives. Yet we count not the cost."[42] Wars of conquest, argued Buffalo Methodist Charles Albertson, were no more justifiable than wars of vengeance, but neither had a place in this war. Rather, this would be a "war of freedom," a "war of merciful intervention."[43]

When the fighting actually started, in late April, and with this dominant interpretation of the issues at stake, even those few periodicals that had remained openly opposed to the war until its beginning came to express their loyalty both to the nation and to the cause of "humanity."[44] And the pervasive celebration of the war among church leaders was on full display when the various denominations gathered in May for their annual meetings. Interest in issues of the war emerged in committee reports, annual addresses, and resolutions of all sorts.[45] None other than the *Nation* took note of this nearly univocal support for the war once begun. In a May 19 column called "The Church in the War," its editor, the same editor who had so recently praised the clergy for their caution and restraint following the *Maine*, lamented their forceful and widespread support for the war, their prayers for divine blessing, and their condemnation of those opposed.[46]

Even American Catholics and African American Protestants subscribed to this new definition of American responsibility. Widely considered outliers on the landscape of public religion at the close of America's "Protestant century," many leaders of these groups embraced the war and something of the dominant Christian nationalism in their understanding of its meaning. Consider, for example, the rhetoric of some African American clergy. If anyone was positioned to scoff at widespread calls for humanitarianism, it was these ministers, and many did use the events of the war as an opportunity to highlight parallels between Spain's treatment of the Cubans and the treatment of black Americans. Yet, perhaps even more than the secular black press, religious leaders often voiced strong support for American intervention in Cuba, and on the same terms articulated by the white clergy.[47] The African American Congregationalist minister H. H. Proctor, for example, offered an important defense of American action as eschewing both vengeance and conquest. Addressing the "Colored Military Companies of Atlanta" gathered at the First Congregational Church in Atlanta, Proctor celebrated the war as a war of "compassion" rather than "passion":

> Not for reasons of greed or vengeance do we justify this war. It rather finds Christian justification on grounds of humanity. Christ said, "I have compassion on the multitude." The state of things that exists in Cuba is terrible. The island is laid waste, homes are desolate, the people are starving, multitudes are dying. And this almost in sight of our shores. This state of things has become a stench in the nostrils of the American people. This destruction is intolerable and in the spirit of Christ they rise up in just indignation and declare their compassion for the multitudes of Cuba. "I have compassion on the multitude." It is not a war of passion against the Spaniard, but of compassion for the Cuban. Are we not our brother's keeper?[48]

Here, in what has survived as one of the most extensive examples of African American religious commentary on the war, Proctor offered an excellent exposition of the themes shared by his colleagues. His sermon began with sympathy for the Cubans and a celebration of the American desire to intervene, followed at length by a consideration of the interests of the African American community that were at stake. Fully aware of arguments about the hypocrisy of fighting oppression abroad when so many remained oppressed at home, he called for duty and loyalty nonetheless. For Proctor and others, the war represented a chance to affirm a worthy national cause and in the process demonstrate the loyalty and quality of African American citizens.

In his early support for the war and in his consideration of the issues in light of implications for the black community, Proctor provides a good representation of the larger perspective of the black religious press, as reflected in the commentary of key periodicals like the *Christian Recorder*, the *National Baptist Magazine*, the *Star of Zion*, and the *AME Church Review*. As in other wars before and since, the predominant theme in African American commentary on the war was the opportunity it provided to prove the quality of black citizens and their loyalty to America and its institutions. And it should come as no surprise that when black troops failed to receive the recognition owed them as the war went on, black support for the war waned in turn.[49] But beginning early and continuing through the months of the war, black religious leaders did affirm the religious significance of the war and America's role in it using the same basic terms as their white counterparts. As early as April 7, two weeks before the war officially began, the Reverend W. H. Marshall invited a war that would punish Spain for its crimes against humanity. "I hope for peace," Marshall wrote, "but not a peace which will leave Spain enact upon humanity such cruelties as are now being endured by a people whose only fault it [*sic*] that that [*sic*] they have wearied of tyranny and seek liberty." "God liveth," he continued, "and right will prevail. If war is the issue, the Negro will be found eager to take up arms against oppression."[50] And take up arms they did. Black ministers, for example, enlisted as chaplains for regiments of black soldiers. The African Methodist Episcopal bishop Reverdy Ransom even raised a troop of soldiers himself.[51]

The resolve of early April met stronger resistance as the war brought further disappointment to black hopes for equality. But some continued to insist on the holiness of America's cause in Cuba and even that the sentiments driving the nation to war there would ultimately be their salvation. No one could write without an appreciation for the inconsistency in American humanitarianism and the treatment of blacks, especially in the South. But some religious leaders continued to insist that patriotism was both justifiable and necessary, while unpatriotic statements only helped confirm white suspicions. Perhaps the best example of this perspective appeared in a July column in the *National Baptist Magazine*. J. M. Henderson wrote his article, "The Position of the Negro towards the Spanish-American War," as a direct response to those in press and pulpit who decried America's treatment of blacks in light of humanitarian pretensions in Cuba. Without disputing the severe problems of the African American position, Henderson's central claim was that the sentiment driving the war in Cuba was right and true and that in it blacks could find hope for their own liberation. In fact, he argued, "the Negro has failed to respond to the influences of American civilization if his heart does not beat in sympathy with the sentiment of brotherly love that has lead [*sic*] America to go to the rescue of the down-trodden people of bleeding Cuba." "All that is said of the injustices done us here is true," Henderson conceded, "but not a single mob was ever composed of men who were swayed by the sentiments that have called the present great army to war. The same great feelings that now lead America to reach out her arm to the oppressed of Cuba will one day lead her to rescue the Negro of America from his oppression, just as it once delivered him from slavery."[52] If anyone was likely to reject the Christian, humanitarian justification for war with Spain and a definition of American national character in that light, it was someone like Henderson. Yet here he affirmed that interpretation of national policy in no uncertain terms.[53]

❖

For American Christians black and white, for Proctor and Henderson as for many others, the war had come to represent an example of altruism on a national scale. The prospect had once seemed to many a product of inflamed passion at best, the evil machinations of warmongers at worst. Now war—this war—seemed the very definition of a Christian humanitarianism. Theirs was a nation willing to sacrifice its own treasure and the lives of its citizens not for vengeance or to display its power or to satisfy its greed for more territory but for the sake of the weak and lowly. America, in short, was responsible for defending the world's oppressed even when its own interests suffered the consequences. "It is for right rather than for her own rights that America is in arms," wrote the *Churchman*.[54] Or, as Tennessee's *Baptist and Reflector* put it, "for ourselves we have everything to lose and very little to gain. But for Cuba there is everything to be gained."[55] None captured the posture of this Christian nationalism faced with the Spanish-American War quite as well as the *Outlook*. This was a righteous war, it argued, nothing less than a "crusade of brotherhood." It was, in effect, "the answer of America to the question of its own conscience: Am I my brother's keeper?"[56]

God's New Israel?
New Biblical Models for American Identity

The focus of the chapter to this point has been the emergence of a new sense of responsibility, resulting in nearly universal public support for the war among Christian leaders, who defined it as righteous and holy. What remains to be explained is the rationale that emerged to bolster this widespread support. Why was intervention necessary, righteous, and holy?

This rationale mattered because not everyone thought the war was so praiseworthy. On one hand, most commentators, religious or otherwise, agreed on the sincerity of America's humanitarianism.[57] In some ways, for example, *Harper's Weekly* understood the war on the same terms as the religious press: both conceded that the United States stood to gain absolutely nothing. But for *Harper's* and other critics this meant that the war was useless, unnecessary, and deeply unfortunate.[58] For those who supported the war in the face of such challenges, perceiving this as a new kind of war for the United States and for the world, new models for understanding the nation's identity and the foundation for its actions were understandably important. Church leaders made their most significant contribution in justifying the altruistic motives that nearly everyone believed drove American intervention. Having long drawn on the resources of biblical Israel as a prototype of their republic, Americans returned to scripture for new models that could justify what they saw as their nation's sacrifice of itself for the sake of others. Two ideas were especially important: the call to love neighbor as self, captured in the parable of the Good Samaritan, and, even more striking, Christ's sacrificial death for humanity. The appeal to these biblical images produced, in effect, a redefinition of what it meant to be a Christian nation.

From Levite to Good Samaritan: Intervention as Neighborly Duty

The parable and principle of the Good Samaritan offered a ready model for justifying military intervention in Cuba to extend the "blessings of liberty" to that island. But what exactly did it mean for America to be the "Good Samaritan among nations," as Texas Baptist B. H. Carroll proclaimed in early April?[59] The story in question appears in the Gospel of Luke, specifically Luke 10:25–37, where Jesus uses the parable to explain the deuteronomic command to love neighbor as self, defining who qualifies as one's neighbor. As the story goes, two haughty religious leaders pass by a man left wounded and helpless by robbers, unwilling to help their fellow Israelite. It is rather a Samaritan—a racial and ethnic other with no natural bond to the man in need—who finally shows compassion, suspending his own journey to bind the man's wounds and carry him to safety. Commentary from the religious press through April and May 1898 illustrates how this principle, love of neighbor, and its parable proved useful for understanding the American intervention. Many writers believed that America offered a prime example of what it meant for a nation to act as neighbor. Consider, for example, the perspective of New York's *Independent*, one of America's most widely circulated publications, whose commentary was often reprinted in excerpts by smaller periodicals across the country. On April 28, just days after the declaration of war, the editor ran a column titled "The Christianity of It." The primary question for all Christians, according to this column, was whether the war was Christian, especially since "it is one in which we are the challenging, attacking party." After all, it claimed later, "we should not need to excuse a defensive war; everybody would say that such a war is right." But, for this editor at least, this was clearly not a defensive war. "The compelling reason is one and single. It is not revenge; it is not greed; it is compassion." As to whether war for such a reason qualifies as a Christian war, the article answered with a question: "Is it Christian to stand still and look on when a ruffian is committing murder? The answer to that simple question settles the matter. There is nothing else to be said. The right of self-defense is Christian, but the duty of defending and rescuing others in danger of wrong is as much more Christian as it is less selfish." For the *Independent*, the war was supremely Christian because it was other-directed, intended to lift up the helpless. It was a Christian war for a Christian nation, a "sacred crusade" even, because in this war America showed what it meant to love neighbor as self:

> We have here the very highest justification for war that can be conceived, a war that rises to the sacredness of a crusade. That we have gone into war for such a purpose, have been willing to suffer and let our people die for it, is evidence that we have not lost the Christian heart—that we feel for our neighbor's wrongs; in short, that we love our neighbor as ourselves. A selfish people would have said that they would not give the life of one Yankee for all the *reconcentrados* of Cuba. We could not say that; our people are a Christian people.[60]

It was precisely this interpretation of the war, as a manifestation of love for neighbor, that the *Independent* would urge ministers to promote from their pulpits in the early days of the war. Writing "A Word to Ministers," it called on them to specifically condemn all appeals to vengeance or conquest as sinful and irrelevant to the nation's purposes. Forced by duty and circumstances into this war, "we must remember, and our ministers should teach our people, that it is solely for purposes of humanity. . . . A people close to us are oppressed and weak. Because they have a right to freedom and are trying to get it, and are our neighbors, we help them." The *Independent* explicitly acknowledged what such an application of love of neighbor to national policy implied, that the laws governing the conduct of individual Christians must govern the conduct of nations as well: "Our national policy in this war is absolutely an unselfish one; it must be in the progress and the conclusion of the war, and always thereafter.

The rule, 'Thou shalt love thy neighbor as thyself,' is for nations as well as individuals, and all questions of public policy must be settled by that rule. If we have good, we are to give it, and not keep it. That is good Christianity, and thank God it is good policy."[61]

Other periodicals were just as quick to identify the importance of the principle captured in the Good Samaritan story. The Disciples' *Christian Evangelist* of April 28, like the *Independent*, justified the intervention as a neighborly duty and added a parable of its own to illustrate the principle. If a father oversteps his legitimate authority and begins abusing his children, as Spain had done in Cuba, do you not have a duty to intervene, protect the children, and ensure the father can no longer harm them? For the *Christian Evangelist*, the answer was an obvious yes, and that was precisely what the United States was doing in Cuba.[62] As Matthew Parkhurst of Chicago's *Northwestern Christian Advocate* argued, this war shifted America from its past "'none of our business' position of the priest and the Levite into that of the good Samaritan."[63]

These references to the principle and parable of love for neighbor and the Good Samaritan through the periodical literature shed some light on their power to explain an unprecedented national policy, but a far more thorough treatment of these themes came in a sermon on Luke 10 by an Episcopal minister, William Rainsford. Titled "Our Duty to Civilization, or Who Is My Neighbor?," the sermon was an extended application of the Good Samaritan story to the nation's decision to go to war and a full-fledged attack on those who would oppose the war on the basis of national self-interest. According to Rainsford, such opposition represented a backward position that failed to recognize new international realities. To love neighbor as self required that America use its strength and resources to aid the weak, the poor, and the oppressed. And the Good Samaritan story was specifically relevant. First, Rainsford noted that the Good Samaritan addressed the needs of the wounded man even though he was of a different and hostile race. Further, responding to those who objected to intervention because it would inevitably involve the United States in a long and costly rebuilding process, he argued that the Good Samaritan cared for the downtrodden even though it cost him both time and money. For Rainsford, the command of Jesus to go and do likewise applied directly to the nation as it faced the crisis in Cuba: "We cannot, as Christian men, tolerate the statement that the unendurable woes of Cuba are no business of these United States." War may be awful, he continued, but worse than war is "the spirit which selfishly, supinely sits at home in comfort and national plenty when the divinely-given right of freedom and justice is denied to our next-door neighbor."[64]

The polemical tone of Rainsford's sermon shows that he too was keenly aware of the unprecedented and, for some, ill-advised nature of military entanglement on foreign soil. But he celebrated the fact that peace-loving Christian ministers stood together in their support of the new policy, and he believed these ministers had a special responsibility to remind the nation of the true meaning of the issue.[65] For exercising this responsibility, the Good Samaritan proved an effective tool. In the priest and the Levite ministers could account for those who argued against the war to preserve American interests, not to mention the nations of the Old World that had watched several years earlier when Turkey massacred its Armenian population. In the wounded man they identified racial others, poor, beaten down, and uncivilized due to centuries of oppression. And in the Good Samaritan they saw the United States, well equipped in power and material resources, spending freely of its own money and the lives of its own citizens to lift up a people to whom they had no connection other than the common brotherhood of humanity. This, they believed, was to love one's neighbor as oneself. And, as another minister later concluded, "The year of our Lord 1898 will be ever memorable as that in which Uncle Sam became the Good Samaritan."[66]

A *"Ransom for Humanity"*: *Intervention as Messianic Sacrifice*

Just as potent as the Good Samaritan imagery, if not even more so, was the connection of this national sacrifice to the sacrifice of Christ.[67] Celebration of death in battle as a kind of martyrdom or a sacrifice on the nation's altar was part and parcel of every war, and such sacrifice was still the dominant category for interpreting the significance of the soldiers' deaths in the Civil War, North and South.[68] What debuted in the justification of this war—and what made the death of Christ such a useful analogy—was that the nation was perceived to be sacrificing itself and its interests for the sake of another people.[69]

As with the Good Samaritan metaphor, the analogy to the death of Christ appeared widely in the religious press but received its fullest development in sermons delivered near the beginning of the war. The *Outlook* of April 16, already resigned to the inevitability of the war, framed the issue as a contest between civilizations, between progress and freedom on one hand and sterility and decay on the other. Such a contest, it continued, is sacred and of world-historical significance just as was the cross of Christ, and it may require similar sacrifice: "When such an issue is presented, the sword may become as sacred as the cross, for it may represent as truly the spirit of self-sacrifice and unselfish service."[70] The *Congregationalist*, too, called for the spirit of one who "takes the symbols of our Lord's sacrifice of himself for humanity" in what could only be described as a "holy war."[71] Similarly drawing on the sacrifice of Christ for humanity, the *Standard* printed a poem celebrating the dead of the *Maine* as retroactively representative of those who would sacrifice themselves in this worthy, redemptive cause. Drawing from language echoing that of Mark 10:45, the poem described the sailors' deaths as a "ransom for humanity."[72] As Christ gave himself to redeem the downtrodden, so now these sailors, and America, must sacrifice for lowly Cuba.

One of the more textured uses of the Christ motif appeared in the Missouri Baptist periodical *Word and Way*, in a column evoking themes of race, gender, and domesticity. Like nearly every religious paper, *Word and Way* included a weekly column titled "The Home," a page targeted at women with advice for their roles as wife, mother, and the backbone of the church. The author of many of the columns signed simply as "Mother Bunch." Immediately after the start of the war, Mother Bunch began to address the conflict from the perspective of the women who would remain at home, and the primary category was sacrifice. She framed one of her more striking columns as the story of the author's experience coming to accept the severe costs the war would bring. The account foregrounds sacrifice for America more clearly than sacrifice for Cuba, but Cuba's plight as a cause for the war is present throughout, and, even more important, the precedent found in the death of Christ remains the same. The story begins with a contrast between Mother Bunch, who speaks of her regret that war has come and her unwillingness to give the blood of her boys, and her young grandson Ted, whose only regret is that he is not yet twenty-one and cannot help deal with Spanish atrocities. The turning point in the story is an exchange between Ted and "our colored boy" Jess, who has no regard for Ted's patriotic fervor. "I aint got no use fur wah," Jess exclaims. "I don't know nothin' about Spain an' Spain don't know nothin' about me. I aint got nothin' agin Spain and Spain aint got nothin' agin me, an' I aint goin to wah agin huh." "Why Jess, they're a fightin for the colored people," Ted retorts. "That's what started the war in Cuba." This argument has no effect on Jess: "I don't know nothin' about that, but I ain't a goin' to no wah, u'less I haf to." As the story goes, what bothers Mother Bunch is that she sees herself in what she understands to be Jess's selfishness. She thinks of "the noble women who had given their sons to bleed and die for the cause of freedom over 100 years ago," realizing that if they had not made those sacrifices she would not now enjoy such liberty. She realizes that here, like Christ, she must be willing to sacrifice herself for the interests of others, or as she puts it, "the few must be sacrificed for the many—even as Christ died for the sins of the world."[73]

If these examples from the religious press indicate the pervasive use of the Christ motif for understanding the national duty to intervene, the meaning of this national messianic sacrifice was more fully developed in several published sermons. Some references were fairly anecdotal, as when ministers added eloquence to their sermons with the famous refrain of the "Battle Hymn of the Republic": "As he died to make men holy, let us die to make men free, while God is marching on."[74] Other sermons were more specific, however, and found the metaphor useful for combating arguments against intervention based on concerns for national interests or concerns about the racial quality of those for whom American lives would be sacrificed. Syracuse minister Edward Packard, for example, took up this theme in his message of April 17, just days before the nation would declare war on Spain. He argued that Christianity often demands war because it is built on the concept of self-sacrifice, laying down one life for another, something modeled in Christ but applied to the Christian life on every level as well. This, he insisted, was a "holy war, because it is the strong helping the weak." Here the "whole nation must lay down its life for the stopping of a wrong," and in "these acts of humanity the nation clothes itself with the majestic garments of God himself." Based on the principle of self-sacrifice, and just as Christ intervened to save sinners through his death, "Christianity means intervention to save everywhere, always, unto the end."[75] One week later, in New York City, David Gregg, a Presbyterian, made a similar case. Against those who protested that the Cubans were not worth the loss of American blood, he argued directly from the sacrifice of Christ for sinful humanity. Christ did not consider the sins of humans against himself or the infinite distance that separated his own divine position from that of lowly, created human beings. Rather, he sacrificed his life freely, and, as that sacrifice was made for our spiritual freedom, he argued, so now we must pay the price for Cuba's freedom. Gregg did not dispute the lower quality of the Cuban people when measured against American lives, merely the notion that this made them unworthy of sacrifice. He argued simply that unity in Christ breaks down national boundaries, making the sorrows of the Alien the sorrows of America as well.[76]

It was Henry van Dyke, Gregg's fellow New York Presbyterian, who offered by far the most important case for intervention as messianic sacrifice. Pastor of New York's prestigious Brick Presbyterian Church, Van Dyke was a leading light of American Protestant liberalism and one of the era's most popular writers.[77] On May 1, the first Sunday after the official beginning of hostilities, he delivered a sermon that would be cited and reprinted in excerpts throughout the religious press as a landmark interpretation of the meaning of the war. As a communion sermon, it was designed to prepare congregants for reflection on the significance of Christ's death and to apply that death to their lives. In essence, it was an extended treatment of the relevance of the cross for understanding the nation's duty in the crisis. Both for the richness of its content and for the breadth of its influence, it is worthy of close consideration.

War was the "heaviest cross that a nation is ever called to bear," Van Dyke argued, and it "must be carried in the same spirit in which Christ bore his Cross and fought his battle on Calvary." According to Van Dyke, that spirit had two components: submission to God's will and devotion to the service of humankind. The call to the cross is essential, he argued, so that the men who fight and the women who weep would learn from Christ to "accept their bitter cup because it is inevitable, and to endure their sacrifice because it is for the sake of others."

It is these two elements of the cross of Christ—submission to God's will and sacrifice for the sake of humanity—that Van Dyke applied specifically to the American action in the Cuban crisis. First, Americans must recognize this war as a providential necessity in an imperfect world. For all their attempts to avoid war, he continued, this is the point to which the force of events had brought them. To argue that Cuba belongs to another and is none of our concern would require "more than a change of national policy. It would mean a change in national character." Granting that the decision to intervene would prove a "costly sacrifice," Van Dyke, quoting Jesus's words from the Gospels, insisted Americans must accept it "in the deep solemnity of submission to God. 'If this cup may not pass away except we drink it, Thy will be done.'"

Beyond submission to God, the second major lesson from the cross was that Jesus accepted his sacrifice willingly because it was "the price of untold blessings for the world." Though no human suffering could match the salvific suffering of Christ, Van Dyke conceded, the precedent set there was worth following: "to suffer for the benefit of others is heroic and Christlike. To bear the cross of war for the sake of delivering men is to be crucified with Christ." Suffering for others is precisely the opportunity the nation faced in Cuba, he argued. Spain's was a long-standing regime of rapine and robbery; America's task was to rid the continent of the "most obstinate barbarians who exist outside of Turkey," to grant liberty to the captives and freedom to the oppressed, to secure peace and order for a broken people while proving to be the friend of the downtrodden. These were "high, generous, Christian aims," he continued, but goals that could not be achieved apart from sacrifice, for even "Christ himself could not win the victory for us over evil, without strife and the shedding of blood." Van Dyke's conclusion, drawing language from Mark 10:45, is a fitting summary of the use of Christ's death to define a messianic, sacrificial role for the nation. Yes, America was approaching the great, heavy, and unwanted cross of war, but "if we bear it in submission to God, in the spirit of Christ and for the sake of humanity, it will be a ransom for many, and a sign of peace unto far-off generations."[78]

The sacrificial death of Christ proved a powerful metaphor for making sense of an unprecedented national policy of intervention. It was especially useful for those trying desperately to exclude appeals to national interests, both for and against the war. However significantly figures like the Congregationalist Lyman Abbot, the Presbyterian Henry van Dyke, and the Baptist Mother Bunch may have disagreed over the theology of Christ's atonement, they found in that sacrifice important principles that helped to clarify the nation's duty in a war they believed would cost more than it paid. Like Christ, America looked down upon a people broken, oppressed, and unable to free themselves. Like Christ, America would be required to sacrifice much on behalf of those who could offer nothing in return. And, like Christ, America by its sacrifice would prove to be a "ransom for many." With such metaphors ready at hand, this was a war American ministers could justify.

This rhetoric, especially the appeal to the Christ motif, also reveals a deeper layer of significance embedded within religious attempts to locate meaning in the war with Spain. It points toward a new understanding of what many believed it meant to be a "Christian" nation. This now involved more than visions of domestic righteousness or purity that had fired the hopes of most nineteenth-century Christian activists. A Christian nation was also a nation that *acted* as Christ did, sacrificially on behalf of the weak. No one recognized this new departure more clearly than yet another New York minister, Thomas Dixon, in his sermon of May 1. Dixon came to greater fame through his series of race novels that would provide the basis for D. W. Griffith's notorious 1915 film, *The Birth of a Nation*. For now, he served as pastor of the liberal People's Church, a relatively new congregation founded on the principles of theological modernism. In America's decision to fight for Cuba, Dixon saw the fulfillment of all he hoped the nation could be. In this war, he argued, "for the first time in modern history, a great nation has accepted the Spirit of Jesus Christ as the motive power of life." Self-interest determined the "old law of nations" as the "supreme standard of life." America, he believed, had recognized that "the law of Christ is sacrificial and redemptive love. This nation has taken up its cross in Cuba. It has begun a holy war, with nothing to gain, and millions of dollars and priceless blood to lose." For Dixon, this action represented the "sublimest incarnation of Christianity of this century," and here, he argued, a new nation was born.[79]

❖

Everyone seemed to recognize that in going to war with Spain America now stood on new ground—new because this war would be fought beyond continental borders; new because the interests involved, as most viewed the stakes, were not America's but those of another, weaker people; new because justifying this action required a new sense of national responsibility in the world. America, a remarkable number of Christian leaders argued, must play the role of Christ in the world. "Seldom in the history of mankind has war been waged for such reasons," concluded the editor of the *New Orleans Christian Advocate*, and he was far from alone.[80] Many believed that a war fought not for national self-interest but for humanity was an altogether new kind of war. What would it mean, for America and for the world? Answering this question would consume the attention of American religious leaders in the coming months, but their answers would not move beyond the deep and pervasive confidence rooted in a precipitating cause they saw as holy and quintessentially Christian. By May 5, the *Congregationalist* had captured the mood: "is it not possible that, though we would have had it otherwise, some gracious, some wonderful purpose of God, not for America only but for the whole world, is being carried out, even though ironclads and marching battalions are the means used . . . ?"[81]

2

Clash of Civilizations

Spain as Enemy and the Crystallization of American Messianism

The first blow of the Spanish-American War was landed nearly ten thousand miles away from Cuba. On what became known as "the glorious first of May," Commodore George Dewey and the U.S. Asiatic Squadron steamed into the Philippines' Manila Bay. And in a span of mere hours they achieved an unqualified victory that set the tone for all that was to follow in the "splendid little war" with Spain. Dewey and his fleet had been stationed in Hong Kong at the outbreak of the war, but British neutrality forced them out of the port city. Too far from home to survive on their current supply of coal and following a strategy sketched hypothetically by Theodore Roosevelt several years earlier, Dewey and his sailors made for the Philippines and the first strike in the war to liberate Cuba. No one expected what was to follow. Manila Bay was guarded by formidable Spanish fortresses armed with long-range batteries and was home to numerous warships. But by the end of the battle the nine ships of the U.S. fleet had destroyed every one of their Spanish counterparts, and all this without the loss of a single sailor.

Dewey's guns still echoed in most hearts and minds when the American Baptists gathered in Rochester for their annual meeting on May 17–18, 1898. They were just one of several denominations to hold annual meetings in mid- to late May, when the euphoria over the American victory was still widespread. As expected, the two days of the program were laced with a strong patriotic flavor, which culminated in the final night of the meeting. The delegates had been expecting an address from the famed A. J. Diaz, a Cuban Baptist pastor funded by their home missions board who had long been active in his island's struggle against Spain. Diaz, however, was already in Florida, preparing to re-enter Cuba as an interpreter on the staff of American general Nelson Miles. Instead, the American Baptists heard from the popular pastor of New York's Calvary Baptist Church, Robert S. MacArthur.[1] They were not disappointed. MacArthur's address, titled "The Hand of God in the Nation's Conflict," be-came one of the two or three most cited sermons on the subject of the war and one of the most powerful interpretations of its significance. In part, the sermon's notoriety stemmed from the fact that MacArthur delivered it on several occa-sions over the course of the war, culminating in a widely celebrated rendition at the annual Christian Endeavor Convention in mid-July. Though apparently the sermon was never published separately as a pamphlet, multiple periodicals reported on it, summarized its contents, or printed the transcript in full.[2] Given this unmatched exposure, MacArthur's address remains one of the most impor-tant interpretations of the meaning of both the nation and its war.

The sermon's title was well chosen. In the wake of America's overwhelming victory in the Philippines, MacArthur was certain the hand of God was with the nation. "If we listen well," he argued, "we shall hear above the booming of cannon, the sighs of the defeated and the shouts of the victorious in Manila Bay, the voice of God saying, 'As I was with Moses, so shall I be with thee, O heroic Commander Dewey. No Spanish ship will long stand before thee, thou leader of victorious Americans, in this triumph of humanity, of liberty and of true Christianity.'"[3] Taking up arguments he and others had made in the days just before and after the war began, MacArthur located the hand of God in the lofty, humanitarian motives that had inspired American intervention. These motives, he believed, set this conflict apart as a "crusade of brotherhood," nothing short of a "holy war for humanity." But celebration of the cause of America's war was not the central thrust of the message. Rather, he saved his most potent language for vilifying the Spanish enemy and his most ambitious speculations for explaining the causes of Spain's downfall. Indeed, he argued, "if there is any nation with which we can engage in war without compunction of conscience and with the approval of the highest Christian conviction, it is with cruel and tyranneous [*sic*] Spain, whose hands are red with innocent blood and whose heart is black with manifold crimes." MacArthur recognized, it seems, that America's character would here be thrown into greater relief be-cause the nation stood "united against a common foe," locked in what he cast as nothing less than a "war between widely differing civilizations." As he saw it, "it is a war between ignorance, bigotry and superstition on the one side, and intelligence, liberty and a true Christianity on the other side . . . ; it is a war between the most despicable civilization of modern times and the most

Christianized civilization of all times; it is a war between the sixteenth and the twentieth centuries."

To this point MacArthur remained on ground publicly disputed by few if any American Christians. But MacArthur did not stop here. Supported by numerous illustrations from Spanish history, most of which centered on the famous Inquisition, he argued that "in its ultimate issues it is a war between Romanism and Protestantism."

As MacArthur's bold rhetoric illustrates, the Spanish-American War offered a prime opportunity for reflection on American national character, defined not only by the reasons the nation went to war but also by *whom* it fought so victoriously against. With a new sense of national purpose defined and justified in the days leading to war, a second question became very important: why should anyone believe America was fit to carry out this new responsibility?[4] Why would America be able to interfere in the affairs of other nations without falling prey to the self-interest that had plagued European colonial powers? This chapter demonstrates how another distinctive feature of the war—Spain as enemy—offered a crucial plank in the foundation of confidence in American ability. Defining their nation in contrast to Spain, Christian ministers found evidence of the precise character qualities necessary to sustain a messianic foreign policy and, later, expansionism. Part one of the argument illustrates the basic categories used to contrast the two nations, categories that mirrored MacArthur's rhetoric very closely. First, most came to view the war as a clash of alternate civilizations, invoking a shared set of terms with near-formulaic consistency and interchangeability. Measured against medieval, barbaric, tyrannous and cruel Spain, the United States appeared progressive, altruistic, humane, the champion of individual liberties. These were qualities that, in sum, identified America as Christian; Spain, then, was something else. These were the categories that explained why America was fit for a world mission Spain had spoiled from the beginning. On this much there was widespread agreement. The second section of the argument addresses one of the few areas of *disagreement* among American Christians over the meaning of the war, namely whether Spain's Catholicism was responsible for its backwardness. Was this a war between Protestantism and Catholicism, as Robert MacArthur had argued? Was the character of American civilization a product of Protestantism and the abuses of Spain a logical progression from Catholic dogma? These questions were the subject of fierce debate between America's Protestants, many of whom blamed Catholicism for Spain's downfall, and American Catholics, who saw the war as a moment both for demonstrating Catholic loyalty to America and for shedding the stereotypes that had once relegated them to the margins of

American public life. Detailing the anti-Catholic take on Spain and the American Catholic response in turn, I argue that in spite of their disagreement on the role of Protestantism and Catholicism in the character of each nation, American Christians even in this very debate showed a common understanding of the categories that defined the American character. The importance of this debate for the development of Christian nationalism, then, is that it only reinforced confidence in America's ability going forward. In establishing the welfare of others as the sole criterion for national policy, in contrast to Spain, Protestants and Catholics alike believed America had proven itself a quintessentially Christian nation.

Spain versus America: "Barbarism" and the "Light of the Twentieth Century"

One of the most venerable explanations for the origins and cultural significance of the Spanish-American War has focused on the existential angst of an American public strained by a lack of cohesive identity. This was a period of identity crisis born out of economic depression, industrialization, immigration, and sectional hostility left over from Reconstruction. The war with Spain, according to this explanation, offered a much-needed "other" against whom a common identity could be defined, an opportunity for, as Frank Ninkovich puts it, "self-validation through denial of the worth of the other."[5] Not all Christian leaders were as quick to vilify the Spanish as some other sectors of the American public sphere, but they too took full advantage of the othering process so basic to all wars. Specifically, drawing a contrast with what they saw as the qualities of the Spanish, they identified the moral attributes they believed would secure national faithfulness as America intervened in the affairs of other nations. I illustrate the power of these character categories first by charting the typical narrative explaining Spain's fall from glory. I then show the image of America that developed by contrast through a group of sermons preached by New York ministers during the earliest weeks of the war.

"The Past History of Our Present Conflict"

In some ways, since the earliest colonial years and especially since their successful revolution against Great Britain, Americans had worked to define themselves in contrast to the nations of Europe. By the close of the nineteenth century, Spain had become their best example of all that was worst in the Old World. Where nations like Great Britain and Germany had advanced to varying degrees, Spain remained a quintessential product of Old World values frozen in time, or so many believed. More than three hundred years earlier, readers on both sides of the Atlantic had welcomed the English-language publication of Bartolome Las Casas's *Tears of the Indians*, a graphic polemical description of mass torture and murder inflicted by Spanish colonists on the innocent, defenseless natives. In the writing of Las Casas, himself both Spaniard and papist, the English found all the confirmation they needed for long-held convictions about the depths of Spanish cruelty and barbarism. As the prefatory remarks of the English translator made plain, this portrait of an old enemy helped reinforce the identity of the English as the holy and righteous people of God in the wake of a bitter, confusing civil war.[6] And so, when in 1898 Las Casas's tract was reprinted in the United States, the symbolic weight of the publication was hard to miss. "The Spaniard of the 19th century," wrote the editor of the reprinted pamphlet, "differs but little from the Spaniard of the 16th."[7] In the minds of many Americans, Spain's character remained firmly moored in a bygone era.[8] Numerous enemies—numerous "others"—had left their marks since Spain had last served as a primary foil for American identity. There were the French of the eighteenth century. There were the British of the Revolutionary period.[9] And of course there were the ever-present Native Americans, with whom the American military had recently waged a series of brutal wars.[10] But now, at the dawn of the twentieth century, as the old nemesis resurfaced, to familiar categories like tyranny, rapacity, and cruelty was added one all-encompassing descriptor: backwardness. In the heady days of the Progressive Era, one could be guilty of few things worse. In the crucible of the Spanish-American War, American self-perception was forged around the notion of progress or modernity in combat with a relic from the medieval world. For many religious observers, progress was equal to liberty, altruism, and universal "brotherhood"—in sum, to Christianity, with America as history's best representative. Backwardness, then, was defined by greed, oppression, and "inhumanity."

Contrasts drawn along these lines appeared from the earliest days leading up to the war, featuring prominently, for example, in the congressional debates over the necessity of intervention.[11] After Dewey's victory in the Philippines, however, when it became clear just how ill equipped Spain was relative to American military power, rhetoric comparing the two nations became even more popular. The task was to identify the reasons for Spain's precipitous fall from its former glory and, by extension, to explain America's simultaneous rise to world supremacy. Many looked to the past as the key to understanding the present, recognizing that Spain's deplorable condition did not emerge overnight. "Spain has been the nursery of brutality and cruelty for many centuries," one editor claimed;[12] argued another, Spain "has been for many years ripening to her death. Her cruelty, superstition and injustice have been antecedents to an inevitable conflict with the forces of modern civilization."[13] Now, it seemed, the "mistakes of the sixteenth century are finding their atonement in nineteenth century calamity."[14]

Efforts to trace what the editor of the *Christian Standard* called "The Past History of Our Present Conflict" tended to follow a common trajectory.[15] The starting point was consistently the sixteenth century, which dawned with Spain as the "light of the world," a place of chivalry and learning.[16] Then, with respect to culture, refinement, and technology, it was Spain that possessed Europe's most advanced civilization. It had the greatest navy, the most invincible army, and the largest empire of New World dependencies providing a constant stream of gold for the national treasury. The turning point came in the midcentury reign of Philip II. First, the Spaniards purged the nation of its long-standing communities of Jews and Moors. In ejecting the Jews, they cast out thousands of their "best subjects—professors, physicians, artists, merchants." And, when persecution drove away the Moors, Spain deprived itself of the "peaceful industry of this remarkable people" responsible for the supremacy of Spanish civilization when the rest of Europe was still emerging from the Dark Ages. The Moors had crafted the palaces and cathedrals, the aqueducts and irrigation systems, the schools and libraries that had made Spain great. Because of these expulsions, the Methodist E. O. Dunton concluded, "the harvest of the garden and field, the product of factory and loom, do not in Spain to-day equal the wealth of four centuries ago."[17]

Then, with the Inquisition came the eighteen-year rule of Inquisitor-general Tomas de Torquemada, whose reign of terror saw tens of thousands of Spain's own best and brightest killed or imprisoned. The result, according to this common narrative, was the disappearance of ambition, of learning and independent thinking, of all elements necessary for progress. What remained was a uniformity imposed by bigotry, a military supremacy turned to cruel militarism, and an unearned and unsustainable luxury based on greedy exploitation of colonial resources. Thus began a long, inevitable decline of a once-glorious nation. "Four centuries of Spanish history," Dunton argued, "reveal a diabolical cruelty quite without parallel; a religious bigotry that effectually throttled freedom of thought; an insatiate greed which blighted the fairest provinces for sake of an immediate return in gold. A catalogue of the crimes of Spain against humanity and civilization is sufficient to doom her to eternal execration. Her perfidy outstrips the Turk; her bigotry outromes Rome; her cruelty outdevels the savage red man of the forest."[18]

Some argued Spain's demise had been foreshadowed by the providential defeat of its mighty Armada that fateful night in the English Channel in 1588. Tragically, one commentator noted, "to the lessons of civilization and Christianity taught then and there, Spain has remained proudly and obstinately blind, as are those who never forgive, seldom learn, and are consequently left far behind in the march of humanity's advance."[19] It was Spain's great pride, its unwillingness to learn and progress, that had produced a nation crippled by poverty, a people hampered by mass illiteracy, a culture of inhumanity evident nowhere more clearly than in the recreation of choice, bullfighting.[20] And so, Americans believed, the Spain of Torquemada, Cortez, and Pizarro had yielded the Spain of General Weyler and his barbaric policy of reconcentration.

American Character in a Spanish Mirror

This was the perspective on Spanish character many ministers took with them into their pulpits in the weeks immediately following soon-to-be Admiral Dewey's triumph in Manila. It was this portrait that their sermons reinforced, and it was against this portrait that they defined American identity and the stakes of their war with Spain. The sermons of ministers across New York City delivered on May 8 and May 15 were especially revealing.[21] The vitriol of the Reverend Henry Frank, pastor of the Metropolitan Independent Church, left little to the imagination. "The Spaniards have become Insane," his sermon of May 8 argued. "Ages of cruelty, barbarism, and bigotry have eaten into their breasts, until their native humanity has been transformed into the basest bestiality." Lest any from pity hesitate to destroy such a "senile monster," Frank continued, "let us not forget how a beautiful isle lies to-day blistering and prostrate because of the brutal blows of that monster whose bloody hands are staid alone by the bayonets of our brave boys and the belching of our shotted guns."[22] That same day, across the East River in Brooklyn, Charles Goodell of the Hanson Place Methodist Church mixed some hope with his arraignment of Spanish brutality, hope that now a "better day is dawning" and that "barbarism has no place in the light of the twentieth century." Goodell, like so many others, chose as his subject "The Story of Spain," and his sermon charted the familiar, tortuous decline of a once-great civilization. A tragic unwillingness to adapt had produced a Spain of the present indistinguishable from the Spain of the medieval past: "The Spaniard in the West is as much a relic of the past as was China in the East. Spain has used the weapons of the Middle Ages, and the spirit of Philip II. and Charles V. lives in the breast of Weyler and his men." In going to war against an enemy such as this, Goodell argued, America had stepped to "a higher level" and had served "notice upon the world that we are the friends of the oppressed everywhere." The true significance of the victory in Manila, he argued, was inseparable from the cruelty and oppression embodied in the defeated enemy: "The thunderous shock of Dewey's cannon blew the rack and the thumb-screw and the whole paraphernalia of medieval persecution off the face of the earth forever. It undermined the intolerance of bigotry and an awful superstition and told the world that a new hour had struck in the history of nations." Here, now, in this war, he concluded, America had proven "that without dispute the flag that presses closest after the crimson cross is the Stars and Stripes."[23]

Goodell's conclusion thus expressed a widely held conviction that in fighting against Spain and all it represented in the world, America had proved its mettle as a distinctly Christian nation. If Spain's deplorable condition could be traced to inseparable traits like cruelty, bigotry, and oppression, America's rise to preeminence must result from its commitment to opposite principles. And these principles—principles like liberty, justice, and self-sacrifice—represented, for many religious leaders, the essence of Christianity. This was the contention of Goodell's Methodist colleague James King in a widely celebrated sermon delivered one week later, on May 15. King preached that evening at the Union Methodist Episcopal Church, not in his normal capacity as a minister but as chaplain to the Empire State Society of the Sons of the American Revolution. On a platform fully decorated with the American colors, King addressed "The Situation and Justification of the Nation at War with Spain. . . ." In many ways his sermon was typical: it celebrated the humanitarian impulse behind America's decision to fight, and in some detail it cast the war as a contest between two irreconcilable civilizations. But the distinguishing feature of King's argument was its emphasis on the Christian character of American national life. "By historic origin and precedent, by principles of legislative action, by the character of our fundamental institutions, by judicial decisions and by the genius of our civilization," King concluded, "we are a Christian nation."[24] It was this Christianity, he continued, that made intervention against Spain nonnegotiable, and as such "it is impossible to minify or narrow the scope and meaning of the contest." Not primarily about commerce, money or politics, not even primarily a "naval and military contest," he argued, "it is a contest in which the character of civilization and the interpretation of the Decalogue and the Sermon on the Mount are involved."[25]

If the nature of America's cause had set this war apart as a holy war, the character of the enemy defined the issues as barely short of apocalyptic. The image of Spain—and by inference the image of America—that emerged in the early days of the war identified this contest not simply as a clash of civilizations but as the culmination of the age-old struggle between barbarism and progress, between tyranny and liberty, between Christianity and the powers of evil. "This war," argued Lyman Abbott's *Outlook*, "is the final outcome of a great historic conflict; it is part of the struggle for freedom which has been going on in the world for centuries."[26] The Presbyterian Samuel McComb, preaching at the Rutgers Riverside Presbyterian Church, echoed Abbott's assessment with even greater specificity. "The fact is," he insisted, "that beneath the outward incidents of the bloody drama being enacted at our doors there lies the battle of principle." Predictably, the "principle" McComb saw at stake was framed in the contrast between the medieval world and the modern world, between tyranny and freedom, corruption and justice. Spain, on the one hand, "belongs to the sixteenth century, is corrupt, moribund, eaten through and through with fraud and chicanery. America belongs to the nineteenth century, is the home of freedom and defender of right. In taking the sword," he concluded, "in appealing to the dread arbitrament of war we are the agent of the Almighty in ridding the Western Hemisphere of the rotten tyranny that has too long cumbered the earth."[27]

Here McComb introduced one of the central themes in the sermons of these New York ministers responding to the victory in Manila: the theme of judgment for Spain, with America as the instrument ordained by God. The scale of the victory, combined with the widespread apocalyptic identification of the combatants, seemed best explained as a direct intervention by God, whose patience had finally reached an end. So preached Heber Newton of the All Souls' Protestant Episcopal Church. Newton was convinced that now, at last, "Spain's Nemesis is overtaking her. The long story of Spain's rapacity and extortion, of her oppression and cruelty, of her treachery and perfidy, is reaching its culmination. The cup of woe is at last filled to overflowing, and is being even now pressed to her lips. And the hand which is ordained to hold that cup to her lips is the hand of America."[28] So also W. F. Anderson, as if reading from a common script, drew the same conclusion for his congregation at the Washington Square Methodist Church. "The Spanish nation is a lesson to remind us that a people who ignore the commands of Almighty God must come to an end. The Spanish people have refused to obey the laws of progress. When the defeat of Spain shall have been accomplished it will not be the United States who accomplished it—it will be done by the will of God. He used America as His instrument." Given the stark contrast between American and Spanish identities heralded in pulpits across America, Anderson spoke for many when he concluded that an American victory was at the same time "a victory for humanity and justice."[29]

For many American church leaders, then, the true meaning and significance of the war derived from the identity of each nation fighting in it. The competing civilizations were themselves produced by centuries of devotion to two disparate sets of principles, and in the cautionary tale that was Spain's rise and fall Americans saw more clearly what it was they stood for—and against. In the throes of an early victory, many found more than sufficient confirmation of American supremacy, a supremacy based not merely on military might but on the strength of a Christian character defined by liberty and self-sacrifice. No one voiced this conviction more clearly than Robert MacArthur, in his famous "Hand of God" sermon. "This war," by his reckoning, "is for the triumph of nations which have the right to survive." Given unparalleled resources and opportunity, "Spain proved herself unworthy of the great possessions alike in the new world and in the old world." Now, at the end of Spain's long and inevitable decline, "God has virtually placed the American people at the portal of the twentieth century, and has given them command not only to refuse admission to the civilization of the sixteenth century, but to drive it utterly from this Western hemisphere." MacArthur saw in Spain's history more reason than ever to believe that by the laws of progress only the fittest survive and that progress— the future—lay with American principles. "The nineteenth century," he was convinced, "will go out with the spirit of humanity, with the note of brotherhood, with the duty of altruism as its diapason, as its inspiring slogan, as its divine bugle call to the nations of the earth."[30]

Patriots All? Protestants, Catholics, and the Spanish-American Divide

There was wide agreement, then, that both Spain's downfall and America's simultaneous rise to power were by-products of the distinct principles upon which each civilization rested. And there was similar agreement that the principles responsible for American greatness were Christian principles. But from this point wide agreement gave way to one of the few significant matters of disagreement as to the meaning of the war—a debate over the place of Catholicism in America. Were Spain's cruelty, tyranny, and bigotry a result of the influence of its Catholicism and America's humanitarianism a product of its Protestant heritage? Was this, as Robert MacArthur claimed, ultimately a "war between Romanism and Protestantism"?[31] Even Protestants themselves were not in total agreement on this question. Some, especially Baptists, Disciples of Christ, Methodists, and select Presbyterians and Congregationalists, were convinced that Spain represented the world's best example of what Catholicism would produce when given free rein in human society. Some others, less vocal, were willing to regard Spain's condition as at worst a perversion of Catholic principles. But those who had the most at stake in this discussion were American Catholics, a rapidly expanding group just carving out a place of public influence on the national level. Their leaders viewed the war as an opportunity to prove their loyalty, affirm common notions of American identity, and distinguish their religion from the religion of Spain. Ultimately, there would be no agreement about the relationship of Catholicism to the respective identities of America and Spain. But the debate itself revolved only around who did and did not warrant a place within an American identity that, at root, Protestants and Catholics seemed to agree upon. As to the terms that defined this identity, the debate served only to reinforce widespread confidence in the nation's Christian moral fiber.

Anti-Catholicism in Protestant Perceptions of Spain

That Catholicism would be a prominent feature in the crisis with Spain became clear even before the war began, in a public relations mishap surrounding the pope's attempt to serve as a mediator between Spain and the United States. As tensions escalated in late March, church authorities in Rome sought any possible means of maintaining peace. Archbishop John Ireland of Saint Paul, Minnesota, a personal friend of William McKinley and several well-placed senators, kept close watch on developments in Washington while the pope, Leo XIII, used his influence to convince Spain to comply with the American demand for an armistice with the Cuban insurgents. McKinley himself, hoping to avoid war, had remained open to anything Ireland or the pope could accomplish with Spain. The problem arose when Spain publicly viewed the pope as acting on a direct request from the American president, which was both false and a politically dangerous prospect for McKinley, faced with a Protestant public clamoring for war.[32] Though the efforts of Leo and Ireland proved fruitless, word of their attempt leaked to the press. The response among religious editors was varied. Some welcomed the negotiations as evidence of a sincere desire to sustain peace.[33] Others, reacting more strongly to the news, claimed to prefer war to any peace for which the pope was responsible.[34] Typically, those who opposed any role for the pope focused on the hypocrisy of his attempt at peace, given years of Spanish brutality in Cuba. "While his best beloved son, Spain, was butchering Cubans by the thousands," one Baptist editor complained, "Spanish bishops were praying for the success of Spanish arms. Now when there is a prospect that the Castilians must go home and behave themselves or be thrashed, the old man of the Tiber plays the role of peacemaker and cries out against the shedding of blood."[35]

Such deep anti-Catholic feeling owned a long past in America. It predated the nation itself, in fact, with roots stretching into a colonial era that saw the British colonists surrounded by the Catholic French to the north and west and the Spanish to the south and west. These passions never burned more intensely than in times of war. Anti-Catholic sentiment was especially strong during the Anglo-French wars of the mid-eighteenth century. It was then, the historian Nathan Hatch has argued, that American Protestants sacralized their notion of individual liberty civil and religious, seeing themselves locked in millennial combat with the tyrannical forces of the popish antichrist.[36] Nearly 150 years later, America's first war with a European Catholic foe witnessed a return of such rhetoric in all its vigor, yet even during the intervening years the absence of an external Catholic threat did little to alleviate Protestant fears of the influence of Rome. Immigration had done more than enough to keep these concerns alive. First came the Irish in droves following the potato famine of the 1840s, which in part inspired the urgency of tracts like Lyman Beecher's famous *Plea for the West*.[37] Following the Civil War, it was waves of Catholic eastern European immigrants that stirred Protestant angst, within a broader context of American nativism that spawned groups like the American Protective Association. It was only a few years before the war with Spain that the Congregationalist minister and activist Josiah Strong published his wildly popular book *Our Country*, in which he identified "Romanism" and immigration as the great threats to the stability of American civilization.[38]

This was the context in which many Protestants interpreted the significance of war with Spain. Such anti-Catholic rhetoric, unsurprisingly, only intensified with the outbreak of the war. On May 5, with the war barely two weeks old, Georgia's *Christian Index* ran a front-page column representing one of the earliest attempts to sum up the essence of the conflict. Written by the Baptist J. G. McCall, the column framed the war as a referendum on two competing visions of Christianity. His premise was simple: "Spain, the oppressor, is directly under the convictions of the Church of Rome. The United States, the liberator, is controlled by the doctrines entertained by Baptists and Protestants." The two governments, he continued, were mirror opposites of each other. Where in the United States citizens enjoyed all the benefits of self-government, Spain had "always been hard and exacting of her subjects," seeking only to enrich its court and courtiers, its clergy, and its officers of state. The point, for McCall, was that it was impossible to separate the quality of a nation's government from the predominant religious convictions of its people. Or, as he put it, "the people of Spain are seventy-five per cent, or over, members of the church of Rome, and as the religious sentiment of the people of every nation always gives shape and character to government, a fact established beyond question by the history of nations, it is fair to conclude that monarchy is the legitimate outgrowth of Romish faith." On the other hand, he argued, "it is likewise just to conclude that a government by the people and for the people is the legitimate fruit of the Christianity of the Baptists and Protestants, as taught and practiced by our people." Now, with these two nations locked in "mortal combat," McCall believed the time was ripe for a final evaluation of each civilization and the religious principles at their respective foundations: "They stand in comparison; let the comparison be made. On the beautiful island of Cuba, for fifty years civil oppression and military despotism have held its people ground into dust for the aggrandizement of the three favored classes. In America, the masses select and elect the classes—and make them the servants. In Spain the classes make the masses the servants." With the comparison thus drawn, McCall offered the words of Christ as the final arbiter, driving home the last nail: "Whosoever is great among you, let him be your servant."[39]

In this early assessment, McCall foreshadowed the two major claims of the anti-Catholic interpretation of the war: that the character of each nation was the direct product of its predominant religion and that the results of the war would offer a final judgment on the merits of each system. Even more than the benefits of American Protestantism, the debilitating effects of Spanish Catholicism were the subject of choice for many Protestant commentators. "Surely Spain is a fair sample of what Romanism can do for a country," another Baptist editor surmised, "for it has had practically undisputed sway there for centuries, and the people have been remarkably submissive to the priests."[40] This editor and many others were convinced that Spain, more than any other nation, was a case study in the social costs—and inevitable implications—of unfettered Catholic influence. Spain's Catholicism, to these observers, was the primary cause of the nation's disastrous decline.

J. H. Garrison, editor of the prominent Disciples of Christ weekly *Christian Evangelist*, offered one of the most thorough treatments of Catholicism's role in the demise of Spain's civilization. Though Garrison conceded that the present war was between two governments and not two religions per se, he insisted that in its ultimate issues it must be understood in line with the historic contest between Roman Catholicism and Protestantism, what he called "the irrepressible conflict." Each religious division had produced a set of "governments, laws, customs and institutions"; thus embodied, they represented "two distinct kinds of civilization." The fundamental principle of Catholicism, he argued, was a hierarchical structure of God-ordained authority, which played out in civil government led by kings who claim to rule by unimpeachable divine right in the state. Protestantism, on the other hand, rested upon the rights of the individual conscience under God, with authority located in the hands of the people. In civil government, this principle secured the right of the people to select their government officers just as they select their pastors and teachers in their churches. The former theory of government, furthermore, must result in "religious and political slavery," discouraging the "diffusion of knowledge" for fear that it would make the people dissatisfied with their condition. The latter theory, then, depended upon its ability to foster intelligence if the people are to rule themselves well. "There can be no truer test or criterion," Garrison argued, "for judging of the two conceptions of religion than in the kind of civilization which they respectively produce." Spain, he believed, offered a "very good illustration of the outcome of Roman Catholicism as respects human government and civilization," having been "intensely loyal to the Papacy for many centuries." "What Spain is," he continued, "is due to Roman Catholicism. What the United States is, is due to that purer and freer conception of Christianity, known as Protestantism." For this reason, Garrison concluded, the war between these nations could be described as a conflict between competing civilizations, and its issues provided all the evidence necessary to judge the merits of the two. Spain's character was obvious from the conditions in Cuba: "Under Roman Catholic influence Spain has, for centuries, oppressed and despoiled Cuba, and for many years has wasted the island with a cruel and desolating war, butchering and starving innocent women and children and other noncombatants." Now to Cuba's rescue came the United States, "whose constitution, whose freedom, whose resentment against oppression and tyranny, whose unselfish interest in the welfare of others are the results of the Protestant form of Christianity."[41] Garrison's Disciples of Christ colleague at the *Christian Standard* echoed this association between religious principles and the character of nations, with an even greater emphasis on the historical details of Catholicism's detrimental influence on Spanish society. "Spain," he concluded, "is bankrupt, not financially only, but politically, morally, and religiously"; the inquisition, he would argue at great length, was both the primary culprit and the fullest embodiment of Catholic principles. By his reckoning, "none but a nation trained in the schools of tyranny, of bull-baiting, and of the inquisition could fall so far behind our age of civility as Spain has done." On the other hand, he insisted, "no

Protestant nation under heaven would treat a subject people as Spain has treated Cuba."[42]

It was only natural that Baptist and Disciples of Christ partisans should deploy the strongest anti-Catholic rhetoric in explaining the origins of Spanish tyranny. These groups, after all, had long viewed their congregational polity, with its emphasis on local autonomy and governance by the entire congregation, as both the fullest expression of Protestant principles and the closest parallel to the American government they believed Protestantism had inspired. But they were far from alone in their identification of the religious undertones of the conflict and its background. Many Methodists, black and white, shared this view; the editor of the African Methodist Episcopal *Christian Recorder*, for example, called for his church to take the lead "in this holy crusade to rescue Cuba from the thraldom [*sic*] of Romish error and superstition."[43] And, further, one of the earliest commentators to blame Catholicism for Spain's demise was S. J. Humphrey, a contributor to the Congregationalist *Advance*. In an article of April 21, Humphrey presented a long, detailed description of the factors leading to Spain's current crisis, noting all the common features from illiteracy to bullfighting. Undergirding it all, and most responsible for "the evils which have afflicted Spain," was that nation's unmatched faithfulness to Roman Catholicism. "The voice of the Pope is more regnant in Spain to-day than that of all Europe besides," Humphrey argued. "It has had its own way in Spain almost unhindered from the beginning. . . . And the condition of Spain to-day is the finished product of Rome's best work."[44] In almost identical language, then, Protestants like Humphrey and Garrison argued that religious principles must work themselves out in the structures of a wider civilization and that nowhere were the alternate values more clearly displayed than in the contrast between America and Spain.

With the two nations defined as products of their respective religious influences, it took little imagination to view their war as, in the words of the *Baptist and Reflector*, a "war of Christianity" that would exchange "light for darkness, hope for despair, joy for sorrow, freedom for tyranny, civilization for barbarism, and," as if in summary of the foregoing, "a pure Christianity for a corrupt, effete and semi-heathen religion."[45] As if more evidence were required, many looked to the results of the war and to America's early success as a clear referendum on the quality of the divergent civilizations and, perhaps, as an omen portending the demise of Catholicism worldwide. At the very least, some concluded, the war would deal a crippling blow to the interests of Catholicism in the islands, where the church could hardly expect to thrive in a religious free market. "The independence of Cuba," argued the editor of the *Alabama Baptist*, "will sound the knell of Romanism in the island. Of course the Catholics will hold on there, after a fashion, but the keenness of contrast between their views and ours will be made so striking by reason of the enforced contact that Romanism will never again flourish."[46] But others saw even more broad implications in America's likely defeat of this Catholic foe. Arkansas minister J. C. Williams, writing for Louisville's Presbyterian *Christian Observer*, placed the war with Spain at the conclusion of three hundred years of fighting between Protestant and Catholic powers. During that time, he argued, Protestant forces had prevailed in every case, often against great odds. England's clash with the Spanish Armada, Europe's Thirty Years' War, the Glorious Revolution in seventeenth-century England, the defeat of Napoleon's France at Waterloo—all these and more suggested an inevitable trend that, for Williams, found explanation only in the providential purposes of God. Now, he concluded, in the present war "Catholic Spain has lost every battle" and with destruction so great that it had to represent the judgment of God, whose "battle cry is not 'Remember the Maine,' but 'Remember the Inquisition and the *Auto da fe.*'"[47]

If more impassioned than most, Williams was far from alone in viewing every victory over Spain as a God-ordained victory over the Church of Rome.[48] As in Elijah's contest with the prophets of Baal, this war, many believed, pitted Spain's idolatrous prayers to the Virgin Mary against America's prayers to the God of the Protestants, and the results were no less clear than in that battle of old.[49] For these observers, the character of America and the character of Spain flowed directly from their respective commitments to Protestantism and Catholicism. The outcome of this war, at the culmination of three hundred years' development, offered conclusive proof for all who would see that the future, secured by God, belonged to Protestant Christianity. And as a nation governed by the principles of Protestant Christianity, America would lead the nations of the world into that future.

Catholics, Loyalty, and American Identity

Needless to say, this anti-Catholic rhetoric was not lost on America's Catholics, accompanied as it often was by accusations of disloyalty. They had been dealing with Protestant suspicions since the nation's earliest days, and were more often than not kept at arm's length from positions of influence by the fears of those who thought it impossible to be loyal both to Rome and to America. Further, the strong ultramontane impulse within global Catholicism of the late nineteenth century—seen preeminently in Vatican I and the declaration of papal infallibility—had done little to aid the public image of the church in America. Many Catholics were perhaps especially sensitive, though, to these renewed charges, given that the war with Spain began at the high point of a decades-old controversy within Catholic ranks over the proper form of their church in America. Defining the nature of the dispute with any precision is quite difficult. In general, according to the historian Patrick Carey, the American church was divided over the proper view of the "modern age and of how the church should relate to it."[50] But the problem does not seem to have involved any theological or dogmatic accommodation to modernity, at least not of the sort condemned by the *Syllabus of Errors* of Pius IX. Rather, the crux of the matter seems to have centered on how "American" Catholicism should become and *could* become without compromising the faith of the worldwide church.[51]

On one side was the group known as the Americanists, native-born for the most part, most well known in American public life, and best connected within the networks of national influence and power. Led primarily by John Ireland of Saint Paul, prominent Americanists also included John Keane, Denis O'Connell at the North American College in Rome, and sometimes-patron James Cardinal Gibbons of Baltimore. This group, extending the ideas of Orestes Brownson a generation earlier, believed that Catholicism was not only compatible with American values but represented the best embodiment of American cultural and institutional values. According to Michael Zoller, Americanists believed that America was "more than a geographical concept, and even more than a political system, and therefore one became an American by adopting the country's way of life and its fundamental convictions."[52] Ireland, O'Connell, and others embraced the prevalent idea that history was progressive, that a new age was coming to the world, and that America was the fullest incarnation of that new age. Ecclesiologically, this meant that global Catholicism would have to adapt to new world conditions, and, the Americanists hoped, it would fall to the American church to lead the way into the future.[53] Practically, it meant that assimilation within American culture represented an unqualified good, and Americanists tirelessly promoted their principles throughout the church, principles like religious liberty, separation of church and state, greater ecumenical cooperation, and increased individualism and lay initiative.[54]

On the opposite side of the debate were the conservatives and the more recent European immigrants, who remained wary of what they believed to be the spirit behind the appeal for accommodation to modernity. Typically positive in their view of American political institutions and grateful for the religious freedom they enjoyed under the Constitution, this group believed that living peacefully in accord with the nation's laws was all that good citizenship required and that this earned them the right to sustain a distinct Catholic, often ethnic, subculture. On a practical level, their philosophical differences with the Americanists played out in several high-profile disputes over the use of the English language for worship and education, the appropriate method for education, and the relationship of the church to pressing social issues of the day, such as the roles of labor and industry.

Ostensibly, the Spanish-American War was a moment that would belong to the Americanists, an opportunity to affirm both their loyalty to the nation faced with a Catholic enemy and their conviction of the supremacy of American civilization. And many did claim the opportunity. But, perhaps as important, the war showed that by this point the bitter divisions in American Catholicism were not based upon any lack of support for the nation or belief in the superiority of American institutions among the conservatives. The weight of Protestant challenges and the suggestion that Spanish abuses were Catholic abuses fell on all American Catholics equally. Across ecclesiological divisions, they moved quickly to voice their support for the nation even before the war began; for obvious reasons, their commentary tended more toward affirmations of loyalty than that of their Protestant counterparts. But, as the war unfolded, Catholic leaders demonstrated more than simple patriotic loyalty. Many revealed an understanding of the war's significance and of American identity in categories that closely followed the commentary of Protestant leaders, diverging only in their insistence that the great gulf separating American and Spanish civilization was not created by Spain's Catholicism.

American Catholics responded to the *Maine* tragedy in much the same way as other religious folk: they held masses for the dead, they warned against too hastily agitating for war, and they praised McKinley and other public leaders for their patience in the face of growing pressure. But within days of that event and more and more as the chance of war increased, they sought to remove any doubt about their national allegiance. They worked hard to assure the public that their loyalty to America would not be tested by a shared Catholicism with their nation's enemy. "No true American Catholic," argued Archbishop John Ireland in a March 19 interview, "will think of espousing the cause of Spain against that of this country because the former is a Catholic nation." To do so, he insisted, would be un-American and a violation of Catholic principle as well. It would be to "set one's self down as traitorously inclined to the teachings of this religion, as well as to the country which it is his bounden duty to defend against all enemies, both internal as well as external."[55] Many others shared Ireland's sentiments. His fellow archbishop in Oregon, for example, issued a letter in late March to the clergy and laity of his diocese on the subject of possible war. "Should a war break out between our Republic and Spain," he instructed his flock, "we are obliged in conscience to be loyal to the flag—the Stars and Stripes." For now, their duty was to pray for peace, but if war should come, he promised, "we will add our prayers that you may rival the splendid record of loyalty, bravery and heroism which your brethren in the faith have won in other wars of our Republic and that an honorable success will crown the flag of our country once more."[56] Barely three weeks later, war did come. And, for his part, the editor of the *Pilot* pledged that "no patriotic American can have any doubt of his duty to support the government, even to the expenditure of the last dollar and the last drop of blood."[57]

With the beginning of the war, similar letters went out from individual archbishops around the nation. Explaining in detail that Catholic teaching identified service to country with service to God, Archbishop William Henry Elder of Cincinnati insisted it would be sinful for Catholics to do anything less than their full duty in wartime. Elder went on to offer an indulgence of forty days to those who would recite Our Fathers and Hail Marys, asking for guidance for the government, protection for fighting men, and mercy for the souls of those who would die.[58] Bishop Thomas Byrne of Nashville, Tennessee, was even more forceful, insisting that the time was past for individual judgment as to the wisdom or justification of the war. "We are all true Americans," he proclaimed, "and as such loyal to our country and to its flag, and obedient to the highest decrees and the supreme authority of our nation." No longer torn section from section, he continued, "we are united as one man, and we have our faces set as flint against a foreign enemy and a common foe." All that remained, then, was to pray for the safety of those fighting and "to beg the God of battles to crown their arms on land and sea with victory and triumph."[59] By mid-May, the American archbishops and bishops embraced collectively what had begun as the individual initiative of leaders like Byrne and Elder. Together, the group drafted a circular letter calling for loyalty during the war and ordered it read in all churches.[60]

The Catholic response to the war did not end with these expressions of loyalty. Like their Protestant compatriots, Catholic leaders also showed great interest in the broader meaning and historical significance of the conflict, along with its implications for American identity. And, like the Protestants, many framed the war as a clash of two disparate civilizations. Naturally, they argued against identifying Spanish brutality, bigotry, and overall backwardness with the Catholicism of its people. Spain, they believed, had fallen to its present state in spite of its Catholicism, at best by neglecting the church's teachings, at worst by abusing them outright.[61] But, with this crucial qualification in place, some had little problem comparing the character of America and the character of Spain through the prevalent terms of analysis. The Americanist leader Denis O'Connell, writing to Ireland near the end of May, was more explicit than most. The war, he wrote, was about more than Cuba. In its ultimate issues, the war raised the "question of two civilizations. It is the question of all that is old and vile and mean and rotten and cruel and false in Europe against all [that] is free and noble and open and true and humane in America. When Spain is swept of[f] the seas," he continued, "much of the meanness and narrowness of old Europe goes with it to be replaced by the freedom and openness of America." "This," O'Connell concluded, "is God's way of developing the world."[62] Ireland himself, if less willing to criticize Spain as freely as some, nevertheless saw "a providential purpose in this war," a purpose he identified with "the avowed mission of humanity which the country takes to itself."[63] Similarly, one Vicar-General Davis, preaching at the cathedral in Davenport, Iowa, celebrated the "noble purpose" at stake in the war, in which America had claimed the right to "defend the sacred cause of humanity, to rescue the oppressed from the thraldom [*sic*] of tyranny."[64] Here was a familiar perspective on the war, one that matched the most partisan of Protestants. This was a war between the forces of liberty and the forces of tyranny, between an America defined by liberty and an altruistic regard for "humanity" and a Spanish enemy wracked by years of cruelty and unrestrained greed.

In this response to the war, American Catholics moved beyond their differences over the role of the church in modern society, affirming a common commitment to America and to what they believed it represented in the world. As the editor of the *Pilot* noted himself, "whatever differences may exist in the episcopate on matters of ecclesiastical polity, there are and can be none on the question of patriotism."[65] There was perhaps no better example of this common ground than in the nearly identical perspectives voiced by two erstwhile foes in the church controversy: Bishop Bernard McQuaid of Rochester, and Father Sylvester Malone, rector of Brooklyn's Church of Saints Peter and Paul. Both men were long-standing vocal proponents of their respective parties within the church, McQuaid a leader among the conservatives and Malone one of the more radical Americanists. That very year, 1898, their paths crossed directly in a public dispute with roots in the Americanist controversy. Both men had been competing candidates for a position with the board of trustees for the State University of New York when Ireland, claiming an opportunity to spite his rival bishop in his own diocese, lobbied forcefully on Malone's behalf. McQuaid responded by condemning Ireland from the pulpit. As a symptom of the larger crisis in the church, the affair drew interest even in Rome.[66] Yet, ecclesiological differences notwithstanding, Malone and McQuaid responded in kind as the war with Spain took shape.

Aside from Malone's individual reputation as an Americanist, the church he served as rector had a well-earned reputation for its very public patriotism. In fact, it had been known as the "Church of the Flag and the Cross" ever since the Civil War, when, after the assault on Fort Sumter, Malone had raised an American flag underneath the church's cross.[67] A few days after the explosion on board the *Maine*, the priest observed a mass for those who had died. He, like most others, held in tension a desire for peace and calm deliberation along with a resolve to die for country if necessary, as the "true American and Catholic principle."[68] By April 18, Malone was convinced that war was in fact necessary, that it was the inevitable course of action for a nation of America's character confronted with the conditions Spain had imposed in Cuba. "Our country is doing to-day what any Christian country should do," he told his congregation. "The starving of thousands of innocent persons, who are not allowed to help themselves, upon the very threshold of our door is a disgrace to modern civilization. In the interest of humanity, this Government has the right to interfere."[69] With the official beginning of the war, Malone grew even more enthusiastic in his praise of the nation and what he believed it represented. "We cannot be too patriotic," he once again told his people. Spain, claiming to be Catholic, had violated the teachings of the church, both in "her method of government and the wholesale annihilation of her subjects." America, by contrast, "is our country and home and in her institutions we are taught that which sustains everything that is right."[70]

This is precisely the sort of rhetoric one might expect from an Americanist Catholic of Malone's pedigree. What is perhaps more remarkable is how closely Bernard McQuaid echoed his sentiments. In mid-May, a banquet held in honor of the bishop was an occasion for explicit displays of patriotism on every hand. With the banquet hall thoroughly decorated with American flags, those preceding him on the program raised the climate of patriotic celebration to a boiling point before McQuaid even took the stage. In his introduction of the guest of honor, one Bishop Farley turned his attention to America and its nascent war with Spain, claiming that America was "the greatest country that man ever lived for, bled for or died for" and that, as it was "engaged in a deadly struggle, the Catholics of this country will be the first to risk their lives in its defense." Inspired by Farley's words, Archbishop John Ryan of Philadelphia, another prominent conservative, spontaneously rose and began to sing a popular patriotic song, "The Red, White and Blue." "Instantly," wrote one reporter, "every prelate and priest was on his feet, the whole five hundred singing with one heart and one voice."[71] Bishop McQuaid's speech would only intensify that enthusiasm. Claiming a "love of country down to the very marrow of my bones," the bishop offered a contrast between America and Europe of which even the most radical Americanist or Catholic-hating Protestant would have been proud:

> When we find that the principles underlying our government are those which make people great and noble, have we not cause to be proud of this country of ours. The nations of Europe have again and again pointed at us the finger of scorn, and have taken pains to blazon our failings to the world. But we are not looking for lessons from Europe. We want a country unshackled by the chains of European customs.

McQuaid, as surely as Malone, Ireland, or any Southern Baptist, saw in the war a clash of two competing civilizations. With them, he affirmed an America defined by liberty and Christianity opposed by, at worst, tyranny and barbaric cruelty. And, like Malone, he sought through his own patriotism to prove that Catholicism was not the issue. "This nation is now at war, and with a Catholic country," he concluded. "This is our country, and we will stand with it, ready to shed our blood, and the Catholics of the United States will be the first in the struggle."[72]

❖

Among Protestants, the response to the patriotic displays of American Catholics was mixed. Some of the more progressive outlets, particularly in the North, welcomed these sentiments wholeheartedly, celebrated Catholic loyalty, and proved fully willing to distinguish Catholic teaching from the flaws in Spanish national character and policy.[73] Many others were less impressed. Loyalty to Rome, these believed, left no room for loyalty to America. Catholic patriotism, then, could be hardly more than skin deep, rooted in a desire to gain power rather than to bring about Spain's fall.[74] Animosities centuries old were not disappearing anytime soon, and the expansion debate that heated up with the summer months only exacerbated these tensions. Many Catholics would oppose American sovereignty in the former Spanish territories; most, at best, viewed the prospect with suspicion, worried that the nation's policies might aid Protestant missionaries in their attempt to rid the islands of Catholicism. Many Protestants, on the other hand, supported American expansion precisely because they believed the Catholics were right and assumed that American control would mean Protestant advance.

For now, however, the debate over the place of Protestantism and Catholicism in American identity served only to reinforce common convictions about the nature of American national character, regardless of who deserved credit for that character. Ultimately, whether or not Protestants took Catholic patriotism at face value was less important than the fact that, for all their differences, the staunchest Catholic conservative and the most virulent Protestant critic of Romanism defined the identity of their nation in the same basic terms. What set America apart in the minds of its religious leaders, what distinguished their nation from the nations of the world and qualified it for an active messianic role, was its thoroughgoing embodiment of Christian principles. At the core of this identity was a commitment to the sacred liberty of the individual, body and soul. But, more than an ideal, the national embodiment of Christianity involved a disposition to extend the benefits of that ideal to others, especially to people who, like those for whom Christ died, were unable to succeed on their own. "What is a Christian nation," asked the *Outlook*, "except a nation which, in its national capacity, acts upon the principles upon which Christ acted in his individual capacity? A Christian is one who believes that the strong should serve the weak, and the rich the poor, and who acts upon that principle. A Christian nation is a nation which so believes and so acts."[75] A Christian nation, by this definition, was a nation willing to act sacrificially, not just to secure its own interests but, like Christ, for the sake of "humanity." Looking to the war with Spain, and especially by contrasting their nation with their nation's enemy, many religious leaders saw more than sufficient evidence of the American character they had long hoped to attain. By their reckoning, Spain had ruled its colonies for centuries with great brutality, concerned only with how best to exploit available resources for national gain. America, by contrast, was even now sacrificing its own resources, even the lives of its best young men, for the sake of those from whom it stood to receive nothing. America was fit to succeed where Spain had failed.

3

"The Hand of God
in the Nation's Victory"

Providence, American Success, and

the Meaning of National History

When measured against the tone set by Dewey's dramatic victory, the following two months of the war were anticlimactic at best. It is difficult to imagine a military operation less organized or efficient than the American mobilization. As one historian summarized the problem, "the last vestiges of nineteenth-century voluntarism and amateurism collided with an incipient twentieth-century military professionalism, creating confusion, mismanagement, and indeed, at times, comic opera."[1] Logistical problems notwithstanding, for those with fresh memories of the Civil War, this conflict was relatively painless. In fact, the defining feature of the war for those observing from home was the ease and unqualified completeness of the American victory. Not until late June were ground operations of any consequence under way. It was then, during the intense battle for the Cuban city of Santiago, that Theodore Roosevelt and his band of Rough Riders won themselves a secure place in American lore with their charge up the San Juan Heights. Far more consequential, if far less famous, was the naval battle outside Santiago harbor on the morning of July 3. With barely any loss, the Americans destroyed Spain's entire Caribbean fleet and, with that fleet, any hope Spain held for a favorable outcome to the war. By war's end, in mid-August, the Americans had seen merely 345 killed in action.

One of the most important distinguishing marks of the Spanish-American War was this unqualified and unprecedented triumph of the American arms, and, this chapter will argue, the scale of their triumph had tremendous influence

60

over the way many located the meaning and historical significance of the war. America's victories in battle, when read through the long-tenured tradition of what Nicholas Guyatt has called "historical providentialism," provided emphatic validation of the activist slant to the nation's sense of purpose. Following an opening section on contemporary trends in the theology of divine providence, I first chart the course of events on the battlefield, framed by the two naval victories at Manila and Santiago, to show why Christian ministers became convinced that God fought for America and the cause he had ordained. Then, in the second major section, I show that this overwhelming success also inspired a providential reading of all American history, with the Spanish-American War as the inevitable point of culmination. To many, a victory so dramatic in a cause so holy proved that God had developed the nation specifically to give liberty to others.

Providence
in American Theology and Culture

The American propensity to read national events as a record of providential activity owned a long history by 1898, a history well described by Nicholas Guyatt in his *Providence and the Invention of the United States, 1620–1876*.[2] Guyatt suggests a helpful distinction among three forms of providentialism ascendant at various times in American history. Apocalyptic providentialism, or the conviction that God was fulfilling a prophetic drama in history through appointed nations, was especially prominent on both sides of the Atlantic during the early years of British North America, as ministers identified prophecy fulfillments in the minutest details of events from the founding of New England to the English Civil War. Judicial providentialism, the most regularly applied form of providential reasoning, represents the conviction that God judges nations on the virtues of their people, rewarding faithfulness and punishing sin as necessary without reference to some larger scheme. Though never out of vogue, this rhetoric was especially useful in times of great crisis, as when apocalyptic predictions about the English Civil War failed to materialize, or during the lean phases of the Seven Years War, or in the American debate over God's view on slavery. The final form, historical providentialism, Guyatt defines as the "belief that God imagined a special role for certain nations in improving the world and tailored their history to prepare them for the achievement of this mission."[3] Like both apocalyptic and judicial providentialism, historical providentialism emerged from various people at various times throughout the seventeenth and eighteenth centuries in both Britain and America. But Guyatt argues that it rose to special prominence in America during the Revolutionary and early national periods, as the young nation sought to carve out a separate identity from its motherland and a unique historical trajectory traced along the progress of liberty. The Civil War, then, posed a severe test as many in the North and many more in the South abandoned a providential destiny for a united American nation.[4] By Guyatt's account, however, it was precisely historical providentialism that paved the way for national reunion after the war, for by interpreting emancipation as the purging of a national sin and the removal of any threat to America's providential destiny in the world, white Americans North and South could return to focus on that destiny without attention to any further responsibility toward—or role for—the freedpeople.

In the years following the Civil War, Guyatt's historical providentialism, the conviction that God works uniquely through certain nations he has prepared for his purposes, only increased in predominance and proved especially useful for understanding the results of war with Spain. Where providentialism of the judicial and apocalyptic varieties worked best to explain times of national suffering, historical providentialism was perfectly suited to the success Americans enjoyed at century's end. Yet even before the war this form of reasoning rose in popularity with the ascendance of a theological sensibility best known as Protestant modernism.[5] At the heart of this prevalent theological outlook was a deep conviction that God was everywhere immanent in humanity, in nature, and in human history and that the divine character and purposes were best revealed there. In turn, belief in the pervasive presence of God in human society fostered a widespread optimism and confidence in the linear, progressive nature of history, which placed these Protestants comfortably amid the social hopes of the Progressive Era. Seeing God at work in their culture all around them, many believed that the Kingdom of God was coming soon and was coming in this world, not the next.[6]

A by-product of this optimistic perspective on divine immanence was renewed confidence in the ability of humans to discern the providential purposes of God. "More and more," one historian has argued, "it was assumed that man as rational creature could know God's plans not only for individuals and by hindsight, but for the whole world of nations and by foresight."[7] There were differences, admittedly, in the ways these thinkers described the goals toward which God was moving history, but all shared convictions about God's rule over history. And, even more significant, there was agreement about the means by which God would accomplish his providential purposes: nations were the primary individual actors upon which history turned, and America was at the helm of history's forward march.[8] It was in this vein, then, that one minister proclaimed in the midst of the war that "over all races, creeds and sects our

Nation looms as the visible incarnation of the coming Kingdom of God." "The Nation," he argued, "is thus the organ of the common consciousness of God, as well as the visible expression of the divine purpose in history."[9]

At the close of the century, the most convinced of theological modernists did not speak for all Protestants, and in the coming years many would grow very uncomfortable with the implications of theological immanentism, especially with regard to the being and nature of God and the medium of divine revelation. But in the 1890s there was far less obvious division along liberal and conservative lines than there would be after 1910 and in the era of the Scopes Trial. There were important differences among distinct groups of Protestants.[10] But an underlying unity remained in place, evident in personal friendships, ecumenical partnerships, and networks of shared influence. And this unity was more than social. More important, Wacker argues, in the 1890s Protestants across theological lines shared a sense of the pregnancy of this moment for divine activity in the world through the Spirit, and with this sense a strong optimism about the shape of the future.[11]

So, on one hand, when the American military met with unexpected success against Spain in 1898, the moment belonged especially to the most progressive of America's ministers and theologians. Much of the strongest and most specific language about the providential significance of the war appeared in their sermons and columns. But, on the other hand, at least in print, their interpretation of the war went largely unopposed, and they were joined across the board in a Christian consensus that American success, like all of American history, was best understood as a work of God and a sign of divine favor. Though not framed precisely in the convenantal terms of their Puritan forbears, America's path from victory to victory in the war with Spain provided more than sufficient evidence for religious interpreters that God was on their side. Success in battle, then, demonstrated the providential significance of the moment and confirmed God's favor for their newly articulated national mission. Furthermore, inspired by the exigencies of the present and bolstered by confidence in the immanence of God in history and their ability to discern the divine intent, these same interpreters used the issues of the war to open a clear window into the providential meaning of the American past.

"The Stars in Their Courses": Providence and the American Naval Victories

The epic battle of Manila Bay, briefly described in chapter 2, would emerge in American popular imagination as the defining event of the war with Spain. Part of its power derived from the sheer shock with which most Americans greeted the news of their victory. In hindsight, the outcome of the battle is far less surprising. The wisdom of such an attack had been affirmed several years earlier, in a series of strategies for hypothetical war with Spain drawn up by faculty and students at the Naval War College. And, as early as late February 1898, authorities in Washington had ordered George Dewey in Hong Kong to begin preparing an attack on the Philippines in case war should result from the *Maine* disaster. So, when Congress declared war in late April, there was little question that Dewey would make for the archipelago immediately.

Though the scale and the swiftness of the American victory surprised even Dewey, the reasons for the victory are not difficult to identify. Manila Bay was hardly the most advantageous location for the Spanish admiral Patricio Montojo to make his stand against the American attackers. And, resigned to inevitable defeat, he and his fellow commanders had done little of the necessary preparation to protect the fleet by land. By far Montojo's biggest mistake, however, was his failure to position his squadron under the cover of formidable land batteries around the bay, a blunder that, according to the historian David Trask, "deprived Spain of any chance for victory."[12] Hamstrung by these strategic errors, the Spanish fleet was an easy target for the Americans, whose ships were greater in number, in speed, and in technological capability. In fact, Dewey's eight-inch guns allowed his squadron to rain merciless fire on their enemies while remaining, for the most part, beyond the range of Spain's inferior weapons. The result was decisive: where the Spanish fleet was completely destroyed, with 371 of its sailors killed or wounded, damage to the Americans was barely cosmetic.

However understandable the victory appears in historical perspective, nothing had prepared the wider American public or its church leaders for the thrill of this triumph. In one respect, the Philippines had never appeared in the lofty rhetoric justifying the war, where Cuba had been the sole point of reference. Most barely knew the location of the islands, much less anything about their history, topography, or population.[13] More significant, for those who had lived through the Civil War barely thirty years prior, nothing in their experience had led them to expect such an unqualified one-sided victory. In that earlier conflict, more than 620,000 Americans had died through four years of fighting, with an incalculable civilian cost in lives and property.[14] The battle of Manila hardly fit the paradigm for those whose memories of war included the battle for Petersburg, Virginia, where nine months of trench warfare brought more than seventy thousand combined casualties. Some of the many critics of jingoism in the spring of 1898 justified their caution by appealing to the Civil War experience as precedent for the suffering war would bring. The editor of Virginia's *Religious Herald*, for example, aware that his readers "do not need to be told that war is a horrible thing," lamented that the "very earth in all this region 'rings hollow to the foot, It is so full of graves.'" Given their experience, he concluded, "it is not to be wondered at that we should shrink from war."[15] Even though few doubted that American arms would prevail against an obviously weaker foe, Americans expected war to be costly. They expected to feel something of the pain borne by hundreds of thousands of American homes a generation earlier. They expected a long, bloody struggle in the dense jungles of Cuba, where heat and disease would be as formidable as Spanish artillery. What they got, at least initially, was an almost bloodless victory on seas a world away.

For the Christian preachers of 1898, as for their predecessors, providential interpretations of events in war made most sense in the context of the unexpected.[16] From his Plymouth Church pulpit, just after the full weight of the Manila victory had been absorbed, Lyman Abbott voiced the sentiments of many. "I venture to say," Abbott concluded, "that not even in the Old Testament history is there a stronger demonstration of the leading of Divine Providence than that most extraordinary victory at Manila—a fleet wiped out of existence, a country set free, the map of the world changed at a stroke, and not a life lost by the victors."[17] Of all the echoes to Abbott's interpretation, perhaps the most articulate belonged to Robert MacArthur, a Baptist, in his well-traveled "Hand of God" sermon. "It is not too much to say," preached MacArthur, "that no battle was ever fought between the Israelites and the Canaanites, or any other foes of Israel's God and God's Israel, whose history is recorded in the Bible, which gives more marked evidence of God's presence, power and approval than the battle in Manila Bay." MacArthur went on to draw what seemed to many an obvious parallel, a parallel between this battle and what for centuries had been cast as one of the most significant interpositions of providence since the biblical era: the sixteenth-century destruction of the Spanish Armada. As the story had been told, England had little hope for victory when faced with the mightiest navy in the world; as that fleet of Spanish Catholics charged into the English Channel, the fate of the Protestant world hung in the balance. But God himself fought for the English that night, sending a powerful storm that destroyed the entire Armada once and for all. Such was the story as remembered by the Anglo-Saxons, and for MacArthur the comparison was unmistakable: "The glorious battle just fought and the superb victory won at Manila Bay was but the continuation and conclusion of the battle begun by Elizabeth, and thus sublimely completed by the heroic Dewey."[18]

Euphoria from this early victory continued to shape the American psyche in the weeks to follow, but this did not altogether remove concern for what many feared would be a long struggle on the ground in Cuba. In fact, some editors warned their readers not to expect a subsequent victory on the scale of Manila. Dewey's conquest was hailed as unparalleled in naval history, so how could they expect a repeat performance?[19] Events on the ground, furthermore, gave ample reason for concern as May turned to June, for the stellar record of the navy was matched by contrast in the debacle that was the mobilization of the United States Army. Forced to accommodate the enthusiastic throngs who responded to President McKinley's call for volunteers, army leadership proved thoroughly unprepared and, at times, simply incompetent. This was only the beginning of a record of mismanagement so severe as to incur an official investigation by war's end. For now, when compared to the swiftness of Dewey's achievement, the logistical process of organizing, supplying, and transporting tens of thousands of soldiers to Cuba seemed to last an eternity. It would be a full month and a half after the battle in Manila before the first transports set sail for Cuba.

While many remained bottled up at embarkation points in Florida, the first U.S. troops landed at Daiquiri, on Cuba's far southeastern tip, on June 22. They met no initial resistance. Theodore Roosevelt, who had resigned his position as assistant secretary of the navy to help organize an elite volunteer cavalry unit, made sure his band of Rough Riders was among the first to land. They would remain near the front and in the headlines throughout the slow march across the island. The target for this first landing force was the port city of Santiago de Cuba, home to a strategic harbor and a garrison of Spanish troops numbering more than ten thousand. The fiercest fighting of the war centered here, in an outlying village called El Caney and on the hills that provided a key to the city's defense. The battle began on July 1, and through seven hours of conflict American casualties numbered 205 killed and 1,180 wounded. By the end, Roosevelt and the Rough Riders had charged their way up Kettle Hill and into the American pantheon. And, firmly ensconced with the rest of the American forces in the San Juan Heights surrounding the city, they settled in to wait for a Spanish surrender now considered inevitable.

Meanwhile, events of even greater—if less famous—significance were developing in the Caribbean Sea. The whereabouts of the Spanish fleet under the command of Admiral Pascual Cervera had been the chief cause of concern for American commanders throughout the month of May and a source of fear for vulnerable residents along the eastern seaboard. The squadron, last seen leaving the Cape Verde Islands on April 29, was the object of a furious search by the American fleet, a search thwarted time and again by miscalculations and faulty intelligence. Finally, on May 29, a Spanish cruiser was spotted in the bay off Santiago. Within twenty-four hours the entire American fleet, under the command of Admiral William Sampson, had the Spanish squadron bottled up in the harbor. The U.S. ships dropped anchor and waited roughly a month for their Spanish counterparts to act. And so the stage was set for the second major naval victory of the war, yet another sabbath rout.

On the morning of July 3, the Spanish fleet found itself surrounded, with American land forces just beyond the city and the navy guarding the open seas. Now pressed in on all sides, Cervera decided to make a desperate run for open waters in broad daylight; the Americans waiting at the harbor entrance were not fooled. The wooden ships in the Spanish fleet were fast but outdated and thoroughly overmatched. One by one the American ships ran them down, a debacle so complete that even the American sailors sympathized with their dying enemies. Within four hours, all six of the Spanish ships were destroyed; of their 2,227 men, 323 were killed and 151 wounded. Only one American sailor died, and not a ship was lost. The battle left Spain with no navy, its remaining ground forces starving and surrounded. Though there would be further skirmishes and the war would officially stretch on for another month, few could miss the obvious meaning of these events: Spain's last sliver of hope had sunk with its ships. The war was over.[20]

For America's religious leaders, a deeper meaning was no less visible. The providential favor that they had described as the controlling theme of American history was never more clearly demonstrated than in this battle. "We predict that this is the most remarkable naval conflict as to results that will ever be fought," wrote the editor of the *Alabama Baptist*.[21] The *United Presbyterian* joined in this assessment, insisting that, along with Dewey's victory at Manila, "our naval record in this war is without parallel in history." And, as in the response to that earlier triumph, parallels to the defeat of the Spanish Armada proved irresistible: "we recognize the hand of God as clearly and as effectively as in the destruction of the Spanish Armada of 1588."[22] Tracing this "hand of God" was the task of column after column in the immediate and overwhelming response to the battle.

Following interpreters of all great victories before them, many saw the hand of God in the details of the battle, fixating on events beyond human control that broke invariably toward the Americans.[23] Superior resources and weaponry, themselves gifts of God, could not explain the scale of the one-sided destruction. It appeared as if even "the stars in their courses fought against Cervera."[24] The *Outlook* argued from history that "the unknown element in war has been on the side of righteousness." Here, the editor insisted, though any number of twists or turns could have thwarted America's best efforts, "events wholly beyond our control have co-operated with us."[25] The *Christian Observer* put the event in biblical and historical context, noting from Old Testament examples that in Israel's great victories God orchestrated the course of events specifically to demonstrate that he, not Israel's military prowess, was the source of Israel's success.[26]

If some looked to the specific details of the battle, others found evidence of providential favor in the scale of American success broadly construed. In its typical way, the *Outlook* saw proof that—Spanish courage notwithstanding—the sixteenth century was no match for the nineteenth. But there was a deeper meaning. "Never in the history of the world have two such naval victories been won as those at Manila and Santiago; never was destruction so complete accomplished with so slight injury to the destroyer." What could a victory so complete indicate if not that God fought for the Americans? Or, as this column more eloquently put it, "The prophetic vision which saw God's guardianship in Gideon's warfare or in Israel's emancipation may well believe that Manila and Santiago have emphasized divine approval of America's mission by the preternatural victory of America's arms."[27] Even the Texas *Baptist Standard*, whose editor had remained cool toward the war from the beginning, could not deny the meaning of these events. A victory such as this must represent divine providence writing "its fiat on the broad face of the world's destiny."[28]

These seers of divine activity found a welcome ally in President William McKinley. Just days after the battle, the president returned to a time-honored tradition and declared a national day of thanksgiving. Fulfilling an almost priestly role, McKinley issued a Thanksgiving Proclamation explicitly affirming divine providence as the key to American success. He urged

> the people of the United States, upon next assembling for divine worship in their respective places of meeting, to offer thanksgiving to Almighty God, who, in His inscrutable ways, now leading our hosts upon the waters to unscathed triumph, now guiding them in a strange land through the dread shadows of death to success, even though at a fearful cost, now bearing them without accident or loss to far distant climes, has watched over our cause and brought nearer the success of the right and the attainment of just and honorable peace.[29]

Support for McKinley's proclamation poured immediately from the press, which typically hailed it as a display of a "higher plane of Christian patriotism" in its humble recognition of God as the giver of victory.[30] Along with his proclamation, McKinley called on churches to set aside Sunday, July 10, for special thanksgiving services. Ministers and congregations all across the country—both Protestant and Catholic—wholeheartedly complied. The services included public readings of the proclamation, plenty of patriotic music, and sermons interpreting the significance of the nation and its victory; flags draped the churches and even some pulpits.[31]

Sermons preached that Sunday echoed many themes familiar since the beginning of the war, contrasting American and Spanish civilization, barbarism and liberty, progress and decline.[32] But perhaps the strongest theme in these thanksgiving sermons was the nation's providential destiny as confirmed in the climactic defeat of Spain.[33] No sermon more prominently features or more fully illustrates this theme than that given by a naval chaplain on board one of the victorious ships in the Caribbean fleet. Chaplain Roswell Randall Hoes of the *Iowa* entitled his sermon "God's Hand at Santiago," leaving little doubt about its trajectory. He wasted no time in making his point: "officers and men in the naval service of a Christian land" should remember "that it was the 'right hand' and the 'holy arm' of Almighty God that gave us this marvellous victory." The course of this battle was not random, he continued, and, like all of history in war and in peace, it represents "the unfolding of God's plans for the government of the universe. Events do not come to pass through blind chance or accident. There is an intelligent purpose that marks all the events of history, and guides the destinies of the human race." Sometimes, Hoes argued, God chooses to use human instruments to carry out his designs, and those who would trace the hand of God in this war must conclude that here God was using America to punish Spain for its crimes. Like so many others, he was especially impressed by the disparity in losses by the two sides in a battle he considered "unique in the naval battles of the world," a disparity unexplainable from "any human point of view" that points only to the "protecting arm of the Almighty." Noting all the remarkable facts of the case, Hoes offered a bold conclusion, remarkable for its intensity but typical in its sentiment: "With all reverence we conscientiously believe that the voice of our guns was the voice of God, and that the awful message uttered was in condemnation of Spanish oppression and cruelty, and a punishment for crimes that have left many indelible stains on the pages of history. Comrades, the Lord of Hosts hath done it!"[34] Of course, given the framing of the war by Hoes and so many others, any condemnation of Spain was at the same time a celebration of America. In the providence of God, they believed, when one nation falls, another rises to take its place.

Many American Catholics located the purposes of God at Santiago in precisely the same way. Preaching in response to the president's call at his cathedral in Saint Paul, Americanist Archbishop John Ireland offered one of the more celebrated reflections on providence, the American victory, and the divine mission of the nation. Ireland began with a show of gratitude to President McKinley, a personal friend, for his pious recognition that "there is a supreme power holding in His hand the destinies of nations and disposing of those nations for His own designs, even beyond the power and valor of their armies and their navies." The same God who created the world, Ireland went on, had not left his handiwork to blind material forces but continued to rule over individuals and nations alike, guiding them all according to his designs. This fact—and this fact alone—could explain the success Americans now enjoyed: "As the great nations of antiquity rose and triumphed under His hand, so today under His hand America triumphs and America moves forward into a new era of greatness, into new possibilities of good for her citizens, for the world at large. Results often come when not foreseen by the human actors who are the instruments, the occasions of the working out of God's great purposes." As he was unwavering in his conviction that God had given greatness to America, so Ireland was certain about why providence had "willed that she conquer." God, he believed, was here advancing his age-old plan for the evolution of humanity, with America as his chosen instrument. "Why has God given to us victory and greatness?" he asked. "It is that Almighty God has assigned to this Republic the mission of putting before the world the ideal of popular liberty, the ideal of the high elevation of all humanity."[35]

Providence, the War, and the Trajectory of American History

Church leaders across the country thus attributed the scale of American success to the handiwork of God, but, as Ireland's sermon illustrates, their interpretations of the providential significance of the moment did not end with that simple acknowledgment. They were even more interested in why God had shown himself strong to save. Inspired by clear, concrete divine activity, many turned to consider what God was seeking to accomplish in the world and how the events of the present could illuminate the meaning of their national past. Even for a people long predisposed to recognize the distinguishing marks of providence in their history, the remarkable events of the war—an indisputable record of providential activity—convinced many that something new, dramatic, even epochal was afoot. Appeals to the past and the workings of providence differed from the Puritan models of two centuries earlier. Those forbears had called hearers back to a mythic past as ideal, a time when founders ruled over holy societies that embodied divine principles more than any community before or since.[36] In 1898, interpreters viewed the Spanish-American War as their primary reference point, explaining the meaning of the past along a progressive continuum leading to this more glorious present and a still untold future, from infancy to adulthood, from isolation to world power, from liberty as possession to liberty as gift. Beginning in earnest around Memorial Day (or Decoration Day, as it was then sometimes called) and culminating with the Fourth of July and the special thanksgiving celebrations, many ministers and editors framed the war in light of American history as evidence of the nation's rise to adulthood. If most agreed that this war represented an unprecedented example of national altruism, a first of its kind in history, they also agreed that it was specifically consistent with the character of the nation as it had developed over the course of America's short life. In this rendering of the nation's story, the Spanish-American War served as the dramatic culminating chapter. The dominant category was national maturity, often labeled manhood, and the guiding theme was a divine providence that had shepherded America from infancy to adulthood for a specific world mission.[37]

On the evening of May 22, Philadelphia minister Stephen Dana addressed his congregation, the Walnut Street Presbyterian Church, with a sermon titled "Our New Place among the Nations." For his text Dana chose Galatians 3:8, "In Thee shall all nations be blessed." Given text and title, it should come as little surprise that the sermon itself was an extended reflection on the implications of the young war for America's role in the purposes of God. "We are making history most rapidly," Dana began, and "it is for us to interpret the spirit and philosophy of this history, if we can." "We believe that God has been behind the great movements of the centuries," he continued, with the rise and fall of all nations corresponding to God's providential design. God remains at work today, and if this war shows anything, it is that America is on the rise beyond the point of return: "the brilliant and marvelous victory of Commodore Dewey and his brave companions in the far-off Pacific has most unexpectedly thrust us into the family of nations in a way never known in the past. Whether we like it or not . . . we can no more go back as a nation to where we were thirty days ago than we can control the tides of the sea." Dana insisted that his duty was to interpret and apply the "Christian meaning" of these irreversible events.

First, Dana located the significance of the war in contrast to America's traditional foreign policy, a policy guided by the advice offered by George Washington in his Farewell Address to avoid entanglements abroad and maintain international isolation. Washington's counsel was wise, Dana conceded, in the "days of our infancy." But, though we should honor the memory of Washington, "we would really dishonor him if we assume that he would give the same advice and pursue the same methods if alive now that he did one hundred years ago." Thirteen small and isolated states had now developed into "one of the first powers of the world," and that power must be used responsibly: "As Christians we know it must be consecrated power, if we work out the high purposes of the living God." Those purposes of God, for Dana, were no less clear: to use America's newfound influence in the world for good, by taking the liberty that Americans enjoyed and giving it to others. Quoting an unnamed author, Dana effectively summarized the shift in America's world purpose: "Our institutions, our freedom have been a lesson to the world, and such liberty is the world's only hope. It is our duty to help the world to such liberty; not to stand behind safe ramparts and give them worthless moral sympathy, but to take part in bestowing human rights on human beings."[38]

Dana's sermon succinctly captures the dominant motif reflected broadly in the religious commentary at this phase of the war: that America had now passed from infancy to adulthood. The sermon also illustrates the two inseparable categories through which many analyzed this overarching narrative of progress. First, America had moved from isolation to world power, to be used by God for the good of the world. The significance of the moment, realized by Dana and many others, appeared most clearly by contrast with America's traditional foreign policy, guided to this point by Washington's counsel and by the Monroe Doctrine. And, second, Dana's sermon captured the operating principle that was to control the exercise of America's newfound power: having developed and perfected liberty at home, the nation would now extend that liberty to others.

From Isolation to World Power

Memorial Day provided a timely occasion for reflection on the meaning of the nation's history. Churches in Dana's Philadelphia joined others across the country in special services of preaching and prayer for the nation and its military.[39] In fact, Philadelphia's First Presbyterian Church hosted a Memorial Day "Union Service" with a program that included ministers from the city's Episcopal, Methodist, Lutheran, Baptist, and Presbyterian churches. The several prayers and addresses sounded familiar notes of patriotism and support for the nation's holy cause, but the overarching sense was that America faced a new and uncertain future role, a role in which it must rely on the same providential guidance that had stabilized its past. Episcopal bishop Ozi Whitaker struck this theme in the opening address. They had come together in prayer to face the future in light of the past, he began, "believing in God, believing that he hears and answers prayer, believing that it is through his guidance and support that this nation has come to the happy condition to which it has attained,—in that faith we come together to pray for his continued blessing and direction." From there Whitaker evoked scenes from the nation's history, especially those centered in Philadelphia, recalling in particular the constitutional convention, in which Benjamin Franklin famously called for daily prayer in the assembly. It was the spirit of Franklin, a spirit of trust in God's guidance, that was most necessary for the nation in its current crisis.[40]

Southerners, just like northerners, claimed the holiday for reflection on providence in America's historical development. The Southern Baptist minister B. H. Carroll, for example, was invited to address a joint memorial service for Union and Confederate veterans in Waco, Texas. Carroll's sermon, on the promise in Ecclesiastes of a "time to heal," focused mostly on the reasons North and South now joined together again. But along the way he charted the many deliverances of providence that had secured the nation's success, culminating in the war with Spain. God had preserved Virginia for British settlement by leading Columbus toward Cuba with a flock of pigeons; he preserved New England during Queen Anne's War by destroying a mighty French fleet in a storm, in direct response to the prayers of his people; he protected the fragile Continental Army after the battle at Cowpens by flooding a river. "All through the past," Carroll concluded, "providences of this kind indicate that Almighty God had a high purpose in view concerning this nation." And so he came to the war with Spain. Not only had the "thunder of Dewey's guns in Manila harbor" driven away "echoes of the guns . . . of the Civil War"; the war itself marked the urging of providence beyond the national boundaries that had sheltered the infant nation in its time of isolation. For years, Carroll argued, as Cuba's oppression continued, the United States had played the role of Saul holding the coats of those who stoned Stephen. Now, he continued, that time was past: "Looking at the government of God as manifested in national development, it seems to me—I do not speak dogmatically, nor presumptuously, but from conviction based upon a profound study of history all my life—that the trend of events, the indications of divine providence, the natural expansion of our national life, call for enlargement beyond the barriers that shut in the sight of our fathers when they occupied a narrow strip on the Atlantic seaboard." Whether this expansion would involve permanently retaining conquered territories was a debate that would continue for months; for now, Carroll simply acknowledged that America had emerged once and for all as a force on the world stage.

His reasons were principled as well as historical: "God raises up no nation for itself. He did not guide ancient Israel through the wilderness because it per se was a great people. When he fenced Israel about, when the pillar of cloud by

day and of fire by night preceded its march or overshadowed its camp, it was
not because of any special excellency in them, but God was using them as the
depositary of great and widely diffusive principles, which must be circulated
and propagated in order to the well-being of not one nation alone, but of all
people." All events of history, America's as well as the world's, are guided by
God's purposes toward the great time of peace when Messiah shall reign, Carroll
insisted. Given that larger perspective and the trajectory along which God's
providence had matured the nation from its inception, continued isolation was
impossible. "How can a mighty nation like this live apart from the divine in-
tentions and circumscribe according to its own option the development of its
being?" Carroll concluded, "The Lord God omnipotent reigneth, and no matter
what traditions beguiled the fancies of our fathers, no matter what things
conduce to our own ease and peace, high above all is the destiny which God,
who planted this American people upon this great strategical point of the
globe's surface, and gave it dynamic influence, and power, appointed not for
itself alone, but for the whole wide world."[41]

From late May through early June, the religious press echoed these sentiments from the pulpits. Editor after editor proclaimed the dawn of a "new
national era."[42] Though articles were usually less detailed than the sermons in
tracing the events of history along a continuum of growth, their language of
"maturity" or "manhood" describing the America of the present implied the
same passage from the infancy of isolation and seclusion to a new status as
world power. Some, like New York's Methodist *Christian Advocate*, were more
critical, rightly seeing in this rhetoric an early foundation for retention of territory in Philippines.[43] But more typical was *Zion's Herald*, the *Christian Advocate*'s
Methodist counterpart in Boston. While warning against a loss of national
purity and righteousness in the lust for world conquest, a June 1 column celebrated America's emergence from the era of Monroe and Washington into a
new sphere of international influence as a nation come of age.[44] That same
day, the Congregationalist *Pacific* proclaimed gladly, "Our nation is no longer a
child. Let us, then, take our rightful place among the great powers of the world,
and announce our intention of doing in every part of the world those things
which will tend to the advancement of mankind."[45] The *United Presbyterian*
captured this general consensus as well as anyone in a June column surveying
the significance of the war on the whole. This was a new kind of war, the editor
explained, beyond American coasts but not a war of aggression, territorial
conquest, or defense. True to the "spirit of our institutions," this war on behalf
of the oppressed represented a long-developing national consciousness now
fully displayed. In short, "by virtue of our growth, we have become a missionary

nation; we stand, the world over, as the embodiment of the idea of freedom, and as the messenger of freedom to all others. We have recognized our mission, to stand for right, and to protect the oppressed."[46]

Liberty Gained, Liberty Purified, Liberty Given

This bold claim by the *United Presbyterian* represents an important facet of the wide reflection on American "growth" from isolation to world power: it was never far removed from more precise definitions of the way in which the "missionary nation" would use its newfound power. Perhaps no one described this vision more clearly than Thomas Dixon, a New York minister and founding pastor of an independent liberal congregation called the People's Church. A quintessential example of the Protestant modernism then in fashion, the church listed among its core principles the immanence of God in the world, the non-existence of any separate "secular" world, the church as a means toward the establishment of God's kingdom rather than an end, and the conviction that "religion has to do with this world not the next."[47] Moreover, it identified the sacrificial love of the incarnate Christ as the only suitable operating principle for individual and society alike. Dixon, for his part, was convinced that the nation as the "visible incarnation of the coming Kingdom of God" represented the "one organ through which we all seek justice and right."[48] If nations broadly conceived were to play a central role in establishing the divine purposes, the war with Spain only reinforced Dixon's confidence in the centrality of America in particular to God's kingdom on earth.

This was the subject of a jubilant Fourth of July sermon in which he drew a direct analogy between the developing consciousness of a maturing individual and that of a maturing nation. Children, he argued, were little more than animals, thoroughly centered on themselves and their own needs. To become an adult was more than a physical process; it was an expansion of soul, a developing interest in the needs of one's fellows. "Such," Dixon suggested, "is the evolution of nations and peoples. We have passed through our childhood isolation, our childhood selfishness." Here, now, in this war, Dixon believed, "we have awakened to-day to a glorious manhood with the consciousness of a soul. Our principles are the same, but we have enlarged the sphere of their application. We have gone outside of self, and have applied these principles to our neighbors." Coming into adulthood as a nation, in his opinion, rendered further isolation impossible because maturity was defined by concern for the interests of others, by the application of the Christ-ethic to national policy. America, at last, had recognized this, and so, on this holiday memorializing the birth of the nation, it could celebrate the "beginning of the new national manhood." In Cuba and in the Philippines, Dixon argued, American fighting men were "struggling to give the blessings and privileges of our flag to the world, and to make that flag a heritage to our neighbors. Never before were men who entered battle more deeply conscious of a divine mission." Taking up such a mission, he concluded, "our flag has ceased to be merely national; its cause is the cause of humanity; its progress marks the footprint of God."[49]

One week later, after the victory at Santiago de Cuba, Dixon and the People's Church recognized the president's call for national thanksgiving, a call in which Dixon believed the president was speaking "under the guidance of the Holy Spirit." In this sermon, even more than in his Fourth of July oration, he connected the significance of the American triumph to the nation's long record of providential blessing. This record of blessing, he believed, demonstrated that America more than any other nation had aligned its values with the will of the true God. History, he believed, offered ample "evidence that as a nation we are so close to His divine purpose." The founding principles of the republic, in Dixon's view, marked the clear inspiration of the Holy Spirit, and the odds against American success in the conflict with the mother country would have been insurmountable absent divine intervention. Thus, he argued, "our early history is the story of the providence of God." The Civil War, then, represented the "supreme test" imposed by God. "The nation," perpetuating the institution of slavery, "had sinned against its own life, and its God." And yet through the fire God had resurrected America to new life, "to solidarity, nationality, fraternity." Now, in the war with Spain, the providential favor of God was marked yet again, as an inexperienced, poorly armed force in an unknown country marched from victory unto victory in the cause of humanity. "Well may the nation uncover its head," Dixon concluded, "and give thanks to God."[50]

As Dixon's sermons illustrate, by mid-July descriptions of the guiding principles for American power and their process of evolution followed a specific narrative trajectory. America in its infancy, under God's protecting providence, had secured and perfected an unprecedented form of civil and religious liberty, the hope of earth through the example its government provided. Now brought by its own organic development and by the course of events into adulthood, the nation stood ready to extend its prized liberty to others. No device was more commonly used to trace this outline of the nation's history than a connection of the American Revolution, the Civil War, and the Spanish-American War as the definitive moments of American history, much as Dixon had suggested in his thanksgiving sermon. Inspired too by Memorial Day and Fourth of July festivities, references to these three wars were rather widespread and, admittedly, not all focused on the same themes.[51] But there was a more common narrative. Here the Revolution always represented the birth of liberty. The Civil War represented the refinement of American liberty, proving that such a government or union could survive. For some northern commentators it represented atonement and purification for the national sin of slavery. But for clergy North and South, the Civil War was a redemptive event consistent with the providential development of the nation, a reification of the values that would be America's gift to the world. The Spanish-American War, then, represented a remarkable culmination: having solidified God-honoring liberty itself, America stood ready to give it to others.[52]

Just a week before Memorial Day, the Reverend Horace Mann of Albany's First Christian Church preached a rousing sermon celebrating America's cause of "pure humanity to down-trodden Cuba." Mann insisted that this war was "more righteous" even than the War of Independence or the Civil War. The latter conflict, for example, was surely righteous, but it was brought on "by our selfishness in trying to keep in slavery a portion of our nation." The war with Spain was "more righteous than that conflict, for the civil war was wholly for America. It was for our gain that the dark blot be erased." Now America stood to gain nothing, Mann argued. Here "we purpose to benefit our neighbors to our present loss."[53] Around this same time Mann's Congregationalist colleagues in Boston celebrated a flag raising at their new Congregational House on Beacon Street. One speaker, echoing the theme of Mann's sermon, suggested a symbolic connection between the three colors of the flag and the purposes of America's three wars. Americans fought first for liberty, then for unity. Now the nation had gone to war for humanity.[54]

Perhaps the most prominent advocate of this perspective on American history, Lyman Abbott, had been reflecting on the significance of America's three wars since early May, both from his pulpit and from the columns of the *Outlook*.[55] The fullest account appeared in a May 28 column titled "The New Duties of the New Hour." The column celebrated America as come of age, concluding that the events of the past months "constitute a summons from the God of nations to this Nation to take its place in the world's councils, and share with other nations in responsibility for the world's well-being." This thesis then unfolded with a thorough interpretation of the nation's historical development, divided into four epochs. First was colonial childhood under the protection of Great Britain; America then secured its own liberty and independence during the Revolution, the second epoch. In the third epoch, the nation had to demonstrate its worthiness of the blessing of liberty and independence by purging slavery from its midst during the Civil War. America had now entered a fourth and final epoch, "perhaps the most significant of all." "Having proved our capacity for freedom by self-emancipation," the editor continued, "and our right to freedom by our emancipation of a subject race, we now have laid on us the responsibilities of freedom, in a call to take our place as a witness to and a defender of freedom among the nations of the earth." Here he spoke for many others when he read in the nation's experience past and present a clear commission from God: "We have been called on this side of the globe, we have been forced on the other, to a crusade which, in its divine meaning and scope, can signify nothing less than justice and liberty to the oppressed."[56]

The Presbyterian John Mayhew Fulton, like Abbott, had little doubt about the significance of America's conflict with Spain. In his Memorial Day sermon, Fulton had laid out in detail a providential reading of world history cast in terms of the advance of liberty through use of the sword. Drawing examples from biblical history and early Christian expansion as well as from the Magna Carta and the Puritan settlement in the New World, Fulton predictably reached his zenith with America and its Revolutionary and Civil Wars. With the Civil War in particular "the great purpose of God that had been running and growing thro. [*sic*] the centuries stood at last consummated! To every member in the Brotherhood of man should forever be guaranteed equal rights and privileges before the laws of our land."[57] It was one month later, in his Fourth of July sermon, that Fulton more fully incorporated the Spanish-American War into this perspective on American history. Following typical lines for interpreting the war and its significance, he focused on the nation's selfless willingness to go to war on behalf of others. In the Revolution and the Civil War, he argued, Americans had shown themselves willing to fight for human rights; the war with Spain to end Cuba's oppression was a logical next step. It was but a culmination of America's unique role in God's providential extension of liberty to all.[58]

By the time Fulton gave this Independence Day sermon, battle lines were already being drawn over the prospect of national expansion. Nonetheless, the strong consensus on the significance of this war in light of American history held true. On one hand, the anti-imperialist *Christian Advocate* founded its warning against those drunk with "broad visions of expansion" by appealing to the principles for which the nation had fought in 1776 and in 1861 and for which it was now fighting in 1898. Americans fought now as then "not for conquest, but to help Cuba to find the freedom which our fathers—with foreign aid—secured for us."[59] On the other hand, the pro-expansion *Independent* celebrated "The New Duties of Patriotism" in light of America's triumphs in the Revolution and in the Civil War. The quest for liberty marked by those struggles had now culminated in the Spanish-American War; Americans fought now so that "other struggling peoples, ground under the heel of tyranny, may be as free as ourselves."[60] This was a narrative that could be used to different ends, but on the meaning of the nation's history and on the significance of this war within that history there remained strong agreement. This was a coming-of-age story that turned on the progress of liberty. Having nurtured a tenuous freedom in infancy and having refined it through a difficult adolescence, a mature America led by the providence of God now embraced a responsibility to extend that freedom to others.

❧

After the naval battle at Santiago, the last remaining military event of any significance was the official surrender of the city, which occurred with barely a skirmish less than three weeks later. Meanwhile, for a time, many of America's religious turned toward Nashville and the national meeting of the Christian Endeavor convention. Reported on widely and in great detail throughout the religious press, the meeting had a dominant patriotic flavor in numerous addresses, most notably a rendition of Robert MacArthur's "Hand of God" sermon.[61]

Editors, too, continued expounding familiar themes on the meaning of the war, its cause, and its implications as a capstone for America's history.[62] The *United Presbyterian* spoke to both the good ends God had effected through the war and to the meaning of the American motives and their success. A July 28 column, reflecting on "Our New Place in the World," began its tale with early American history and the young nation's initial desire for isolation. Now, "as in a moment, all is changed," and changed not because the nation had moved beyond the purity of its earlier years and into the greed or pride of its European predecessors. Rather, the national course had changed because "we were deeply moved by the cry of a suffering people near to our coast." "They were not a people for whom we had admiration," the article continued, "to whom we were bound by race ties or to whom we were under obligations other than those common to humanity." In short, "they were our neighbors." The remainder of the editorial charted the dramatic course of the war, which had left the nation in an entirely "new position" and with a new sense of purpose that would certainly outlive the war itself. Far removed from the isolation of its youth, America had entered uncharted waters with confidence in the goodness of an all-seeing providence: "we are the defender of the oppressed beyond our own territory; we have intervened in the internal administration of the affairs of another nation, and there is nothing in the nature of the case to limit the application of the principle involved to the present emergency. . . . We have come to our maturity and take our place as a power, and we do so, not in the spirit of conquest or aggrandizement, but for humanity and right, for God and his truth as the rights of men."[63]

As the fighting drew to a close, this article returned to the very themes that had guided interpretation of the war from the beginning: America, pure and humanitarian in motivation, protected now as always by the providence of God. Perhaps nothing served to crystallize this reading of events more widely or more clearly than the words and actions of one of the war's most celebrated heroes. Captain J. W. Philip was in command of the battleship *Texas* during the July 3 naval battle at Santiago. On the surface, his performance in the battle was entirely unexceptional; there was no reference to remarkable bravery or any action that had a direct impact on the course of the battle. It was rather two statements immediately following the victory that won him praise in articles, sermons, and even poems all across the country, as well as in numerous histories of the war published over the next several years.[64] First, as the *Texas* drew alongside one of the sinking Spanish ships, the crew members understandably shouted with joy over their triumph. But, seeing the plight of the Spanish sailors, Philip had commented simply, "Don't cheer, the poor devils are dying." Second, at the end of the battle, the captain assembled his crew on the ship's deck and solemnly acknowledged God as the giver of victory. He declared, "I wish to make confession that I have implicit faith in God and in the officers and crew of the Texas, but my faith in you is secondary only to my faith in God. We have seen what He has done for us, in allowing us to achieve so great a victory, and I want to ask you all, or at least every man who has no scruples, to uncover his head with me and silently offer a word of thanks to God for his goodness toward us all."[65] It is nearly impossible to explain Philip's immense popularity, his almost universal acclaim, without concluding that he served as a type of the true Christian, American warrior.

For so many, his simple words captured the humanitarianism and the faith in providence that made America what it was. His first statement confirmed that humanity, not vengeance, lay behind the American cause. The *Congregationalist*, like many others, ran a lengthy article that paid close attention to Philip's background and career, taking special pride in identifying the hero as a Congregationalist. But some of its strongest praise was reserved for his sympathy with the dying Spaniards. His sympathy, so this writer argued, represents "humanity at its highest. It is the Christ spirit displayed in war."[66] This typical celebration of Philip's humanity fit within a larger context of reflection on the contrast between the humane treatment of the vanquished Spanish by the Americans and the actions of the Cuban insurgents, who were cast as barbaric. Where the Cubans sought to kill surrendering Spanish soldiers, the Americans not only preserved their lives but paid for their return to Spain. America, like Captain Philip, displayed what the *Churchman* called the "Magnanimity of Strength."[67] From this common perspective, by showing the same selfless sympathy for the Spanish that they had shown toward the plight of the Cubans themselves, the Americans in victory proved the true character from which they had been fighting all along, not vengeance but humanity.[68]

Even more than his humane words, it was Philip's simple faith in providence and his thanksgiving for the victory that featured most prominently in the many accounts of his heroism. The symbolic function of Philip's confession is best captured in an article written for the *Methodist Review* of the Methodist Episcopal Church, South, by the Reverend George Winton. Titled "Was the War Providential?," the article took a broad retrospective view of the war, its causes, and its events. The battle for Santiago was especially important in shaping the public interpretation of the war, Winton argued, for here "the impression of providential leading was deepened. There was a sort of awe in the presence of these stupendous successes. It was not the fact of victory that caused it, for that was expected; it was the unexampled manner of the victory." Nothing captured the public sentiment in response to the dramatic victory better than Captain Philip's words, Winton continued. In fact, it was as if Philip had spoken for the nation: "All felt that when Captain Philip bared his head among his begrimed and perspiring sailors to make confession of his faith, he was but obeying a universal impulse and voicing a universal sentiment. The tremendous sway of this conviction among the American people is a phenomenon to be reckoned with quite apart from any opinion as to its soundness. It prepared them to accept the results of the war in the same way that they had already accepted the war itself, as manifest destiny."[69]

With remarkable prescience, Winton recognized the substantial implications of widespread confidence in America's providential destiny. After a few brief skirmishes in Cuba, Puerto Rico, and the Philippines, the war effectively decided on the waters off Santiago July 3 came to an official end with a peace protocol signed August 12. The following months would be devoted to one all-consuming question: what was America to do with the liberated territories? As Winton's assessment of the response to Captain Philip indicates, this was a question many Americans were prepared to answer. They were prepared by pervasive assessments of the meaning of their national history offered in light of their experience in the war. Success at Santiago, the exploits of Captain Philip, even the war itself—all made sense when viewed in the context of America's long tradition of historical providentialism. America, providentially developed as liberty's incubator, had now been clearly—supernaturally—launched to world supremacy. How could such a nation, guarded as ever by divine favor, fail to execute its new duties? How could a nation made of brave citizens like Captain Philip, humanitarian and confident in divine providence, fail to benefit all it touched?

4

To Anglo-Saxonize the World

Racial Providentialism and
the American Mission

George Winton's confidence in America's God-ordained, messianic destiny rested on more than the nation's remarkable success in battle. There was another crucial dimension to the war and its results to which his article turned in its conclusion. By this war, he believed, God had drawn together Anglo-Saxons at home and abroad. In fact, Winton suggested, "there are those who will say that the war is worth all that it has cost if as a result of it the North and the South are once more bound indissolubly together, and motherland and daughter have clasped each other across the seas in the embrace of final reconciliation." For Winton, this racial reunion suggested a providential purpose just as clearly as the victories at Manila and Santiago:

> For myself, believing as I do that the drawing together of England and America portends the spread of that type of civilization and religion which for a lack of a better name we call Anglo-Saxon, and which hinges on the liberty, development, and salvation of the individual man, white, brown, or black, I hail it with all my heart. The mission which promises to call it into being seems to me the very noblest possible vocation for a race, and the splendid achievements of the Anglo-Saxon in the past are a fit preparation for the innumerable and stubborn difficulties which beset the pathway to this new goal.[1]

The providentialism through which many Christians viewed the events of 1898 bore the deep imprint of a phenomenon known as Anglo-Saxonism. Long before the war with Spain, one crucial reason many came to identify millennial hopes with America was the simple fact that the nation was home to a predominant Anglo-Saxon population, with an environment perfectly suited to the flourishing of the race. Anglo-Saxon theorists on both sides of the Atlantic believed God had developed their race for a glorious global purpose. Viewed through this lens, the events of the war seemed unmistakable signs that long-held hopes were finally to be realized.[2]

The chapter begins with an analysis of the writings of Josiah Strong, which offer the best example of the content of Anglo-Saxonism during this period. But the crux of the chapter is its middle section, which describes the unique features of the war and its implications that meshed so well with the hopes and expectations of Anglo-Saxonism. Specifically, the war with Spain came to represent the union of the race's divergent branches around a common mission. It marked the dissolution of the internal squabbles that were viewed as the greatest challenge to the effectiveness of the race in world redemption. A final section then briefly illustrates the distinctly racial providentialism that emerged in the wake of these events and reinforced the sense that a new interventionist mission was born of God.

Josiah Strong and the Shape of Christian Anglo-Saxonism

Seldom has race been a subject of such great popular and scholarly fascination as in 1890s America. Far from just an amateur's hobby, scientists, eugenicists, and sociologists from elite universities across the nation divided the world's peoples into sharp categories (e.g., Slavs, Teutons, Latins), assigned certain attributes to distinguish each category, and then arranged them in a hierarchy based on the qualities assigned to each group. The Anglo-Saxon race or category, which routinely emerged at the top of every hierarchy, received the greatest attention. Locating precise boundaries around the concept "Anglo-Saxon" as then used is difficult; it could serve as a catch-all for almost any physical characteristic or element of civilization deemed worthy or superior. But, at the very least, "Anglo-Saxon" referred to descendants of Britain's ancient tribes, those who used the English language, and, more often than not, those whose societies built upon some notion of civil liberty. However the precise content of the Anglo-Saxon race might be defined, the constant was an all-pervasive commitment to Anglo-Saxonism, or the belief in the innate superiority of the race. The roots of this conviction ran deep in English historiography and the emergence of modern nationalism, predating any connection to modern biology. But it found its greatest ally in the social application of Darwin's theory that only the fittest survive. In this social Darwinism, Anglo-Saxonism located a scientific explanation for the numerical and political dominion of the race in the world, and, so bolstered, Anglo-Saxonism "became the chief element in American racism in the imperial era."[3] It would be decades, in fact, before threats from Asian immigration and growing tension with the African American community created a place for eastern Europeans within the dominant group, when "Caucasian" replaced Anglo-Saxon as the marker of supremacy.[4]

Anglo-Saxonism of a distinctly religious variety also boasted a prestigious lineage, with such early proponents as Lyman Beecher and Horace Bushnell. But no one else so fully represented this view or so effectively propagated it as the Congregationalist minister and activist Josiah Strong. Himself a graduate of Beecher's Lane Theological Seminary, Strong spent time pastoring and working as a missionary in the American West before turning his efforts toward social and political reform. A tireless proponent of the Social Gospel, Strong also served for a time as general secretary of a long-tenured activist group called the Evangelical Alliance.[5] His work was wide-ranging in focus and varied in effect, including, for example, a strong lobbying attempt to convince the U.S. government to enact a political intervention in the Ottoman Empire, given threats both to the Armenian population and to American missionary interests there.[6] But what cements Strong's lasting legacy is his influential series of monographs commenting on American society and the place of religion in American national identity. And a consistent theme throughout these texts, especially those written between 1885 and 1900, is the significance and destiny of the Anglo-Saxon race. Indeed, one historian concludes, "a feeling of superiority about the Anglo-Saxon way of life . . . infused all his works and was the key presupposition behind virtually all his thought about both expansion and reform."[7] Both for the breadth of his influence and for the clarity with which he expressed his views, Strong, in his writing on Anglo-Saxonism, offers a useful window into the thought of the period and the lens through which many came to view the events of 1898.

In 1885 Strong published the book that would put him indelibly on the map, his first book, titled *Our Country: Its Possible Future and Present Crisis*.[8] Published in multiple editions to incorporate new census data, *Our Country* would go on to sell nearly two hundred thousand copies and was printed in excerpts in periodicals across the nation. Its analysis—one of the first to make extensive use of sociological statistics—was a tour de force, offering a dramatic account of the "perils" facing the nation as incentive for Strong's call to domestic reform and renewed home missionary zeal. It was in the penultimate chapter, a chapter entitled "Anglo-Saxons and the World's Future," that the data from earlier chapters found their most robust interpretation, and it was here that Strong most thoroughly explained the theory of Anglo-Saxonism that would remain his consistent theme.

The argument had three primary components, the first two representing "facts" as Strong perceived them and the third his projection based on those facts. The first component related to the innate character of the Anglo-Saxon race. According to Strong, all influential races throughout history have embodied some great idea that came to define their collective life and civilization. The Egyptians had life, the Hebrews purity, the Greeks beauty, and the Romans law. The Anglo-Saxons, he argued, represented two great, interrelated ideas: civil liberty and pure spiritual Christianity.[9] Neither liberty nor "spiritual" Christianity was unique to Anglo-Saxons, of course. All the "noblest races" were "lovers of liberty," and Strong conceded that spiritual Christianity—that is, Protestantism—was first born among Germanic Teutons. But it was left to Anglo-Saxons to "fully recognize the right of the individual to himself" and to make this the founding principle of government. And Protestantism, nearly dead in Germany, sustained its greatest vitality in the English-speaking world. In the United States, the Anglo-Saxons had only enhanced these central ideas, more nearly perfecting civil liberty through their revolutionary system of government and best preserving spiritual Christianity through the separation of church and state. These improvements, along with the physical advances fostered in the frontier environment, elevated the race to new heights and established North America as the seat of its power. Even more important, Strong argued, these two Anglo-Saxon ideas corresponded precisely to the greatest needs of humanity.[10]

The second component of Strong's argument was the numerical dominance of Anglo-Saxons relative to the world's other races. This is where the author put his beloved statistics to use with greatest effect. Strong's complicated analysis built upon past rates of increase to argue that in one century the number of Anglo-Saxons would surpass the entire population of Continental Europe and by a century after that perhaps the number of all other civilized peoples combined. As with Anglo-Saxon character, the numerical growth of the race would reach new heights in the United States. Strong calculated that America was already home to more than half of the world's Anglo-Saxons and if past rates of increase remained steady, the proportion would be much larger in the following century. More important than the mathematical formulas and even the specific numbers themselves, the dominance of Anglo-Saxons relative to the world's other races was not a matter of chance. For Strong, this dominance was directly related to the quality of their character and civilization.[11]

The third and most consequential component of Strong's analysis was his attempt to fix the meaning of these facts, facts he believed to be "the mighty alphabet with which God writes his prophecies." Here he found the divine intent easily discernible: "God, with infinite wisdom and skill, is training the Anglo-Saxon race for an hour sure to come in the world's future."[12] That future hour, furthermore, he framed in the stark terms of social Darwinism: the race had been schooled for a great competition with the races of the world, a competition not of arms but "of vitality and of civilization," where only the fittest would survive. The history of the world was littered with the remains of "barbarous" nations supplanted by the more civilized, as if those "inferior tribes were only precursors of a superior race, voices in the wilderness crying: 'Prepare ye the way of the Lord!'" Now, it seemed to Strong, God was working with "two hands," preparing the Anglo-Saxon race to place its civilizing stamp on the nations of the world and preparing humankind to receive that stamp. "Is there any room for reasonable doubt," he concluded, that the race "is destined to dispossess many weaker races, assimilate others, and mold the remainder, until, in a very true and important sense, it has Anglo-Saxonized mankind?"[13]

This language, powerful as it is, must be qualified somewhat. Strong did not believe that the Anglo-Saxon race was inherently more dear to God than other races or that its impact on the world would necessarily be for the better. That the race would influence the world's future he regarded as inevitable, given the numbers, but it was by no means certain what the shape of that influence would be. The race could yet abandon the principles of liberty and Christianity that had powered its success so far, replacing these with baser motives, and this possibility was the driving force of his call to Christian activism. Strong saw races, like individuals, as mutable in quality: the powerful and the civilized could abandon their principles and collapse, and the inferior, by adopting higher principles, could strengthen themselves. Indeed, his vision for Anglo-Saxon world power had less to do with eliminating "inferior" peoples than with elevating them, incorporating them into the best that Anglo-Saxon civilization could offer and creating unity from diversity.[14] Yet there is no avoiding the fact that, at the very least, Strong's language could be easily misunderstood. As one historian framed the realities of the period, when professors called for maintaining the benefits of Caucasian civilization and stump speakers waxed eloquent on the subject of white supremacy, they offered but slight variations on a theme. Here was a distinction without a difference.[15] And ultimately, for Strong, the thought that many races would be obliterated even as others were raised through contact with Anglo-Saxons concerned him but little: "Whether the extinction of inferior races before the advancing Anglo-Saxon seems to the reader sad or otherwise, it certainly appears probable."[16] This was Anglo-Saxonism at its finest. And this was the lens through which many came to understand the dramatic events of 1898.

A Race United:
Anglo-Saxon Solidarity and the War with Spain

In light of the commitments of Anglo-Saxonism, the Spanish-American War had remarkable significance in several of its details. But here my focus is the providential indicators that the time for expansive international influence had come. Specifically, the war seemed to have secured the unification of the race in preparation for the mission America had now taken up.

The numerical dominance of Anglo-Saxons demonstrated by Strong was not sufficient on its own to secure the high hopes many held for the race and its role in the world. Far greater than any external threat was the cycle of dissension and violence that pitted Anglo-Saxon against Anglo-Saxon. Solidarity and unity would be the necessary foundation for any successful effort to uplift the world's lower races, but common purpose likely seemed far-fetched to many given more than a century of conflict between the United States and Britain and given the long and bloody American Civil War fought just a generation past. But with the Spanish-American War, at least on the level of perception, many witnessed these bitter divisions melt away and, with them, one major obstacle to Anglo-Saxon influence over the world's future.

An Anglo-American "Alliance"

The earth-moving intranational conflict that was the Civil War did little to obscure the long-standing tension between Great Britain and its former colonies. Besides the fact that the two nations had gone to war in 1776 and again in 1812, many in Washington resented the British sympathy—and sometimes outright support—for the Confederacy during the Civil War. Furthermore, a politically powerful contingent of Irish Americans fought hard to incite conflict with Britain in the years after the war, and the large number of free-silver proponents in the last quarter of the nineteenth century resented Britain's unwillingness to abandon the gold standard. But surely the biggest crisis of the period revolved around a boundary dispute between Venezuela and British Guiana in South America. In 1895, just three years before the war with Spain, U.S. Secretary of State Richard Olney demanded that Britain arbitrate the dispute, claiming that it violated the Monroe Doctrine's venerable principle of self-determination for the Americas. When Britain predictably responded that the Monroe Doctrine was irrelevant to the case, an irate President Grover Cleveland asked for authority from Congress to appoint a commission to investigate the boundary. Most recognized that this would be but a short step from outright war, and not a few relished the thought. Though the clamoring for war was short lived and drowned out by cooler voices on both sides of the Atlantic, the episode revealed the hostility many cultivated just below the surface.[17]

It was Great Britain that first sought to heal these old wounds, and not for sentimental reasons. The British had long ruled a lion's share of the prized China markets, but by century's end Russia, Germany, and France posed significant threats to their hegemony. Because they favored open-door trading over the exclusive colonial models of other European powers, the British hoped to find a natural ally in the United States to shore up their interests in the Far East. Just before the war with Spain broke out, in fact, British diplomats had in effect asked for some form of alliance, a request McKinley refused to grant. It was clear that Britain stood to gain most from a transatlantic friendship. The Spanish-American War, then, according to the historian Charles Campbell, marked the turning point at which Americans began to reciprocate this affection.[18]

As the path to war with Spain took shape in the spring months of 1898, Britain participated with other European nations in diplomatic efforts to persuade the United States not to go to war with Spain. It refused, however, to join the strong denunciations of intervention issued by the Continental powers. When the war began, it quickly became clear that Britain alone favored the Americans. Officially, Britain would remain neutral through the course of the war; unofficially, the British public was swept up in a wave of unprecedented pro-American sentiment, celebrating both the humanitarianism of the war and the fact that victory in Manila had forced the United States to look eastward. The Stars and Stripes went up all over London, as ceremonial tributes were held through the course of the war, even celebrations of American independence on July 4. Prominent leaders, including Rudyard Kipling, James Bryce, and the Archbishop of Canterbury, formed the Anglo-American League, devoted to fostering the transatlantic friendship, and the British press joined political figures in public expressions of good feeling.[19] A speech by Joseph Chamberlain, Britain's colonial secretary, was by far the most popular example. Given May 13 in Birmingham, the speech eloquently described the many ties of culture, history, and lineage that created a natural bond between the two nations. Chamberlain's conclusion, then, left little to the imagination: "terrible as war may be, even war itself would be cheaply purchased if in a great and noble cause the Stars and Stripes and the Union Jack should wave together over an Anglo-Saxon Alliance."[20]

The effect of this good will was not lost on the Americans, who came to believe Great Britain—neutrality notwithstanding—was the only force preventing the European powers from joining the war against the United States. In the religious press, most at least noted the prevailing sentiment on both sides of the Atlantic, while others held high hopes for the meaning and implications of a potential alliance. Such commentary appeared from the earliest days of the war. On May 4, just days after Admiral Dewey's victory announced America's arrival on the world stage, the Methodist *Western Christian Advocate* considered the significance of recent events in light of the new friendliness between the United States and Britain. "'America' and 'God Save the Queen' are sung to the same air and by the same voices," the editor noted. "Deep in American hearts is the hope that the destinies of England and America may become identical." The shape of that common destiny would be unlike anything the world had seen, or so this editor was convinced: "Mother and son, standing together, could dictate humanity and peace to the world. . . . Not for war, but for peace and humanity, for the good of mankind and the glory of God, England and the United States should be in alliance, holy and perpetual."[21] Similarly, the *Congregationalist* ran a column the following day suggesting that an Anglo-Saxon alliance could be a hinge for world history: "If these relations shall be secured, and cemented by Christian faith and common purpose, this result will compensate for all its loss and will be a turning point in the history of the world."[22]

Some ministers were even more explicit in their hopes for what such a racial alliance could accomplish, none more so than the New York Baptist Robert MacArthur, who in May preached sermons behind a pulpit draped with the Union Jack.[23] In his celebrated "Hand of God" sermon, inspired in part by the content of Joseph Chamberlain's recent speech, MacArthur identified the possible Anglo-Saxon alliance as one of the chief markers of the divine hand at work in the conflict with Spain. Such an alliance, he insisted, would be "an alliance for peace and not for war; an alliance for liberty and not for tyranny; an alliance for all that is noblest in human government and divinest in human liberty and progress." MacArthur was only just beginning. His conclusion, full to the brim with millennial fervor, speaks for itself:

> The Union Jack and the stars and stripes entwined in loving and inseparable friendship and fellowship, and waving over an Anglo-American alliance will be the crowning glory of the closing century. It will be one of the great factors in the evangelization of the heathen, the humanization of all governments and the divinization of all peoples. It will be a sight which will rejoice the hearts of saints

and seraphs, of angels and archangels. When this alliance shall have been recognized, then the eastern sky will be radiant with the crimson and gold of the millennial dawn.[24]

Without question, MacArthur's soaring rhetoric was more the exception than the rule, and support for an official alliance was short lived. The majority of writers in the religious press remained wary of any codified agreement from the beginning. Here the editor of the Texas *Baptist Standard* was more typical in his assessment. Commenting on the growing popularity of such an alliance, he was honest about the substantial grounds for hope in such an agreement: both nations shared a strong Christian character, an affinity for civil liberties, and a "visibly strong" racial tie, all of which promised a potential "magnificent destiny" for the "united aspirations of the Anglo-Saxon race." But this alliance such as it was, he concluded, should remain at the level of sympathy and common purpose, rather than be codified in an actual treaty.[25] What MacArthur and the editor of the *Baptist Standard* shared, however broad their differences over policy, was the fundamental conviction that Anglo-Saxons, possessing the precise character qualities needed by the world, could achieve tremendous good if only they shared a common purpose. That common purpose, portended on every hand by displays of "friendly feeling" between the two nations, was destined to be one of the great results of the war with Spain. On this point, virtually all Protestants agreed.[26]

"Domestic Strife . . . Forever Past"

For all the talk of Anglo-American unity, the war with Spain also helped to bridge an even deeper, more bitter Anglo-Saxon divide. Faced with a common, "foreign" enemy, Americans North and South came together. Historians have long identified the final decades of the nineteenth century as a time when Civil War wounds began to heal, especially as white Northerners themselves came to regret many of the policies of the Reconstruction experiment. This was a healing process with a strong Anglo-Saxon flavor, fostered by a common fear that both immigration and black suffrage posed imminent threats. The Spanish-American War, then, became a crucial moment for codifying these gradual gains, providing both a common external enemy and a revived sense of a shared national mission. The significance of the war for that purpose, noted widely by subsequent historians, was not lost on contemporary observers.[27]

Commentators across the nation located symbolic details on every hand. At the outset of the war, to wide acclaim, McKinley appointed two former

Confederate luminaries as U.S. generals: "Fighting" Joe Wheeler, from Alabama, and Fitzhugh Lee, nephew and celebrated biographer of Robert E. Lee
himself. During the Civil War, Baltimore residents had greeted the occupying
troops of the Sixth Massachusetts with clubs and bats; now, when the unit
passed through the same city en route to the Gulf Coast, it was met with flags
and flowers and cheering crowds.[28] Others noted that the first fatality of the
war, naval ensign Worth Bagley, was a North Carolinian. One editor captured
the symbolic significance: with this life, "given in defense of a united country,
were buried forever all the differences of a generation ago."[29] In this climate, a
southern editor could cite his Chicago colleague without reservation: "It is
well that we pause, in the midst of a foreign war, to seal with our affection the
compact of brotherhood among all Americans. Domestic strife, please God,
is forever past." This year—this war—could mark the point at which "the old
bitterness was finally and entirely buried, leaving only a true Anglo-Saxon
reverence for the courage and devotion of those to whom tribute is still to be
paid, so long as their name endures—the boys of '61."[30]

Perhaps nothing better illustrates the prevalent good will—and the foundation of that good will in a new sense of common mission—than an address
given just after the war by J. B. Hawthorne, pastor of Nashville's First Baptist
Church. That fall, on October 19, Hawthorne had traveled north for an engage-
ment with the Boston Baptist Social Union. In Boston, he delivered a speech
titled "Present Feeling in the South Towards the Federal Union and the People
of the North."[31] By Hawthorne's reckoning, the Civil War emerged as a redemptive event, and the Spanish-American War marked the moment the South fully
embraced reunion around a common vision for America's Anglo-Saxon mission.
Hawthorne freely admitted that the antebellum South had held its delusions
about the supremacy of a strictly agricultural, slave-based economy. The collapse
of this misconception represented for him the true legacy of the Civil War:
"Whether the men who followed the victorious flag of the Union did or did not
contemplate such a result, the truth is that the triumphs which they achieved
brought to the white race of the South a deliverance immeasurably greater
than that which came to the enslaved negroes."[32] Thus finally able to appreciate
their own deliverance, Hawthorne further argued, Southerners greeted the war
with Spain as an opportunity to demonstrate their own loyalty to the nation's
God-given destiny, even as the shape of that destiny now appeared in more
expansive form. His conclusion made this abundantly clear: "Our country will,
henceforth, extend the benediction of her beneficent influence and power, until
all despotisms are demolished, all governments democratized, and the wide
world is free. In loving, struggling, and sacrificing for a country to which God

has given a mission so sublime, the sons of the South will prove themselves worthy of the admiration, the confidence, and the comradeship of the sons of the North."[33]

As Hawthorne was giving his speech to the Baptists of Boston, President William McKinley was in the midst of a vaunted speaking tour through the Midwest, celebrating the war and selling expansion in towns across Iowa, Missouri, Illinois, Nebraska, and Ohio. At nearly every stop, national unity was a guiding theme in his tribute to the nation's conduct in the late war.[34] "During all these trying months the people of the United States have stood together as one man," he told a crowd in Clinton, Iowa. "North and South have been united as never before."[35] McKinley brought this theme to a crescendo in mid-December, as he took a similar speaking tour through parts of Georgia and Alabama. Not surprisingly, his tribute to national unity in these speeches tended to focus on Southern loyalty as displayed in the war with Spain, but in a famous speech delivered at the state capitol in Atlanta, the president went one step further. In a gesture of tremendous symbolic power, McKinley declared that the time had come for the entire nation to aid in the care of Confederate graves.[36] In this speech the president described the "unfortunate Civil War," of which he was a veteran, as a "tribute to American valor." Though the graves were made when the nation was bitterly divided over the proper course for the future, he went on, now, "in the evolution of sentiment and feeling under the providence of God," the time had come when "in the spirit of fraternity we should share with you in the care of the graves of the Confederate soldiers."[37]

Not all shared McKinley's unqualified excitement over the development of sectional reunion or the renewed friendship with Great Britain, even among those who supported the war to liberate Cuba. Some recognized that these displays of fraternity came with a price; they required that important errors of the past be forgotten, episodes that would clash with the prevalent descriptions of Anglo-Saxon character as liberty-loving, humanitarian, Christian. The powerful Irish immigrant community, for example, loudly objected to talk of an Anglo-Saxon alliance, rightly recognizing that these shows of solidarity often included positive assessments of Great Britain's imperial career.[38] Black Americans too sought more prominent recognition of their loyalty in the war and their accomplishments on the ground in Cuba, contributions largely passed over in the euphoria of national reunion. But these voices had little noticeable effect. Through the end of 1898, and almost invariably in retrospective accounts of the significance of the war, Anglo-American friendship and American national reunion emerged side by side as central features of the conflict's ultimate meaning.[39] And so, as perceived by those already enamored of Anglo-Saxonism, the

Spanish-American War came to mark the birth of an unprecedented racial solidarity, yet another harbinger of providential designs for America's messianic
future.

"A New Commandment, a New Mission for the World"

Thus, in the events of 1898, a pre-existent Anglo-Saxonism found fertile soil for
growth and an even more powerful resonance. Many, like Josiah Strong, were
already committed to their belief that the Anglo-Saxon race was preeminent in
the global hierarchy—the most free, the most humanitarian, the most Christian.
Now, in this war, the contentious branches of the race had come together,
removing what many believed to be the most debilitating obstacle to its potential
role for good in the world. Taught to affirm what "is" as what God intends,
Christian interpreters took it upon themselves to locate the significance of these
developments as the will of providence. Given the unique contours of Anglo-
Saxon character and the close correspondence of that character to the world's
greatest needs, many concluded from the events of 1898 that it must be God's
intent for this race to "bring the world to him."[40] This racial cast on American
destiny was reflected widely in the religious press, but select sermons provide
the best examples of how the idea took shape.[41]

Before the close of the war and just following the naval victory off the coast
of Santiago, an Episcopal minister on Long Island, William Gardam, joined
many others in considering the theme of "America's Mission." His sermon was
a discourse on liberty as a unique possession of the Anglo-Saxon race and on
the duty of the race to define it and present it to the world. America, for Gardam
as for many others, had been the incubator, settled in the providence of God by
the only group from the Old World with any sense of individual liberties. The
sermon charted a familiar course as it surveyed the nation's history, a history
now culminating in a new resolve to abandon isolation and take up a "political
crusade." "The heart and mind of this nation are centred [*sic*] upon one thing,"
Gardam assured his congregation, "and its strong right arm is lifted for the
vindication of what it believes to be common human rights."[42] Where Gardam's
sermon differed from similar interpretations described in earlier chapters is in
his formulation of this development as a "race problem," placed in the context
of a struggle for supremacy among competing civilizations. The war with
Spain, by his account, was most significant for forcing the question of "whether
the world shall be led and governed and fashioned by the Latin or the Slav or
the Anglo-Saxon." In the war America had dealt its first blow in that all-
important struggle, but, having removed tyranny, now the nation faced the

more daunting task of cultivating liberty. Gardam saw no cause for concern: "to the Anglo-Saxon race, Anglo-Saxon gifts, Anglo-Saxon civilization, God Almighty seems literally to be giving a new commandment, a new mission for the world."[43]

One of the most detailed explanations of the importance of Anglo-Saxons in the world's future came, in fact, from an Englishman, the Baptist minister John Clifford. In late September, 1898, Clifford and George Lorimer, a Boston minister, arranged a pulpit exchange, building no doubt on the groundswell of sympathy between Americans and Britons. On September 25, Clifford addressed the congregation at Boston's Tremont Temple, making a strong case for the providential significance of the race and a strong appeal for an alliance between the two nations as the next and necessary step "in the higher progress of mankind." In the bulk of the sermon Clifford offered his reasons for confidence that the race had been developed by God for a task that such an alliance could help fulfill. The British and the Americans shared a common racial stock, a common language, a common commitment to individual liberty in government, a common Christianity, and, as a result, a common concern for the welfare of others. In fact, Clifford argued, "the Anglo-Saxon people are the depository of the greatest store of altruism—that is unselfishness—of the race. . . . And because we share together this spirit of enthusiastic endeavor to help our fellows, therefore it is that we must come together."[44] For Clifford, Anglo-Saxons were no less than "joint custodians of the principles upon which the order and the progress of mankind depend," principles like liberty of conscience, justice in government and social relations, education, and concern for truth. Surveying the facts as they appeared in 1898, Clifford saw that Anglo-Saxons possessed the precise qualities needed by the primitive world, they now enjoyed unprecedented unity of sentiment and purpose, and they had now before them a wide field of need and opportunity in the East. Given these data, he argued, "it is not outside the revelation of his predestined purposes, as it lies on the face of facts, to say, God has elected us." Indeed, he continued, "the God who chose Abraham, the God who chose Saul of Tarsus, has chosen the Anglo-Saxon people for the carrying forward of these great principles."[45] The only question that remained was whether the race on both sides of the Atlantic would embrace this destiny and work as a people for the good of the world rather than for the narrow interests that had so often derailed its progress.

❖

Anglo-Saxonism of the Josiah Strong variety therefore helps to explain why so many greeted messianic intervention with such enthusiasm in the context of

the war with Spain. Strong and his ilk had insisted that Anglo-Saxons possessed the exact principles on which depended the "progress of mankind." The
Spanish-American War, it seemed, was the providential stroke that removed
barriers within the race and united Anglo-Saxons around a common activist
impulse. But this same Anglo-Saxon lens also had a dramatic effect on the way
many Americans viewed the other peoples in question.[46] Indeed, the perspective
on the quality of Spain's former subjects, when filtered through the predominant
Anglo-Saxonism, only reinforced a sense of urgency for what a united race could
provide.

The conviction that the former Spanish colonies were not prepared for
responsible self-government began to emerge in force as the popular perception
of the Cuban insurgents turned sour. In the debate leading to up to the war
through March and April, many had glamorized the insurgency, casting the
Cubans as freedom fighters in the mold of America's Revolutionary generation
and their cause as a direct parallel to America's struggle for independence. In
fact, even when McKinley consented to intervention, some members of Congress and others in the press protested the president's unwillingness to officially
recognize the existence of a Cuban republic.[47] But this perception changed
dramatically when American troops began to interact with their ostensible allies,
especially in late June and July. As one editor would come to conclude, "The
African, Indian or Insurgent of sentiment, a noble creature of patriotic imagination, is one thing, the real, live African, Indian or Insurgent is very different."[48]
During ground operations against Spain, Cuban troops served as guides and in
supporting positions through some of the fighting, but, for example, American
commanders denied their Cuban counterparts any role in negotiations for the
surrender of Santiago. Negative accounts of the insurgents' performance in
battle began to circulate, too; when compared to the charge of the Rough Riders
up San Juan Hill, the Cubans' guerrilla tactics appeared cowardly. Even worse,
many were outraged at reports of the abuse of Spanish prisoners.[49] By war's
end, New York's *Christian Advocate* was in doubt as to whether "the Cubans will
be able for years, if ever, to govern themselves."[50] So too the editor of the *Watchman*, who argued that "for the United States to interfere in Cuba out of motives
of humanity, and then install a government which would be dominated by
savage impulses would be the height of absurdity." Yes, the editor conceded,
the legislature had bound the nation to a promise not to retain Cuba as a result
of the war, but "there is nothing in that ordinance to prevent us from keeping
our hands on the island until the conditions of what Webster used to call 'respect-
able government' are established."[51]

The conviction about native incapacity was even more pronounced in
discussions of the Philippines. "Half savage" was a typical description of the

Filipinos and "anarchy" a typical assessment of the likely result should the United States lift its steady hand. "They certainly are not free and independent," Lyman Abbott's *Outlook* would later conclude, "and it is very doubtful whether they have as yet the character which entitles them to freedom and independence."[52] True, the *Christian Evangelist* conceded, "the people of these islands do need our civilization, and the civil and religious liberty which we enjoy."[53] But the United States must first teach them how to enjoy such liberty, how to sustain such a civilization, and this would mean ruling over them until they had gained the necessary ability lacking in their natural condition.

Nearly all agreed, in the end, that, as a result of the war for liberation, America had thrust upon them a people utterly unprepared by race, culture, or historical development to sustain a healthy representative government. On this point there was no substantial debate.[54] Much more contentious, however, was the matter of the nation's appropriate response to the situation given the poor condition of those living in Spain's former colonies. The quality of the races in question grounded some of the most pervasive anti-imperialist arguments. Stanford's David Starr Jordan, writing in the Unitarian *New World*, suggested these non-Anglo-Saxons would never be able to self-govern or embrace American institutions. Others pointed to America's checkered past dealing with "inferiors" such as American Indians, Negroes, and Asian immigrants, insisting that there was no reason to expect a different result in this case.[55] The inferior quality of the Cubans and the Filipinos, then, was precisely the reason America should avoid ongoing responsibility in those territories or at the least abandon any thought of permanent retention of the islands. But this racial argument against empire suffered from important, perhaps debilitating weaknesses in the heady days of 1898 and early 1899. This era of unparalleled optimism, stoked by the thrill of absolute victory over Spain, was hardly conducive to arguments based on American incapacity, about the nation's inability to do anything. Even more, though the fact that these non-Anglo-Saxons were not prepared for self-government might have supported a case against assimilating these territories on the path to American statehood, the prospect of statehood represented a straw man that few if any seriously considered. Permanent retention of Cuba and the Philippines wasn't at issue, at least for most religious commentators. What was at issue was the nation's responsibility to rule over those now imposed upon it by providence, until they were prepared to govern themselves. Liberty, by this reckoning, was about more than self-government; it was about good government, a government free from oppression that secured basic civil and religious freedoms. Given the innate capacity of these races, many argued, their only present hope for such a government—for liberty—was American tutelage.

5

Duty and Destiny

Messianic Interventionism and the Ideology of American Expansion

The lopsided naval contest at Santiago had, in effect, ended the Spanish-American War. Through the end of July, all that remained were a few minor skirmishes—most notably the occupation of Manila and Puerto Rico by American ground forces—before a provisional peace protocol brought the dramatic little war to a close. That ceasefire came on August 12, barely one hundred days after the fighting began. In some ways, though, the more lasting battle, representing the real legacy of the war, was just beginning. Already the lines of debate had been drawn over what to do with the territories now liberated from Spain's grasp. As summer turned to fall, the American military settled into occupation mode, investigators appointed by the president set out to pin blame on someone for bungling so many wartime logistics, and soldiers watched helplessly as more of their comrades died of disease than had fallen to Spanish bullets. Meanwhile, public-opinion leaders in America were busy wrangling national responsibilities out of new and unforeseen possibilities yielded by the war. The religious among them did at least their share of the ideological heavy lifting; tracing their contribution is the purpose of this chapter.

The Philippine Islands emerged early and remained consistently at the center of the debate. Most recognized that America's relationship with Cuba had been determined by Congress at the outset of the war, when Congress explicitly denied that acquisition of the island was a relevant motivation for or possible result of the imminent conflict. The United States would play the role of "stronger older brother," securing order and protecting the island until the Cubans showed themselves ready for responsible self-government. Remarkably, there was just as little debate over the opposite course in Puerto Rico and Guam; nearly everyone agreed these islands would remain permanent possessions of the United States. The Philippines—more populated, more distant, but more relevant to the great China markets—were at once both more troubling and more promising.

Before proceeding, I must clarify the terms I will use to refer to the issue in question. The terminology for the subject of debate—American policy in the former Spanish territories—was and is fraught with political implications. Nearly all today would recognize the policy as imperialism, and contemporary observers were sensitive to that possible perception. Christian leaders typically opposed "imperialism" because they opposed the permanent possession of the territories that they saw implied in the term. "Annexation" had similar connotations for most, if it was not considered as sinister as "imperialism," for this term reminded them of past annexations that had led to statehood, something very few wanted to see for the Philippines or Puerto Rico. "Expansion" was by far the most frequently used term, and it will be the term used in this chapter, in part because it best reflects the dominant, ambiguous outlook on open-ended future policy in the former Spanish colonies.[1] It could mean expansion of territory, as it had with the nation's early westward expansion across the continent. But it could also—and more often did—refer more generically to the expansion of American foreign policy and international influence—in short, America's more expansive role in the world.[2]

Studies of the perspective of religious leaders on American policy in the Philippines have described the issue in terms too polarizing. The earliest examples tend to emphasize a select group of jingoistic ministers widely publicized precisely because of their extreme views in favor of American expansion.[3] Winthrop Hudson's brief treatment offers an important corrective, but only by highlighting prominent opponents of imperialism, leaving intact the impression that the issues were drawn starkly in black and white.[4] In fact, arguments in favor of permanent retention of the Philippines were nearly as rare in Christian circles as arguments for immediate and complete removal from the islands. There was some disagreement—mostly just uncertainty—about the appropriate level of American involvement, but a strong majority was in favor of some form of ongoing responsibility, which is to say American control.[5] Given the lack of definitive policy proposals among these church leaders, the widespread support for the idea of American control of the Philippines was more significant than the nebulous disputes about the precise extent of that control. Realizing the nation faced a new era of foreign policy—an era as yet ill defined and full of uncertainty—most looked to the future with an attitude best described by one contemporary as "fatalistic optimism."[6] And this is the posture I wish to investigate here. My intent is to focus on the shared foundation of the general support for ongoing American sovereignty in the former Spanish territories. I hope to explain why so many believed this sovereignty was necessary and justifiable and, even more, why so few were concerned that even provisional control would be fraught with problems. I argue that the same notions of Christian duty and providential destiny that framed the meaning of the war itself grounded an even more expansive form of messianic interventionism faced with the war's unexpected results.

Another way to frame the question driving this discussion is, How could those Christian commentators, so proud of their promise not to fight for territorial conquest, justify annexing Puerto Rico and the Philippines? One answer is that many were swept up with the missionary opportunities American control would surely provide. Even before the end of the war the religious press was full of articles on the need for missions to assume the mantle of civilization where soldiers could carry it no further. Catholics and Protestants—often bitterly divided over the implications of the islands' existing Catholicism—shared an all-consuming interest in mobilizing their resources to meet the needs of the natives.[7] Numerous studies document the prominence of missionary interests in this critical year, and these interests provided at least a crossbeam in the support for American expansion.[8] These interests were no doubt embedded in the mosaic of motives driving support for expansion. But here I am interested in public justifications of ongoing American control in the islands, not precisely those motives that might have rendered such justifications desirable. In public religious rhetoric, many did assume and celebrate the positive effect American sovereignty would have on missions prospects, and several studies have illustrated what could be known almost intuitively, that missionary hopes inspired support for expansion. But in justifying expansion, benefits to missions, when mentioned, were cast as by-products or as reasons to hope for good results, not as themselves reasons to expand. It was assumed that the missions' interests would be served by the course of events one way or another.

Other explanations for the turn to expansion have emphasized the hypocrisy of earlier promises disavowing any interest in territorial acquisition. Though describing the "real" interests from different angles—whether economic, political, or otherwise—these explanations agree that expressions of religious and humanitarian sympathy were the thin veneer covering the underlying intention to take and exploit the islands.[9] However accurately this may describe some influential figures in American politics, it fails to account for certain features in the early commentary of many Christian leaders. First, all the focus of early justifications for war was on Cuba. Puerto Rico was mentioned only occasionally and the Philippines barely at all. Had these islands been the original endgame, one would expect some public outcry over humanitarian abuses there as a pretext for taking control. Even more revealing is the nature of the response to Dewey's Manila victory throughout the religious press, as discussed briefly in chapter 3. Many editors admitted barely knowing the location of the Philippines, much less any relevant demographic information, and they expected that readers shared their ignorance. May columns included article after article describing everything from topography to racial characteristics and population numbers to the history of the islands. Granted, there was a swift and strong reaction to Dewey's victory in favor of ongoing U.S. responsibility for the islands, but there is very little evidence in the religious press for a preexistent plan to colonize.[10] Something else must explain the early, almost instinctive openness toward American control there. Explanations that focus on a blatant desire of most Americans to consciously exploit the people of these islands fail to appreciate the more nuanced—if not less troubling—reality in the religious commentary on territorial expansion. Vociferously condemning any exploitation of the islands for American interests, the dominant Christian perspective was at once more benevolent and, perhaps, just as dangerous. Implicitly, many refused to believe such exploitation was possible. They were not Spaniards, after all; they were Americans.

What even more sympathetic perspectives have failed to recognize is that expansion became justifiable precisely because of the ideology with which so many had originally made sense of their war and its success. Hudson describes the shift in rhetoric from support for what he calls a "war for liberation" to support for a "war of territorial acquisition" as a "tortuous reversal."[11] In fact, most came to grips with the new American policy through the exact terms they had used to celebrate the war itself. The war was a war for humanity, they had reasoned, and, like all of American history, it had been signally blessed by divine providence. Now, in coping with the results of the war, America would pursue identical humanitarian goals, motivated by claims to the same altruism that had first propelled the nation against Spain. In pursuing this duty imposed upon the nation by a wise providence, Americans could be confident that the same divine favor would secure for them a glorious, if unforeseeable, destiny. In short, as earlier chapters have described, a justification for messianic interventionism rooted in notions of Christian duty received ample reinforcement, both in an anti-Spanish definition of American national character and in evidence of providential favor noted on every hand. Now these same ideas served to justify America's turn to empire.

The chapter's argument is arranged chronologically rather than thematically, which aims to show how the rationale for expansion settled in over time in response to the unfolding course of events. The first section traces the emergence and foundation of support for American control of the Philippines in the religious press and its development over the brief course of the war. The second section then examines the rhetoric of William McKinley through the early fall of 1898. In the roughly three months between the end of the war and the president's official announcement that he had decided to demand cession of the Philippines, McKinley took a speaking tour through the Midwest to sell expansion to the American public. And he sold his policy using the same opaque terms of Christian duty and providential destiny hammered out in the religious press and pulpits throughout the summer. Finally, the third section unpacks an important group of Thanksgiving Day sermons delivered in November 1898. They are important because the occasion yielded an unusual number of surviving sermons; because, given the occasion, the sermons address common subjects and offer an unusual depth of commentary; and, most of all, because this group of sermons claimed the first opportunity to celebrate a policy of expansion that had just become concrete. These sermons, then, represent the case for an ever more expansive messianic interventionism in its fullest development.

Justifying Expansion:
Early Themes Emerge in Wartime

News of Admiral Dewey's triumph in Manila Bay had barely reached American shores when support for ongoing control of the islands began to emerge in the religious press. Through May, this support continued to grow in periodicals spanning all regions and denominations.[12] Some, including several major journals, were more cautious and not a little uncomfortable with this early enthusiasm, advocating instead a wait-and-see approach. So, for example, the Boston Baptist *Watchman* of May 26 viciously satirized the "new spirit" possessing the nation, only to conclude, "We do not know, and nobody else knows, what may be our duty. . . . We hold our judgment in suspense until we know the facts."[13] Even those sharing the *Watchman*'s sense of caution typically admitted provisional government by the United States was a strong possibility.[14]

The month of May saw celebrations of the selfless and humanitarian cause of the war reach their peak. Little surprise, therefore, that the early terms of debate over U.S. control of the Philippines were set over the relationship of such a policy to the highly touted motives for liberating Cuba in the first place.

This was precisely where the editorial critics at the *Standard* focused their attack. The *Standard* began considering options for the Philippines with the same uncertainty about final decisions as early as May 14, and on May 21 it began condemning those who were already arguing for permanent possession.[15] A June 11 column called "The War and the 'New Policy'" pulled no punches: arguments for acquisition of the Philippines represented a turn from the high altruistic motives with which the war was joined toward immoral self-aggrandizement. In the end, this argument remained unconvincing. It fell victim to a powerful conviction that ongoing responsibility in the Philippines was consistent with—even necessary for—America's original humanitarian goals. In this framing of the issue, which took shape in the religious press through the months of the war, the dictates of "humanity" and the deliverances of divine providence were to define appropriate policy for an uncertain future. This potent mixture—humanitarianism and providentialism—would have two important, inseparable functions in the effort to justify expansion. They made expansion necessary, and they made it benign. To put it differently, these currents explain how many became convinced both that America *must* control the territories and that America *could* control the territories while avoiding the errors of others. As the appeal to humanity and providence took shape, it made ongoing control of the Philippines necessary because any other course would fail to achieve the humanitarian goals of the war; circumstances and the clear course of events—that is, providence—demanded it. This appeal made expansion benign because altruistic Americans guided by humanitarian sentiment could only be for the good of the natives, and, guided now as in the past by divine providence, America's mission would succeed where others had failed.

Expansion as Necessary

As early as May 19 the South Carolina *Baptist Courier* was arguing that America might be forced to assume responsibility for the well-being of the Philippine islands. The editorial that day was primarily a celebration of Dewey's victory, a victory here described as unequaled in the history of naval warfare. But the editor turned also to the future and the question of new responsibilities toward the islands. "This was a benevolent war at the outset," he began, "justified on the grounds of intervention in behalf of the oppressed at our very doors with no thought of territorial acquisition." But faithfulness to these same grounds for intervention might require still more: "it may become equally as benevolent to the colonies of Spain for us to retain some sort of possession and control of them when the war is over."[16] The editor was more prescient than he realized; by June, what here he held as possibility had become the decided conviction of periodicals across the nation.

The *Independent*, for example, was one of the most consistent and enthusiastic supporters of a more extensive American foreign policy framed by the dictates of humanity and civilization. Perhaps unique among its peers for its willingness to apply "imperial" to "America," a taboo association for many others, this periodical set about connecting likely results of the war to the lofty principles that inspired it. A June 9 column traced the surprising development of a new national self-consciousness, beginning with the first signs of war for Cuban liberation through the unexpected victory at Manila and culminating in a new set of duties. Americans might be forced to retain what was conquered, it concluded, on the same grounds for which it was conquered originally: freedom from Spanish tyranny. "What we gain in the cause of humanity, we must control in the name of civilization."[17] Demanding the islands as an indemnity from Spain would be nothing short of unchristian, but America might be required to keep them for their own good, in the cause of humanity, "as a matter of pure philanthropy. We are fighting for nothing but philanthropy."[18] The precise form of American involvement in the Philippines remained uncertain, the editor conceded on June 30, but the righteous principles that would determine that involvement were already in place. What these long-oppressed peoples need, what they deserve, he argued, is "freedom and good government," either "by themselves or over them which will allow freedom and prosperity. If we drive Spain's flag from over them, with its shadow of unrighteousness, we must give them full freedom in the hallowed shadow of ours."[19] Freedom, by this definition, meant good government, not necessarily self-government. Where self-government would make good government impossible, self-government was incompatible with freedom.

The argument as framed by the *Independent* would remain a widely used mantra through the end of hostilities. The Presbyterian *New York Observer*, responding to the peace protocol signed in mid-August, discussed new duties in the Philippines with an air of inevitability, a deliverance of the "fortunes of war."[20] Granted, the war was begun on behalf of Cuba, but "this government entered upon war for humanitarian reasons, to rescue a suffering people from misrule and oppression. The widening of the conflict has placed it in our power, if it has not made it our duty, to render a like service to another people suffering from the same intolerable tyranny."[21] In the view of the Disciples' *Christian Evangelist*, similarly, the prospect of expanding national obligations should be viewed in contrast with contraction of the nation's moral mission. The only question worth asking was whether expansion was consistent with America's God-given obligation to impart civil and religious liberty to these islands. If it was consistent, to refuse would be a contraction of the nation's mission and a turn to a policy of national selfishness. And, at this point, the question was merely rhetorical.[22]

By far the most commonly used device for establishing the necessity of expansion and the point at which arguments from humanity and providence most closely interacted was the formulaic review and dismissal of all other options for government of the territories. Outlets of religious commentary joined secular counterparts in recognizing three general alternatives to U.S. retention of the territories after the war.[23] America could return the territories to Spain, cede or sell them to some other European power, or leave them to self-government. The latter option was almost universally rejected from the beginning because of deep convictions about the poor racial quality of the Filipinos. Perhaps Spain was responsible for their backward condition given the many years of cruel oppression, but the fact remained that Filipinos were not seen as prepared for democracy. As the argument typically went, leaving them to themselves would guarantee anarchy and worse conditions than had prevailed under Spanish rule.[24] In addition to allowing self-government, handing the islands over to another power received some brief support, especially the thought that Great Britain might be interested, but this option too was widely dismissed by June 1898. There was some concern that allowing the islands to fall to another power could subject the people to more oppression, but the primary fear was that this would upset the fragile balance of power among Russia, Germany, and Britain in their pursuit of Asian markets. The option that received by far the most attention and the one that was most thoroughly denounced was the prospect of returning the islands to Spain.

Through May and into early June definitions of the war as an epic clash of civilizations reached their apex. In this battle—the battle for the meaning of the war—most Americans agreed that Spain fared even worse than its navy had at Manila. As the terms were set, Spain represented the medieval world, full of tyranny, cruelty, and barbarism best illustrated by the Inquisition or Spaniards' beloved bullfights. If this was Spain's identity, so the argument ran, how could liberty-loving Christian Americans justify concluding a war joined for freedom by returning those liberated to their original oppressors? "To give back to Spain any people not Spaniards," Georgia's *Christian Index* argued, "is to give them back to oppression. We have no right to permit Spain to have any territory to mistreat and tyrannize as she has Cuba, if we can prevent it."[25] The *New York Observer* drew a nearly identical conclusion: "owing to the misrule and oppression of Spain in the archipelago, to retrocede it to her would be simply to belie the humanitarian motives which, we insist, impelled the emancipation of Cuba."[26] Given the Spanish national character and the nation's undeniable track record of brutality, faithfulness to America's prized humanitarian principles rendered a return of the territories unthinkable.[27]

Lacking any other viable option for disposing of the islands in a manner consistent with the humanitarian goals of the war and the demands of a Christian civilization, many concluded that a new responsibility had been "thrust" upon the nation, however much it might wish to avoid it. For a people trained from their own history to locate the will of God in the course of events, divine providence was the only explanation for an unsought, unprecedented, and (many claimed) unwanted set of circumstances. How could they resist such an imposition? The Methodist *Zion's Herald* was one of the first of many to frame the issue in this way, beginning with a June 8 column titled "What to Do with Them?" This was a question the progress of the war had rendered inevitable, it began, since dependencies would now fall to the United States despite the unselfishness with which it had entered the war. The Filipinos are "little removed from barbarism," and the islands cannot be restored to Spain, so, as much as Americans might like to avoid a departure from their cherished isolationism, it now seemed inevitable. All things considered, "an unexpected providence has thrust responsibility upon this nation, and we are compelled to consider duty not in light of national honor or glory, but in relation to the welfare of feeble and oppressed races."[28] Just one week later the Congregationalist *Advance* of Chicago addressed the issue of the Philippines in almost identical language, tempered a bit by sensitivity to arguments that America was now abandoning the altruism of the war's early justifications. "Any possible course seems attended with difficulty and danger," the editor conceded. But "we fail to see the justice of imputing bad faith to this country in case we should decide to retain control over the islands. We did not seek to conquer the islands; in a sense they were thrust upon us by presenting the opportunity of striking a blow at Spain. But now that we have obtained control—if we have—the question presented ought to be decided in the interests of justice and humanity."[29]

As implied in descriptions of the islands as "imposed" or "thrust" upon them, many emphasized that this new responsibility came to America unsought and unwanted. Here they saw further convincing evidence of providential necessity. As one *Pacific* contributor put it, the situation was "clearly of the Lord's planning, not ours," explainable only by the hand of a "marvelous providence."[30] Nothing illustrates this common perspective quite so well as the Texas *Baptist Standard*, one of the few early opponents of entering the war with

Spain. Throughout June and July, the editor frequently reminded his readers of his early opposition to the war, an opposition based on a prescient appreciation of the foreign policy problems it would create, now developing precisely as predicted. A June 9 column inspired by the annexation of Hawaii and applying its lessons to the Philippine situation began as if setting up a strong anti-imperialist argument. It recounted the nation's historic and well-justified refusal to allow entanglement with affairs beyond its borders, lamenting the fact that now "all at once and altogether we seem to have cast behind us the approved principles and policies of the past, and to have entered upon a new and none too promising era of national and international complications." Then, turning on a dime, he conceded "this may be our 'manifest destiny,' against which it is foolish, if not sinful to protest. God reigns and rules the destinies of men and nations according to plans of practical and prophetic wisdom that we may not understand."[31] The editor continued to develop this providential reading of events in his July columns. Debating the propriety of this or that policy on the theoretical level is one thing, but accomplished facts—facts like Dewey's victory in Manila—irreversibly move the discussion from the realm of what should be to the realm of what is. And the realm of what is—of accomplished facts—represents nothing short of divine providence writing "its fiat on the broad face of the world's destiny," making any protest against the new reality a protest against the decrees of the Almighty.[32] So, by the end of July, the *Baptist Standard* was criticizing opponents of expansion, gleefully noting the irony that some among them were the very figures who had pushed the president into war in the first place. Now the editor rejoiced to see that support for annexation was "taking wider root."[33]

What this common sense of conviction implied early on was that the specific policies necessary remained unclear, that those policies would be determined by the nation's humanitarian principles, and that, with those principles intact, they could be confident that circumstances and the exigencies of the moment represented the will of God. The *Outlook* expressed this tension as clearly as anyone: to what policy in the Philippines "events—that is, Providence—will lead us, no one can now judge; but, whatever the method of our policy, the governing principle is clear—justice and liberty to others, not aggrandizement for ourselves."[34] Writing in Lyman Abbott's *Outlook*, the Social Gospeler Washington Gladden similarly located the nation's duty in the uncertain terrain between a hands-off retreat from responsibility to the islands and permanent possession of the territories. From his perspective, what these extreme views shared was a prime commitment to national interest and an unwillingness to see the nation put others first: "I, for my part, believe that the motto 'Every nation for itself' is just as immoral as the motto 'Every man for himself.' Nations as well as men have relations and obligations to others which they must own and fulfill in the fear of God. . . . We will not go forth to rob, neither will we stay at home and look out of the window while the robbers are breaking into our neighbor's house."[35]

For Gladden, the *Outlook*, and many others who mirrored their perspective, an uncertain future was no disincentive when "duty" was clear. Duty became a commonly used term, best defined as the product of humanitarian principles married to a providential reading of concrete, historical circumstances. None could tell where duty might lead; Abbott, for his part, favored some form of protectorate over the islands on the model of the British Empire in Egypt, but the terms remained up for debate. What was settled, for him as for others, was that withdrawal from the Philippines would be a cruel refusal to recognize the deliverances of providence. Foreshadowing what would become a common line of argument, Abbott conceded that taking on responsibility for Spain's colonies went beyond the original purpose of the war for Cuban liberation. But wars are often begun for reasons other than those for which they are finished. Doubters need look no further than the Revolution, where soldiers at Lexington and Concord did not fight for independence, or the Civil War, where at Sumter emancipation was hardly in view.[36] "It is true that we entered on this war only for the emancipation of Cuba. . . . Nations as well as individuals are bore on upon a current which they cannot control, to accomplish results which they did not foresee. This is but to say that it is true of nations as of individuals that 'there's a divinity which shapes our ends, rough hew them as we may.'"[37]

By the time the peace protocol was signed, in mid-August, many agreed that America's duty was clear. Not knowing what the future would hold did not imply that the nation's modus operandi was any less set. Humanity and the providence of God as revealed in events made ongoing U.S. responsibility for the former Spanish colonies necessary. "The only answer we can see," the Georgia Baptist *Christian Index* concluded, "is that now contemplated to hold on to Manila, see that order is brought out of chaos, and then do our duty to humanity, in the light of our traditions as a nation, as that duty is made plain to us. In the providence of God we have as clearly been brought to the side of the Filipinos as was the Good Samaritan to the man on the Jericho road. It is for us to be the neighbor, whether the Philippines come under our flag or no."[38]

Expansion as Benign

By the end of the war a powerful case had emerged for a vaguely defined American control of the Spanish colonies as both a moral and a providential necessity. Faced with this argument, the unavoidable question must be why so many were able to look to a vaguely defined but clearly unprecedented future with such optimism. Why were they able to equate whatever happens so unequivocally with the purposes of God, identifying what was now possible as necessary? To put it differently, why were they so confident they could avoid the errors of the European colonizers they had so long condemned, especially Spain? Perhaps anticipating this line of questioning and after arguments for the necessity of expansion were largely in place, supporters of ongoing American involvement in the islands moved to defend their conclusions with arguments for why they would succeed where others had failed. Here too they drew from the convergence of "humanity" and providence that had emerged in their attempts to interpret the war itself. Their rule of distant territories would be benign because of the unique Christian character of the nation, a conviction reinforced by their interpretation of the humanitarian, altruistic cause of the war. And they would succeed in this new venture because of the favor of providence for the nation made visible throughout its history, nowhere more dramatically than in the events of the war. So America's strong moral character, bolstered by the guiding hand of providence, served as a pledge for an uncertain future.

Both in the initial justifications for going to war and in the interpretation of America's early success, the humanitarian, Christian moral character of the nation remained a central feature. Spain's precipitous fall from its sixteenth-century glory was attributed directly to its tyrannous, medieval, barbaric national character. America's simultaneous, meteoric rise from colonial infancy to world power was explainable only in terms of its liberty-loving moral fiber. This conviction helped define the argument for expansion and allay fears that it would not end well. And it was here that an interesting self-supporting circle emerged for justifying expansion. Arguments in favor drew heavily from definitions of American national character deployed from the earliest days of the war, but these early definitions grounded their assessment of America's altruistic moral quality precisely in the nation's unwillingness to fight for additional territory. Now many argued that America was capable of ruling additional territory because of its moral character as displayed in going to war.

The *Independent* and *Zion's Herald*, two of the earliest strong supporters of the expansion trajectory, were among the first to insist that the high moral character shown in the path to war would ensure American fidelity in this new responsibility. Citing what in early July was still a very uncertain future, the *Independent* showed no fear: "the American people, having undertaken this great work for civilization and human freedom, will stand in the line of their duty until the boundaries of civilization and freedom are enlarged. If that means a new departure, a new policy, and a new national career, they will enter it with stout hearts and, as Bismarck once said, in the fear of God and nothing else."[39] The editor of *Zion's Herald*, writing one week later, was more open about the dangers that attend responsibilities like those facing the United States, especially the nationalism centered on conquest that had eaten away at great nations of the past. America would avoid the mistakes of these European predecessors, he believed, because its Christians and their churches had the ability to sanctify desires for conquest. This war was for him a case in point: "The nation entered upon this war with profession of highest Christian purpose and unselfish sacrifice for human good. There is need that every follower of the Christ, every lover of humanity, should repeat and proclaim this creed and purpose by word and deed continually."[40]

It would be unfair to conclude that this editor or the many who would adopt arguments like his believed that America was above the possibility of moral failure. This column, after all, was an appeal to readers to work hard to ensure that their high moral values continued to flavor national policy. And the widespread concern for national ills such as liquor, prostitution, and urban violence showed that there were fears that American society could be threatened from within.[41] What we can safely conclude is that the possibility of moral collapse on the Spanish model was widely considered small at best. As the saying goes, politics ends at the water's edge; so too, apparently, did concerns about the security of America's Christian civilization. Its new foreign policy would succeed where others had failed because it moved into these uncharted waters with the purest of motives, putting the interests of others above its own. Perhaps the *Christian Standard* best captured the prevailing sentiment: "Men and nations do not blunder when they follow their unselfish impulses."[42]

Inseparably joined to this confidence in the purity of American motives was a strong conviction that God had ordained the task and would necessarily secure its success. Granted, the job of nation building would require "self-control, self-poise, absolute unselfishness, and infinite patience," one editor conceded, but this job was "divinely appointed." So, "if we are destined to a kind of imperialism, let us pray that it may be the imperialism that comes through the loftiness of our Christian ideals and the constraining power of our Christian influence and example." But there was no reason to doubt that these prayers would be answered. "With God's help," he concluded, "we shall meet the responsibility and fulfill the task."[43] The appeal to divine providence, reinforced by popular conceptions of American history, served as the primary ground of confidence in the success of an unprecedented foreign policy.

Three periodicals from different denominations and different locations provide useful examples of the appeal to providence as a source of confidence even as the future remained unclear. The *Baptist Argus* of Louisville began to use this line of reasoning in early July. Flush with joy over the incredible naval victory at Santiago just a few days earlier, the editor celebrated the prospect of a "Greater America" and unseen goals toward which God was guiding the nation. Insisting that this "is no time to dogmatize," he simply concluded, "The Nation Maker and Nation Overthrower has bared his right arm. The drama he is inspiring is too deep for us to see its closing act. We are content to await its unfolding."[44] By September the *Argus* was still waiting for the future to unfold, but the lines of immediate duty had emerged more clearly around an ongoing protectorate in the Philippines. Here it adopted the resolve of the *Standard*'s J. S. Dickerson, who concluded America must "stand ready to give the Philippine Islands civilization and religion until another sort of 'manifest destiny' . . . shall prove to us that our duty lies not here." Following Dickerson's lead, an editorial in this same September 8 issue marveled at how widespread the conviction of a new national destiny had become, asking, "how did we ever exist in the old state of things? We wonder what will be our next leap. Whatever it may be, we will not wonder about it very long after the leap is taken."[45] If the actual shape of future U.S. policy remained unclear, if words like "empire" and "expansion" remained abstractions, the security of the future remained above dispute for this editor. God, through events, would lead the way.

The *United Presbyterian*, by early August, had come down decisively against permanent retention of the islands, but it had also conceded that Spain could not keep them and that they were hardly ready for self-government. Given the circumstances, some sort of provisional government seemed necessary; the editor concluded that duty required "we take charge of the lands which may come under our control, and hold them as trustees for the people."[46] The shape of such a government and where it might lead were far from certain. But, writing one week later, he insisted Americans could rely on the same providential favor that had shepherded them through the late war: "God has been ruling in the direction given to our military management and movement since the beginning of the trouble. God will continue to rule. If we as a people constantly seek his guidance and follow the leadings of his providence all will be well."[47] By September 1, commentary on these themes had grown only more confident. There was no doubt God had created an opportunity, even a duty, for ongoing involvement in the Spanish colonies. Accepting this God-given responsibility, Americans could be certain of divine guidance and blessing. As for responsibility, "We have opened the way under the hand of God; now to close it and shut out the people of these islands from the blessings we have brought within their reach would be to resist God and close the door against the greater work and power now before us." And as for guidance, "How we shall meet this responsibility we must find out as we go along; we can know it only by going forward. He who calls to duty gives wisdom to the faithful."[48]

Perhaps even more than the *Baptist Argus* or the *United Presbyterian*, Boston's *Congregationalist* embodied a *que sera sera* perspective on the U.S. involvement in the Philippines. From the mid-August ceasefire through the peace treaty signing in early December, the editor reflected again and again on the need for some ongoing control of the islands. A firm providentialism grounded his confidence that the success of the nation's mission was more certain than its shape was well defined. Like the *United Presbyterian* and so many other publications, the *Congregationalist* did not favor permanent possession of the islands, opting instead for a vaguely conceived and possibly long-term protectorate. Unfazed by the uncertainty, the editor argued that the nation's confidence should stand in direct proportion to its conviction that God had imposed this new duty: "with the same conviction that we are summoned by Providence to meet and master the situation, we ought to face it with courage and confidence."[49] Column after column developed this theme, as the editor became more and more open to the idea of American expansion. By October he was arguing that the purity of America's motives, the prevailing interest in helping those who need it, was all that Americans could know for certain. Guided by this character, the country would develop national policies in response to new circumstances as they unfolded; beyond this point, only providence could secure a good result. An editorial note of October 13 captured the journal's outlook best. Facing new responsibilities in Puerto Rico, Cuba, and the Philippines, all

> must feel a deep responsibility and not a little sense of mystery concerning the meaning of it all in the divine plan. Conscience, duty, opportunity all say, "Go and carry what you believe to be vital principles of good government for all men, namely, universal education, freedom of religious belief, so much of political liberty as is prudent, government as a means, not an end." History says, "Are you sure you will bless rather than curse?" The nation can only reply as individuals do in like cases: "God knows. My motives are pure. The mystery and the duty are of God's ordering."[50]

This column, even more than others, shows a profound awareness of potential objections to U.S. policy in the Philippines, objections rooted in a long past full of abuses of which even America had been guilty. But when pure, humanitarian motives meet opportunity, trust in providence demands action. Desperate calls for America's return to its former isolation were, to the *Congregationalist*, simply unworthy of a people with "faith in divine Providence and an overruling destiny which calls upon nations to arise and go forth whither they know not."[51]

For these three periodicals—the *Baptist Argus*, the *United Presbyterian*, and the *Congregationalist*—as for the many others their commentary echoes, the same providence that had shaped America's history would prove faithful once again. It was this deep conviction, combined with a strong confidence in the moral character of the nation, that made possible a seamless transition from a pious disdain toward colonial government to widespread support for an American version in some form.

Granted, this widespread support for expansion and the providential language in which it was cloaked was not without critics. One of the most famous attacks, a sermon by the Presbyterian Henry van Dyke, attacked precisely the forms of providential arguments we have just traced through the religious press. Van Dyke insisted that many were peddling two contradictory justifications for American expansion, one of desperation and the other of destiny. Arguments from desperation described expansion as a difficult, unwanted, but necessary responsibility imposed upon the nation for lack of any viable alternative. Arguments from destiny cast expansion as a glorious accomplishment for a nation now come to adulthood, as one further step toward world civilization.[52] For Van Dyke, annexation could not be both an unwanted last resort and a glorious, inevitable destiny. But what his critique failed to grasp was the ability of providentialism to bridge this gap in a way secular notions of destiny could not. As the argument took shape in the religious press over the waning months of the war, U.S. involvement in distant islands with primitive peoples was not what anyone desired at the outset of the conflict. But, given the course of events, there now seemed no other option. The task—however unsought, even because it was unsought—must have been assigned by God. And, as providentially ordained, what was an unwanted responsibility would doubtless end in a glorious destiny, however unforeseeable.

This prominent reading of events was captured with great depth and clarity by the Reverend George Winton, a contributor to the Southern Methodists' *Methodist Review*. Writing near the end of the war an article that would be published later in the fall, Winton addressed one simple question: "Was the war providential?"[53] He began by tracing the major events of the war, noting the shift in the American people from sympathy for the Cubans, to wholehearted support for a war most originally believed unnecessary, to acceptance of some form of ongoing responsibility in the Philippines following Dewey's dramatic victory. He noted how quickly so many Americans had gone from not knowing where the Philippines were to generally believing it was America's destiny to control them, abandoning along the way all opposition to the annexation of Hawaii or concomitant concerns about preserving the Monroe Doctrine. Faced with this incredible turn of events, he concluded, "hardly anything in history equals the lightning-like change of public sentiment in regard to territorial expansion which followed the battle of Manila."[54] Some might choose to explain this change as an attack of the European "greed of territory," Winton conceded, but he embraced a quite different explanation: "More than anything else it was the feeling of destiny, which being interpreted means, to the vast majority of Americans, Providence." The overwhelming victories following Manila, especially that at Santiago, only served to deepen "the impression of providential leading." "There was a sort of awe in the presence of these stupendous successes," Winton noted. "It was not the fact of victory that caused it, for that was expected; it was the unexampled manner of the victory." So, many found here clear evidence of providential destiny, but for Winton the most important feature of this response was the precedent it set for facing the results of the war. As he put it in a passage previously cited, "the tremendous sway of this conviction among the American people is a phenomenon to be reckoned with quite apart from any opinion as to its soundness. *It prepared them to accept the results of the war in the same way that they had already accepted the war itself, as manifest destiny.*"[55]

The remainder of Winton's article moved beyond his account of public opinion to consider whether anything in the war's results justified "this general conviction of the interference of that Will which is over all." Unsurprisingly, he was thoroughly convinced. His argument followed familiar lines, charting the downfall of Spain and its despotic empire along with increased sympathies between England and America. But his primary argument rested on the new opportunities for America to influence the world for good. This was a task for which the United States was uniquely suited. In both religion and government, it could not be more opposite Spain, he argued, and the triumph of the individual in popular government has given the American a "very sensitive regard for the rights of others. His unfaltering allegiance to justice fits him in a peculiar manner for the governing of subject nations."[56] This new opportunity—governing subject nations—would surely prove difficult, but Americans pure in motive would rather face it than "transfer them to the dominion of others less scrupulous." And they would face it with a confidence rooted in their "faith in the God of nations and the persuasion that he is leading us." It was this conviction, Winton concluded, that secured the "invincible American confidence in our ability to meet national issues as they arise."[57] And it was this conviction that grounded a distinctly Christian "might makes right" ideology. In the words of B. W. Featherston, a minister from Meridian, Mississippi, "The measure of *opportunity* is to the Christian always the measure of his *obligation.*"[58]

Selling Expansion:
William McKinley on Duty and Destiny

When religious leaders like Winton and Featherston framed U.S. responsibility in the Philippines as necessary under God for humanity's sake, their appeal to providentialism did not fall on deaf ears. Beginning in the fall of 1898, no less than President William McKinley himself would become the most consistent public proponent of expansion as a divinely imposed responsibility. McKinley was widely known to be a devout Methodist and a faithful worshipper at Washington's Metropolitan Methodist Episcopal Church. It was here that he had heard his new minister, F. M. Bristol, preach eloquently on the providence of God in the events of history and on America's unique role in the world's future.[59] When McKinley brought his decision to annex the islands before the public from October through December, he did so primarily using the terms worked out months earlier in the religious press. America, true to its humanitarian character, would follow the logic of events as the revealed will of God.

McKinley's role in America's progress toward empire has been the subject of vigorous debate among later observers. Historians' descriptions of the president's posture toward the new foreign policy decisions have run the gamut from heroic leader to spineless follower to calculated imperialist, depending on who was writing the biography and when.[60] John Dobson's 1988 study offers a more nuanced account. Aptly titled *Reticent Expansionism*, Dobson's volume portrays McKinley not as a "dynamic empire builder" but as a capable administrator who typically sought the "path of least resistance to his conscience." He was able to perceive what others wanted and was willing to go along as far as his principles allowed. By Dobson's reckoning, McKinley led the country to war not by calculated design but as a consequence of "historical forces and external conditions that converged while he was at the nation's helm."[61] Dobson explains McKinley's decision to annex the islands similarly. Denying that any evidence exists to suggest McKinley planned this move in advance, he describes the president as guided by the course of events. The decision to retain the Philippines may have been shaped more by the fact that "no more attractive alternative ever emerged" than by anything else.[62] Whether or not Dobson is correct about McKinley's private plans and ambitions, his public rhetoric through the fall of 1898 certainly reflected the *que sera sera* approach to events that Dobson describes.

Perhaps the most famous anecdote regarding the religious dimensions of McKinley's decision to annex the Philippines is his reputed conversation with a delegation of Methodists received at the White House. The following represents the conversation as originally reported:

> I walked the floor of the White House night after night until midnight; and I am not ashamed to tell you, gentlemen, that I went down on my knees and prayed Almighty God for light and guidance more than one night. And one night it came to me this way—I don't know how it was, but it came: (1) That we could not give them back to Spain—that would be cowardly and dishonorable; (2) that we could not turn them over to France or Germany—our commercial rivals in the Orient—that would be bad business and discreditable; (3) that we could not leave them to themselves—they were unfit for self-government—and they would soon have anarchy and misrule over there worse than Spain's was; and (4) that there was nothing left for us to do but to take them all, and to educate the Filipinos, and uplift and civilize and Christianize them, and by God's grace do the very best we could by them, as our fellow-men for whom Christ also died. And then I went to bed, and went to sleep, and slept soundly, and the next morning I sent for the chief engineer of the War Department (our mapmaker), and I told him to put the Philippines on the map of the United States, and there they are, and there they will stay while I am President![63]

It is not difficult to understand why this episode has received so much attention. However, historians since have posed serious challenges to its authenticity.[64] And, even if authentic, the conversation is far from a dependable measure of the president's thinking at the time of the original decision. It is said to have occurred on November 21, 1899, a full year after he gave instructions to retain the islands, and the report itself was not published until 1903.[65] With such a significant time lapse, the accuracy of the account is suspicious at best, even if the conversation did occur.

A far better barometer of McKinley's reasoning is the collection of speeches he gave on a tour of the Midwest, a tour that spanned the three weeks leading up to his official directive to the peace commissioners in Paris that they demand cession of the Philippines. Some suggest the president had made his decision as early as September, but at the very least the enthusiastic response to his rhetoric provided all the confirmation he needed.[66] He would lead his people forward, but only where they wanted to go. Framing the issue precisely as had the religious press, McKinley consistently referred to vague U.S. policy in the Philippines as "responsibility" or "duty," a duty imposed upon the nation by the course of events but one that it would surely fulfill thanks to its strength of character and the blessing of divine providence.[67]

The tour began on October 11, with stops in many small towns throughout Iowa. The brief stump speeches that day carried signs of things to come. Certain elements featured prominently with every stop—thanks for volunteers, celebration of new levels of patriotism and national unity, gratitude to God for the nation's victories. Other references looked to the future, always to strong applause. McKinley assured a Clinton, Iowa, crowd that America possessed a "good national conscience, and we have the courage of destiny."[68] "We have accepted a war for humanity," he told residents of Cedar Rapids. "We can accept no terms of peace which shall not be in the interest of humanity."[69] His final speech of the day, in Missouri Valley, was even more specific about future prospects, a future filled with "grave problems." To meet the challenge, Americans must "act together not only for the good of our own country, but for the good of other peoples, in relation to whom the war has imposed a duty upon us."[70]

The following day McKinley arrived in Omaha for the Trans-Mississippi Exposition, the original occasion for the trip. His speech at the Exposition represents one of the most complete explanations of his perspective on the new national "duty." He began by celebrating the progress of the nation in material prosperity as well as in education, science, and invention, national progress that had included periods of expansion defined by the spirit of the Constitution rather than by "temptations of conquest." Faced now with new "international responsibilities," the nation must "follow duty even if desire opposes," avoiding along the way any "temptation of aggression."[71] The body of the speech was a dramatic recounting of the course of the war, emphasizing in particular the deeper bond it had forged between North and South. But McKinley saved the strongest language for his conclusion; it was language any number of religious editors had supplied months earlier. The nation had been led thus far by providence; its guiding principles and deepest motives were concern for humanity. America would take whatever action those principles required; facing divinely imposed circumstances and acting faithfully, Americans could be certain of divine favor in the future. In short, they could not fail. McKinley's conclusions are worth quoting at length:

> The faith of a Christian nation recognizes the hand of Almighty God in the ordeal through which we have passed. Divine favor seemed manifest everywhere. In fighting for humanity's sake we have been signally blessed. We did not seek war. To avoid it, if this could be done in honor and justice to the rights of our neighbors and ourselves, was our constant prayer. The war was no more invited by us than were the questions which are laid at our door by its results. Now as then we will do our duty.[72]

Having clarified the nature and origin of America's national duty, McKinley then offered his reasons for confidence in future success:

The problems will not be solved in a day. Patience will be required—patience combined with sincerity of purpose and unshaken resolution to do right, seeking only the highest good of the nation, and recognizing no other obligation, pursuing no other path, but that of duty.

Right action follows right purpose. We may not at all times be able to divine the future, the way may not always seem clear; but if our aims are high and unselfish, somehow and in some way the right end will be reached. The genius of the nation, its freedom, its wisdom, its humanity, its courage, its justice, favored by divine Providence, will make it equal to every task and the master of every emergency.[73]

These themes appeared regularly over the following days as McKinley spoke at stops in various Iowa and Illinois towns en route to Chicago. To great applause, the president assured a Chariton, Iowa, crowd that "territory sometimes comes to us when we go to war in a holy cause, and whenever it does the banner of liberty will float over it and bring, I trust, blessings and benefits to all the people."[74] Divine guidance joined American altruism as a theme during a stop in Monmouth, Illinois: "May God give us the wisdom to perform our part with fidelity, not only to our own interests, but to the interests of those who, by the fortunes of war, are brought within the radius of our influence."[75] And, echoing Lincoln, McKinley made an even more explicit appeal to providence in an October 14 speech at Saint Louis. "We must pursue duty step by step," he concluded. "We must follow the light as God has given us to see the light, and he has singularly guided us, not only from the beginning of our great government, but down through every crisis to the present hour; and I am sure it is the prayer of every American that he shall still guide and direct us."[76]

McKinley's nexus of humanitarian duty and providential destiny reached its culmination in an October 19 speech to the Citizen's Banquet in Chicago. The occasion was a Peace Jubilee celebration, Chicago's rendition of an event held in many major American cities through the fall. The president's widely publicized speech that night came to define the content and significance of the entire speaking tour. His opening was quite typical: sober thanksgiving for the events of the war and a call for "calm reason" in facing future responsibilities the war had "put upon" the nation. These responsibilities "could not have been well foreseen," he argued, but "we cannot escape the obligations of victory." As he had so often before, so now he insisted that the nature of these obligations must be defined by the same liberating and humanitarian goals that had inspired the war: "The war with Spain was undertaken, not that the United States should increase its territory, but that oppression at our very doors should be stopped. This noble sentiment must continue to animate us, and we must give to the world the full demonstration of the sincerity of our purpose."[77]

Then came the line that would define the speech: "Duty determines destiny." Duty, for McKinley, represented what must be done, the action demanded of a nation governed by humanitarian principles when confronted with specific circumstances. Destiny, then, referred to the results of one's actions. The shape of the nation's destiny could not be known with certainty, but, if faithful in their duty, Americans could know their future would not lead to "failure and dishonor." This argument the president grounded firmly in the precedent of American history, where time and again God had led the nation to glorious results beyond the comprehension of its human leaders. Such was the case with the Revolution, again with the Civil War, and so it would be with the results of this war: "The war with Spain was not of our seeking, and some of its consequences may not be to our liking. Our vision is often defective. Short-sightedness is a common malady, but the closer we get to things or they get to us, the clearer our view and the less obscure our duty."[78] Americans, in short, could face an uncertain future with confidence because their character, their principles, would ensure fulfillment of the duty imposed by providence. And, its duty fulfilled, the nation could rely on the same providential guidance seen clearly at Lexington and Concord, at Sumter and Gettysburg, and at Manila and Santiago. They could not fail.

The tour of the Midwest went on for several more days, and from the beginning McKinley framed the Philippines question as an open one, to be determined by the will of the people and the decision of the peace commissioners.[79] The decision, though, was his, and he had already made it. Less than ten days after his Chicago speech, he officially instructed the peace commissioners to demand cession of the entire archipelago. The grounds for the decision were stated simply and concisely. The United States was in control of all the Philippines, a false claim but pivotal for justifying annexation. And, more important, the nation had no alternative but to accept the grave responsibilities imposed by duty and destiny.[80]

Celebrating Expansion: Thanksgiving, 1898

Christian editors followed McKinley's speaking tour with great interest. Attention to the war and its results had waned noticeably in the religious press over the months since the fighting had ended, but sight of their Christian president framing the nation's identity and purpose in their religious terms brought a renewed focus to the expansion issue. This interest tended to center on McKinley's "duty" and "destiny" formulation. Not all were enthusiastic about the terms, particularly the idea that the national destiny would be inevitably positive, but such concerns were the exception rather than the rule.[81] Most likely saw here an explicit endorsement of their long-standing views on expansion.[82] "Duty" affirmed inevitability, given the nation's guiding character and the circumstances now imposed upon it. "Destiny" affirmed that, whatever shape American expansion might assume, the results would be beneficial to all involved. They could be as sure of this as they were of the nation's moral fiber and the divine providence whose favor it had always enjoyed. Given this formulation, according to the *Congregationalist*, to refuse to support the president and the policy he deemed necessary would be no less than to "repudiate our faith in God."[83]

Celebration of McKinley's policy reached its fullest expression during the festivities surrounding Thanksgiving Day in late November 1898. By then, news of the president's demands for cession of the entire Philippine archipelago had circulated widely. That Spain would honor these demands was considered a mere formality, weak as Spain was and lacking any international support. All that remained, then, was to frame the meaning of America's new international position. A group of Thanksgiving sermons, published and unpublished, provides a fine illustration of the ways some Christian ministers did just that. When compared as a group to the arguments made by the religious press over the summer, they reveal very little that is surprising. The arguments were basically the same; only conviction had grown.

The overlap in content among these sermons is dramatic, little short of formulaic. Naturally, the occasion inspired reflection on the events of the past year and the various reasons for national thanksgiving. This year, references to industrial and agricultural prosperity and material abundance were vastly overshadowed by the details of the war with Spain. The sermons as a group serve as a compendium of interpretive themes that had emerged several months earlier. Nearly all, for example, gave thanks for the blessing of unity inspired by the war, both national unity and renewed friendliness with Mother England. The Knoxville minister Robert Bachman had been a Confederate sympathizer during the Civil War. Now, he hailed the new union between North and South that even after thirty years had still required something more to perfect it. "In the providence of God," he concluded, "that something came in our war with Spain."[84] Edward Noyes of the First Church of Newton, Massachusetts, saw the war as a blow to the division on economic theories that had separated East and West: "When the New York millionaire and the cowboy from the plains charged together up San Juan hill, and shared together the privations of the march and the camp, they did not talk financial theories!"[85] As much as if not more than national unity, ministers celebrated their newfound unity of sentiment and purpose with Great Britain. New York Baptist Robert MacArthur even preached his Thanksgiving sermon with his pulpit once again draped with the Union Jack, flanked by two American flags.[86]

Thanksgiving celebrations also provided an opportunity to reflect on the nation's history, cast along the lines set during the summer, tracing America's progress from infancy to maturity. MacArthur was hardly the only one to conclude that "we have grown more in the last six months than ordinarily we would grow in a hundred years."[87] The Presbyterian luminary George Pentecost looked back to the nation's infancy, when it lived as if in a "nursery" as an "insular republic." But now, almost instantly, America had been called to enter the world stage as a great power, however reluctantly. In short, he argued, "we have had to accept the providence of God and recognize the fact that we have come of age."[88] One of the more extensive treatments of this national coming of age was a sermon by the New England minister George Whitefield Stone, which charted the nation's early years of preparation, years consumed by the quest for material prosperity and political stability. The war revealed what he called a "new force" throughout America, variously called "altruism" or the "Brotherhood of Man," which was in essence a conviction by one with power that others will have the same rights, privileges, and opportunities. This awareness, this force, constituted national adulthood, and that was the time of testing the nation was facing in 1898. For Stone, the results of the test were clear: "This great American Republic, we call the United States, has reached its years of discretion, has reached its manhood. It must now disclose to the world the nature and quality of the education it has acquired in its years of preparation for the responsibility which has been suddenly thrust upon it. Whether for weal or for woe it is undeniably true that this Republic to-day, holds the national leadership of one half of the world."[89]

If the central themes of the Thanksgiving sermons were unremarkable, what set them apart from sermons earlier in the year was their polemical nature, bent as they were on defending a policy that was now more concrete, at least for the short term. The die had been cast, and America would have control over the Philippines. Though firm advocacy for permanent retention of the Philippines was the exception rather than the rule, nearly all favored ongoing, open-ended control in the islands and supported the administration's decision.[90] The ministers' defense of this policy involved some familiar elements, beginning with the dismissal of would-be alternatives such as allowing self-government in the islands, returning them to Spain, or leaving them to another power.[91] But the crux of their defense came in an almost formulaic response to a set of common objections to expansion. First, there was the objection that expansion was inconsistent with historical American policy. The stock response here was by this time well worn: America had been expanding since its inception. Control of the Philippines was the same in kind as control of the Northwest Territory, Louisiana, California, or Alaska, however much it might differ in form or degree.[92] Second, some argued that expansion of influence in the Philippines would represent a change in national character and political values. Response to this objection was less uniform. On the one hand, most were conceding some change in character as the nation moved from its isolationism into international activism; this much had occurred with the decision to intervene in Cuba. But all strongly denied any change in the humanitarian, liberty-loving principles that defined the nation, casting the new responsibilities in the Philippines as a fulfillment of those principles. Ruling an unwilling people along the path to self-government would represent an "admitted inconsistency" with America's democratic principles, Marcus Brownson conceded, but a necessary and benign inconsistency because adopted in the interests of humanity.[93] Finally, these sermons clearly felt the weight of the objection to expansion based on its inconsistency with the original liberating goals of the war. The most common device for meeting this challenge was a comparison of this war with the American Revolution and the Civil War. Inspired perhaps by McKinley's use of this line of argument, several ministers reminded their congregants that the Revolution did not begin to secure outright independence from Great Britain, nor did the Civil War begin as a contest over emancipation. The providence of God expanded the original goals of those wars beyond all expectations, and that is precisely what God had done through the war with Spain. Americans had begun the war to liberate Cuba, but the victory in Manila opened a vast new horizon for extending that same liberation to more peoples than they could have imagined.[94]

This view of the war's results through the lenses of humanity and providence extended beyond the defensive posture just outlined. It formed the basis of the positive message of most sermons as well. As a group, they showed yet again that the results of the war, especially the policy of expansion, would be viewed directly through the prism of the war itself. As a composite, the argument took the following shape. In going to war on behalf of an oppressed people, even when national interests dictated isolation, America had proved its humanitarian, Christian character. The success of the American military, with every conceivable detail favoring the American cause, proved that the providence of God so familiar in the nation's history remained firmly on their side. Now faithfulness to its character demanded further action on behalf of those Spain had long tyrannized, and in fulfilling their duty to humanity Americans could be confident of the continued favor of God. They were God's nation, doing God's work.

These themes pervaded this group of Thanksgiving sermons. So, for example, many gave thanks for the humanitarian concerns that had driven the nation to war, now invoked with a view to the purity of American motives facing future responsibilities. The Reverend George van de Water recalled that the nation had tried in vain by other methods to end "Spain's merciless tyranny in Cuba," but in the end it was forced into an "unavoidable," "honorable," "holy war." This same desire to end tyranny and establish liberty would sanctify the nation's actions in a venture that had led others, like Spain, to their downfall. "To spread the blessings of freedom," he concluded, "is a motive that must be pleasing to God. . . . Fears for the future do not haunt me. Our ability to govern our own children and any that God puts in our way to adopt is certain."[95]

"Fears for the future do not haunt me"—with these words Van de Water captured the prevailing sentiment as well as anyone else. What cause for fear when, as another claimed, "God has called this nation to a Messianic trust," having "made our consciences too sensitive" to "enslave," "loot," or "despoil" the islands.[96] Far from exploitation, the American presence in the islands would constitute a "splendid service to humanity," according to George Whitefield Stone, a service "truly Christian in character." "This war was begun in the interest of humanity," he concluded. "Let us keep it directed to that single end; let us make it 'God's missionary,' as some one has called it, to uplift the living."[97]

The roots of this widespread confidence—confidence in America's ability to govern well, to govern for the benefit of others—were firmly planted in the rich soil of national righteousness, a righteousness displayed clearly in the late war and now preserved by God for his purposes. Edward Noyes described it well:

[A]s new occasions bring new duties, and our giant strength may righteously be put forth, without menace to the rights of others, God grant that this liberty-loving and tyrant-hating nation may again be used of Him to the pulling down of strongholds and the demolishing of the citadels of infamy. And as we hesitate in the face of the unknown future, we sing again the old words of the prophet, "Open ye gates, that the righteous nation which keepeth the truth may enter in." So may God keep the heart of the nation fixed on righteousness and truth, and we may not fear to enter any door He opens before us.[98]

America could—would—rule righteously. For Noyes there was no doubt; America would not abuse its strength, and the rights of others would remain secure, no matter the twists and turns of the uncertain future.

As one can see even in Noyes's reflection, this unbridled optimism rested on more than confidence in the nation's character. Undergirding and stabilizing national righteousness was an omnipotent providence, displayed nowhere more clearly than the events of the war with Spain as a pledge for future guidance. Not surprisingly, the two major naval victories held center stage. Several preachers described these battles as better fit for the book of Joshua than for modern history or as "the Miracle of Moses at the Red Sea wrought again for the emancipator of the reconcentrados."[99] For George Pentecost, Admiral Dewey's victory in particular was an "epoch-making event," and "the turning point of American destiny has been there" ever since. The voice of God speaks through the course of events, Pentecost believed, and here it spoke clearly: "The very voice of God called to us through the mouth of Dewey's guns and told us that there was a wider and greater work for us to do than to free one island from tyranny and a million and one-half of people from cruelty and death."[100] Like Pentecost, Marcus Brownson specifically grounded future responsibility in the providential course of the war. "The dawn of a new day was in the far east," he began, "where the thundering guns of our noble ships awoke the world to the realization that American freedom would share her glorious privileges with the oppressed and the enslaved of the earth. And from that early morning hour of the new day, on to its height at Santiago and El Caney, there seemed to be—there was—the special protection and the particular help of the omnipotent God given to our cause." Given this record of providential blessing and faced with the dangers and duties of a new "national destiny," Brownson asked and definitively answered one simple question: "shall we lose faith in the guidance of God? These perplexities are the result of the war into which 'the pillar of cloud and fire' led us. These responsibilities were not of our seeking. Nor can they be laid arbitrarily aside. God had in store for us a greater mission than we had mapped for ourselves. Until now by *isolation*, and now by *expansion*, it is ours to brighten and to bless the world. No nation liveth unto itself."[101]

The favor of God toward America throughout its history, and especially during the war with Spain, convinced these ministers that they need not know—or fear—what the future might bring. Because God was continuing to work out his purposes for the world through this nation, the future would bring only good both to America and to those under its sway. Knoxville's Robert Bachman, citing President McKinley, spoke for many:

> in view of all that He [God] has done for us as a land and people, we hopefully and trustingly place our confidence in Him for the future. We know not into what seas our Ship of State shall sail. We know not what storms and perils may confront her in her onward voyage. We know not the harbor in which she shall finally drop anchor. But we do know that God is at the helm. He is a wise and good pilot. As such, He will surely bring our Ship of State to His desired

haven. It is for us to obey His orders. It is for us to follow the leadings of His providence.[102]

It is true that not all shared the optimism or imbibed the same providential reasoning predominant at the time. In fact, two of the most widely noted anti-imperialist sermons were preached that same Thanksgiving, and they reserved their most pungent criticism for the widespread appeals to providence. Besides the aforementioned sermon by Henry van Dyke, Charles Parkhurst, a fellow New York Presbyterian, preached a sermon every bit as critical if slightly less famous. Like Van Dyke, he celebrated the war and remained grateful for America's success, but he lamented the "abruptness with which established convictions a century old were instantly knocked to pieces by the discharge of American guns in Manila Bay." Parkhurst would go on to list most of the major objections to which other ministers were responding in sermons across America, but what seemed to bother Parkhurst most was the swift and, to him, thoughtless ease with which Americans embraced the idea of an expanded foreign policy. He insisted he was not necessarily opposed to moving beyond isolation; he merely opposed doing so without proper consideration and in the heat of battles won. And his sharpest rebuke came down on those religious folk who discovered "in Dewey's victory a new edition of the old pillar of fire that used to blaze in front of the Hebrews on their way to the Promised Land."[103] Van Dyke, too, framed his comprehensive attack on the arguments for annexation of the Philippines by foregrounding what he saw as the contradictory appeals to desperation and destiny.[104]

Besides their sharp invective, what is remarkable about these sermons by Parkhurst and Van Dyke is the underlying and often overlooked commonality they share with most of their pro-expansion counterparts.[105] Their arguments are thoroughgoing condemnations of a policy of permanent retention, but few in the religious press or the pulpits were actually advocating such a policy. Many never specified a preference for one policy over another, and of those who did most supported some sort of provisional, albeit open-ended, government by the United States until the Filipinos were equipped to govern themselves. But both Parkhurst and Van Dyke also conceded that some provisional responsibility was inevitable to prevent anarchy and to prepare the islands for democracy. In fact, Van Dyke included a preface to the published edition of his sermon in which he drew explicit boundaries between what he was and was not condemning. "Please do not mistake the purpose of this sermon," he wrote. "It is not against the war of 1898. That is ended. It is not against the avowed object of that war—the liberation of Cuba. That is accomplished." Then came the crucial distinction: "It is not against the full discharge of our responsibilities to the inhabitants of the Philippines. These must be met by doing our best to help them to secure liberty, order, and justice. The sermon is against the assumption that the only way to meet our responsibilities is to annex the Philippine Islands as a permanent portion of our National domain."[106] In his preference for provisional government over permanent retention, Van Dyke was in good company. None other than Lyman Abbott of the *Outlook*, who has been treated as a leading figure among the supporters of expansion, openly favored a protectorate in his own Thanksgiving sermon.[107]

What set Van Dyke and Parkhurst apart, then, was less their policy preferences than that they did not share the prevailing optimism of their colleagues. They did not believe that one providential deliverance led inevitably to another or that the good motives that had led to the war with Spain would certainly guide the nation through the results of that war. Looking back to America's experience with its subject Indian and African populations, they warned of what could happen in the Philippines. And they argued that debilitating, unaddressed problems at home would cripple American efforts to reform the world abroad. But their case proved unpersuasive; given the dramatic events of the past year, this was no time for pessimism.

❖

That Henry van Dyke's concerns were not widely shared is evident in the response to the treaty of peace signed less than two weeks after his Thanksgiving sermon.[108] Spain had little choice but to sign an agreement that stripped the nation of its entire presence in the West Indies and in the Philippines. As if to avoid the impression that it was treating its beaten foe too severely, the American government compensated Spain for the Philippines in the amount of $20 million. Of course, many were quick to celebrate this as a gesture of utmost humanity toward an erstwhile enemy, most definitely not a purchase of the islands. McKinley, for his part, had privately decided against the propriety of a merely provisional government and moved quickly after the treaty to annex the islands through executive order. By this maneuver, he ensured that the congressional debate over ratification of the treaty would be a debate not over whether to annex the Philippines but over whether to revoke the gains made at great cost to the military. This was a debate he knew he could win, and he was right. The Filipino insurgents had been working since June to establish their own representative government and would officially adopt a constitution in January 1899. Moreover, they controlled the vast majority of the island territory. But McKinley remained convinced that no viable government existed there, a conviction that would cost him dearly in the months to come.[109]

Few Christian voices in press or pulpit took any notice of McKinley's actions through December. They were swallowed up by end-of-year retrospectives that marveled at recent events and at what glories might be yet to come. Their optimism was in part a product of their Progressive Era environment, but it was also more specific. Their sense of purpose was deeply rooted in convictions about the nation's character and the meaning of its history. America, in spite of its sins, was a righteous nation concerned most for the interests of humanity, molded under the watchful care of God into a potent force for good in the world. The war with Spain had proven that America was at the forefront of God's providential purposes, riding the crest of history's wave. So one Reverend Arthur Ackerman, writing for the Congregationalist *Pacific*, offered his perspective on "the significance of 1898." He located the meaning of American action as part of a continuum that included Luther at Wittenburg, the Pilgrims at Plymouth, and Lincoln during the Civil War. All were examples, he argued, of men who "swung into the current of God's purposes," and in this year past America "has swung into the line of God's wishes for the good of humanity."[110] Located thus securely in the current of God's unstoppable purposes, the nation's future, however it might take shape, would be even greater than its past. This perspective, forged during the months of the war, determined the way many responded—or failed to respond—to the decisions McKinley and his peace commission made in December. The editor of the *United Presbyterian* spoke for most when he argued that the cession of the Philippines did not represent the much-maligned "territorial aggrandizement." Rather, "we believe that our President and the peace commission desire to follow, as they have been following, the leadings of divine providence in their negotiations with Spain. And we also believe that the great Jehovah, who has so manifestly 'gone forth with our hosts' and 'covered their heads in the day of battle,' will lead on until 'His way shall be known upon the earth, his saving health among all nations.'"[111] It was this reading of events, of the nation's character, history, and purpose, that empowered the *Outlook* to conclude, fatefully, that "the campaign initiated for freedom must not be, will not be, cannot be, allowed to end in despotism."[112]

Conclusion

For the cover of their December 1, 1898, issue, the editors of the *Evangelist* chose a full-page extended quotation from Psalm 2, the first of the so-called Messianic Psalms.

> Yet I have set my king
> Upon my holy hill of Zion.
> I will tell of the decree:
> Jehovah said unto me, Thou art my son;
> This day have I begotten thee.
> Ask of me, and I will give thee the nations for thine inheritance,
> And the uttermost parts of the earth for thy possession.[1]

This has been a study of what I have called messianic interventionism. I chose the term primarily because it captures the prevailing sense that America could intervene in the affairs of others nations not to advance America's national interests but on behalf of the weak. But selfless sacrifice is only one piece of the complex biblical portrait of the messiah. Etymologically, the word speaks of the anointed one, the world's true and conquering king. If America, playing the role of Christ in the world, had lain upon the cross for those who longed for freedom, the time would soon come for taking up the rod of iron.[2]

The scope of messianic interventionism—encompassing both self-sacrifice and kingly rule—emerges in another poem written by Rudyard Kipling shortly after the conclusion of the war.

> Take up the White Man's burden—
> Send forth the best ye breed—
> Go bind your sons to exile
> To serve your captives' need;
> To wait in heavy harness,
> On fluttered folk and wild—

> Your new-caught, sullen peoples,
> Half-devil and half-child.

So began Kipling's hymn welcoming America to the imperial enterprise, published in *McClure's Magazine* in February 1899 under the title "The White Man's Burden."[3] Kipling would go on to use stronger, more explicitly imperialistic language than that used by most supporters of American expansion, so it should come as little surprise that the poem became a rallying point for anti-imperialists and earned strong condemnation among African Americans who had supported the war with Spain.[4] Nevertheless, Kipling's lines meshed perfectly with the now-prominent conviction that the nation's duty was defined by the dictates of humanity, imposed by the trajectory of history, and therefore set by the will of Providence, which had prepared the nation for such a time as this. So, in this vein, the *Christian Evangelist* offered a wholehearted endorsement of the poem: "There is, in our judgment, more genuine, pure, unselfish religion in the following poem by Rudyard Kipling—his latest message to America—than in all the anti-imperialistic, sermon literature with which the country has been flooded. It recognizes such a thing as the moral obligation of stronger nations in lifting up the weaker and helpless peoples to a higher civilization and to a condition of self-help."[5]

Kipling did in fact present his readers with the obligation to "seek another's profit / And work another's gain," but the tone of his celebration was hardly celebratory. It is no accident that Kipling spoke of the white man's "burden"; nearly half the poem reflects on the severe costs of fulfilling this duty toward lower races, promising Americans they could expect from their subjects ingratitude at best, outright hostility at worst:

> Take up the White Man's burden—
> And reap his old reward:
> The blame of those ye better,
> The hate of those ye guard—
> The cry of hosts ye humour
> (Ah, slowly!) toward the light:—
> "Why brought he us from bondage,
> Our loved Egyptian night?"[6]

Kipling's warning was more prescient than perhaps even he realized. Soon after the poem was published and just before the final ratification of the peace treaty with Spain, Filipino troops made their first attack in what would be a long, bloody struggle with American occupying forces in the Philippines. This was a turn of events Kipling had led his readers to expect. If anything, the realism embedded in his poem served to refine the prevailing optimism, preparing Americans to endure expected temporary setbacks in service of a mission that was ultimately worth the cost.

Indeed, theirs was a sense of divine calling to international intervention sharpened in the concrete circumstances of 1898. Given the nature of America's cause, a Christlike sacrifice on behalf of the weak and oppressed; given the national self-conception refined by contrast with the Spanish enemy; given the unprecedented scale of the American victory and the long-awaited union of the Anglo-Saxon race around a common sense of international responsibility; given the clear faithfulness to Christian duty and the overwhelming testimony to providential favor, expansion of American influence in the Philippines and wherever in the world circumstances might allow seemed to many church leaders inviolably right. For Josiah Strong, perhaps the era's most articulate voice for Christian nationalism in America, these were "God's great alphabet with which he spells for man his providential purposes."[7] To turn aside from such an expansion, he argued, would be "treason to ourselves, to the Anglo-Saxon race, to humanity, and to Western civilization."[8] This commitment to messianic interventionism, the foregoing chapters have argued, was inseparable from the distinctive features of the largely forgotten war with Spain. In fact, this commitment emerged from the war strong enough to weather the ironic brutalities of the Filipino insurgency and lived on to shape popular interpretations of the far more consequential and cataclysmic conflict twenty years later. In some ways, this conception of American responsibility, forged in the fires of 1898, lives on today.

A Tragic Irony: Messianic Interventionism and the Filipino Insurgency

The treaty of peace signed with Spain on December 10 determined that the Philippines, like the Caribbean islands, would come under American control for an indefinite period of time. The only remaining ambiguity surrounded whether the Senate would ratify the treaty in early February 1899. There were vocal opponents of the treaty's provisions in Congress and in American culture at large, where the Anti-Imperialist League was beginning to find its stride in the public case against expansion. The Filipinos, for their part, led by the insurgent military hero Emilio Aguinaldo, had no intention of enduring what they saw as yet another colonial regime. They determined to settle for nothing short of self-government. Recognizing that the Americans had no plans for leaving the islands anytime soon, Filipinos felt enormous hostility toward the occupiers, hostility that reached a boiling point by late January 1899. On the night of February 4, the first shots were fired in a war that stretched on for three bloody years. This turn of events, perhaps more than anything else, secured ratification of the treaty when Congress met to vote just forty hours later.[9]

There is perhaps no greater testimony to the strength of the interventionist ideology forged in the circumstances of 1898 than the fact that widespread support for it held firm even as the circumstances shifted in 1899. Christian leaders favoring expansion proved remarkably able to accommodate these unfortunate developments with little cost to their prevailing optimism. So certain were they that the will of God was in the events that had brought them to this place that they balked little at brushing aside the claims of the Filipinos to autonomy. These natives were not prepared for the responsibility, and American tutelage would be for their good even if they failed to recognize that fact at the time and even if it must be bought with blood. This was a perspective for which nearly a year of public commentary had well prepared the American clergy. Writing for the Episcopal *Churchman* in an article published on the day fighting began in the Philippines, Bishop William Doane defended U.S. policy against the charges of the anti-imperialist camp. "The fact is," Doane argued, "that whatever enlargement may come from the present position is not active and intentional land-grabbing, but the passive acceptance of the care of certain people and certain races thrust upon us by the unexpected and unintended outcome of the war." Perceiving the hand of God in the unexpected course of events, he believed Americans could rely on that same guidance in the days to come. Or, as he put it, "for the future, I am disposed to trust this great overruling, believing that, step by step, the way will be pointed out in which we ought to go."[10]

The outbreak of violence instigated by insurgent forces did little to change the conviction of the *Churchman* editor that the United States had a duty to perform in the Philippines, that the islands represented a "trust which must be discharged with an eye single to the interests of the ward." Control was essential, he believed, no matter the cost; subjugation was for the good of the subject: "The flowing tide of national sentiment and conviction has been slowly rising to a conception of its full position not as the owner of the Philippines, but as the trustee of its future."[11] The editor of the *Christian Evangelist* echoed this perspective, writing after more than two months of conflict. As Doane's column showed a resolve sharpened by attacks from the anti-imperialists, this editor revealed that Filipino resistance was having a similar effect. "If our possession and control of the archipelago are but the fulfillment of our duty," he wrote on

April 13, "then we cannot allow the course of destiny to be blocked by the reluctance of these savages to receive our aid."[12] This steely resolve, rooted in the unbounded optimism fostered by the experience of the past year, proved impossible to shake. And understanding this resolve remains crucial for explaining the church leaders' response or lack thereof to events as they escalated in coming years.

Several decisive American victories marked the opening months of the Philippine-American War, from February through May, leaving many to hope they were witnessing only the birth pangs of what would become a loving and fruitful familial relationship. The following months helped dispel such hopes. The rainy season, from May through September, saw little fighting, but in the fall American advances deep into the island of Luzon spawned a fateful turning point in the war. In November 1899, Aguinaldo disbanded the centralized army and called for guerrilla warfare against the invaders in every island province. From here the war followed the course of most conflicts between dominant powers and guerrilla forces, with unmistakable similarities to the later American experiences in Vietnam and in Iraq.[13]

A brief review of the guerrilla phase of the war must set the stage for a discussion of the response to these events in the American public.[14] American leaders in Washington and military leaders on the ground had been firmly convinced from the beginning that Aguinaldo represented an isolated threat, that he did not represent the interests or enjoy the sympathies of the majority of the Filipinos, and that once he was removed the islands would welcome American sovereignty. So, even though concentrated efforts to capture the insurgent general throughout 1899 had failed, American leaders hailed Aguinaldo's dissolution of the central army in November as a sign that the insurgency was over. The Filipinos had no government, they had no army, and their leader was hiding in isolation somewhere in the mountains. Still convinced that many if not most Filipinos disapproved of Aguinaldo, the American commanders assumed it would be only a matter of time before someone somewhere handed him over. Months stretched into years, and this never happened. Instead, at Aguinaldo's bidding, all across the islands the line between civilian and insurgent warrior collapsed. For months on end guerrilla bands of all sizes terrorized American troops throughout the Philippines, even in areas formerly thought to be securely under U.S. control. All the while, as commanding General Elwell Otis offered promise after promise that the insurgency was defeated, American losses continued to rise, with little to show for them. They were losses of the most demoralizing variety. Major battles were few; instead, unsuspecting soldiers fell prey to booby traps or snipers' bullets, marching endlessly through dense terrain in bad weather with inadequate supplies.

These conditions, among others, created an ideal environment for the kind of abuses still to come among American troops. As has been true in all such conflicts, American soldiers cultivated a deep resentment for their enemies that ultimately dehumanized the Filipinos in their eyes. Stories circulated about Filipino abuse of American prisoners, claiming that they were being castrated, buried alive, or "boloed," sliced to pieces with the trademark Filipino machete. Racial difference became central as well: the insurgents seemed short, strangely colored, unable and unwilling to fight fair. And so the Americans began referring to them as "niggers," and ordinary farm boys grew willing to attack these "others" in ways unimaginable with fellow whites back home. Brutality governed conduct on both sides as the fighting drew on and frustration escalated. The "water cure" would emerge from the war with special public distinction. In this interrogation method, which the Americans learned from Filipino guides, a prisoner is bound with mouth forced open while an interrogator pours water down the throat until the prisoner breaks. But this was hardly the only—or the most common—form of torture. Welch's study of at least fifty-seven confirmed cases of abuse identified incidences of rape and murder of soldiers and civilians alongside other abuses.[15] The remarkable ratio of killed to wounded offers perhaps the most telling indicator of the brutal state to which the conduct of the war had descended even by 1900. According to a report that year by a War Department official, 14,643 Filipinos had been killed and 3,297 wounded to date, a ratio of nearly five to one.[16]

Tragically, these instances of individual abuse pale in comparison to the carnage unleashed by official military policy once they had deemed pacification necessary at any cost. Through 1900 and into 1901, American leadership recognized how wrong they had been about what they perceived as fragile solidarity among the wider population. It became clear that the insurgency continued to thrive, even after Aguinaldo's capture, because of supplies and cover offered by the civilian population. The Americans were forced to leave garrisons behind in every village cleared; otherwise, as soon as they had moved forward, they would find the village once again infested with insurgent activity. Frustration and resentment reached a boiling point in September 1901. It was then, at Balangiga, on the Philippines' Samar Island, that Filipino fighters, with help from civilians, surprised a band of unarmed American soldiers waiting in line for breakfast, killing forty-five and wounding eleven others. Described widely as a massacre, the attack spurred a devastating response from military leaders intent on wiping out the civilian sources of insurgent sustenance. Through the following year, the Americans swept through the islands burning crops, killing livestock, and herding civilian populations into concentration camps not unlike those used to such humanitarian ire in Cuba three years earlier.

The tragic irony in this turn of events is mitigated only slightly by the fact that few in America realized the full extent of the regnant tactics in the Philippines. The primary contribution of Richard Welch's work is its explanation of what the American public knew, why it knew so little, and why it responded in the ways that it did to what it knew. First, information about abuses was slow in coming, in part because of the geographical distance and also because of government censorship imposed during the late stages of the war. Moreover, there was some fear within the press of being discredited. The *New York Evening Post*, an anti-imperialist paper, had reported the murder of prisoners after an early battle in the spring of 1899, only to have its source discredited by a military investigation. The Anti-Imperialist League, made up of an elite group of political and intellectual leaders that included several ministers, kept up a constant barrage of criticism of the McKinley administration and of the policy in the Philippines, eagerly promoting any news of abuse as confirmation of its concerns. But, according to Welch, their efforts failed to sway the wider public, in part due to disagreements within the League over how radical their dissent should be and even more because their claims failed to resonate with popular conceptions of American identity.[17] Supporters of expansion successfully portrayed much of the anti-imperialist case as pessimistic, partisan, and, at worst, even treasonous, an outright failure to appreciate the sacrifices of American troops in the cause of humanity.

When more detailed reports of the severe policies of 1901–1902 began to circulate, condemnations of the atrocities reached their peak in influence and attention. But even then, there remained some in the press who defended the policies, even the internment of civilians, insisting that this was different from and more humane than the hated policy of Spanish general Valeriano Weyler. Except for the already committed anti-imperialists, Welch argues, even those critical of American abuses remained committed to U.S. policy in the Philippines and saw the abuses as nothing more than aberrations, however unfortunate. By the summer of 1902, only the most committed anti-imperialist papers gave any further attention to the matter.[18]

It is this lack of interest in American abuses among the wider public, this unwillingness to consider that the nation or its soldiers had gone off course in the Philippines, that represents the most striking feature of the public response. And it is here that Welch's conclusions most directly intersect with the Christian nationalism described throughout this book. The dominant optimism described by Welch as so pervasive within American society and as so decisive in shaping the response to events in the Philippines was at the very least bolstered by the full-throated celebration of American identity offered by Christian leaders during the war with Spain. For Welch, the most important contributing factor in the lack of attention to abuse was the "large reserve of national patriotism" in the aftermath of the war with Spain, which "convinced the American people anew of the superiority as well as the uniqueness of America and its redemptive mission." And, as he concludes, "One cannot begin to understand the failure of Americans to exhibit a strong concern with military outrages in the Philippines if one anachronistically transfers the psychological uncertainties and political unrest of a later generation to American society at the turn of the century."[19] In building a foundation of optimism impervious to psychological uncertainty and political unrest, a wide swath of America's religious leadership had done at least its part. Providence, after all, had ordained the duty; the Filipinos would ultimately benefit from the benevolent sovereignty of a selfless, Christian America.

Continuity and Change: Messianic Interventionism and the First World War

One of the most significant implications of the Philippine-American War, according to Ernest May's venerable study, was that it helped remove whatever taste for active imperialism existed among American political and cultural leaders. Even as early as 1900, seeking to gain reelection, McKinley had been forced to run toward the anti-imperialist presidential challenger William Jennings Bryan, promising a swift transfer of sovereignty in Cuba and abandoning any reference to the permanent retention of the Philippines.[20] Of course, this kind of active territorial acquisition had never been the goal of many Christian supporters of expansion anyway. What did survive the war in the Philippines was a prevalent conviction among religious leaders that America, under the providence of God, had moved once and for all into a sphere of international activity, bent on spreading the divine blessings already embodied in its unique society. What survived was the belief that America could—and should—sustain an altruistic, interventionist foreign policy. It would take another war, with carnage on an unprecedented scale, to faze this confident assessment of the nation's significance. American participation in that next conflict, known as the Great War, came with the full endorsement of the Christian nationalism framed in 1898.

President Woodrow Wilson became one of the chief proponents of this view of American identity and purpose in the decades after the experiment in the Philippines.[21] Like McKinley before him, Wilson was a devout Christian, the son and grandson of Presbyterian ministers. His providentialist worldview bore all the marks of the optimistic view of history and of America's place in its progress reinforced by religious commentary on the war with Spain. Moreover, Wilson himself acknowledged the precedent set in 1898, viewed through the precise hermeneutical lens offered so meticulously in sermons and the religious press. Through the 1910s, Wilson orchestrated a series of interventions in Latin America, most notably in Mexico in 1916, which he framed explicitly as an attempt to help a struggling neighbor achieve liberty. In a speech to a business association in New York in January 1916, he justified the intervention by direct appeal to U.S. action in Cuba in 1898. It was there, he argued, that America demonstrated that "a nation can sacrifice its own interests and its own blood for the sake of the liberty and happiness of another people."[22]

Meanwhile, Europe was already at war on an unprecedented scale. World War I exploded out of a complex web of historical antipathies and national alliances, with a conflict between Austria-Hungary and Serbia initiating a domino effect that, by 1915, had all of Europe engulfed in the conflict. Fighting intensified for nearly three years before America joined the war. During that time, American society remained bitterly divided over the proper course of action. Debate focused, for example, on whether and why to intervene, on the extent to which the nation should prepare its military resources for possible war, and on whether it was best to remain free of the European mess as a matter of principle. Wilson, for his part, seemed to the last moment genuinely opposed to plunging the nation into the war. But maintaining neutrality grew more difficult as American civilians and shipping interests became caught in the crossfire. Tensions heightened further when the United States intercepted a letter from Germany to the Mexican government, proposing an alliance against the Americans. Ultimately, a host of factors contributed to the final decision to enter the war. But, according to the historian David Kennedy, one of the most important features of this shift, for Wilson and for the wider public, was the ability of the leadership to cast American participation in terms "congenial to the American mind, and particularly appealing to the progressives."[23]

In his "War Message" to Congress just prior to the declaration of war, Wilson emphasized that the nation did not seek this war; forced into it nonetheless, its motives would remain unselfish, focused only on the freedom of the world. "We have no selfish ends to serve," he promised. "We desire no conquest, no dominion. We seek no indemnities for ourselves, no material compensation for the sacrifices we shall freely make. We are but one of the champions of the rights of mankind."[24] This would be a war for the survival of liberty and democracy, a fight against rampant militarism, a crusade to redeem Europe itself, a war to end all wars. These were the terms Wilson used to sell the war to the American public; they were terms supplied in full twenty years earlier.

Christian commentary on the war in Europe and on America's relationship to the war followed a trajectory that mirrored the divisions of the broader society. Up through 1917, all commentators expressed a primary regard for peace, but there remained significant disagreement about what policy would best serve the interests of peace. Many regarded the war as the unfortunate by-product of European customs, a clear result of an unfettered lust for power on the continent, and most likely a tragic step backward in the progress of civilization. But by the time America joined the fray, and to an even greater extent after the fact, this interpretation of the war had been reversed dramatically. As one early historian observed, "all the church organizations and nationalistic groups vied with each other in flowery resolutions of patriotism—the Jews, the Catholics, the Protestants, the various Irish, German, Lutheran societies and the Mormons."[25] Now, in Richard Gamble's apt phrase, "What in August 1914 had been interpreted as a 'retrograde step in civilization' became a war of deliverance, achievement, and renewal, a cause for hope rather than fear, a catalyst for fundamental change."[26]

Richard Gamble's study of what he calls "progressive" clergy during the First World War, a detailed analysis of the religious significance attached to this conflict, is a most useful account that illustrates how closely this interpretation matched the meaning assigned to the war with Spain.[27] His consistent emphasis rests on the ideas that made unprecedented total war feasible, those that elevated the conflict to absolute, apocalyptic terms. As in 1898, these church leaders understood American intervention as a selfless disavowal of national interests, a Christlike service to humanity, and therefore a holy war.[28] No patron of these themes appears more prominently or with more force in Gamble's account than Lyman Abbott of the *Outlook*, perhaps the most celebrated Christian interpreter of the Spanish-American War. The terms with which he promoted American identity and national purpose in the later war remained nearly identical to those used in 1898. As with the war twenty years earlier, Abbott understood this latest struggle as part of the age-old progress of the kingdom of God and its inevitable triumph over the forces of evil. In one especially illustrative column, he framed the war as a conflict between the principles and powers of paganism and Christianity: "in paganism the poor serve the rich, the weak serve the strong, the ignorant serve the wise. In the Kingdom of God the rich serve the poor, the strong serve the weak, the wise serve the ignorant. This is the divine order; and the Son of God himself illustrates this order by his own life and death." Little wonder, then, which order each side represented: America, motivated by Christ's spirit of self-sacrifice, represented "organized Christianity"; Germany, ignoring the divine will in the quest for absolute power, represented "organized paganism."[29] As Gamble goes on to illustrate, Abbott would later frame the stakes of this war in even more explicitly apocalyptic terms. In a 1918 speech delivered to the National Convention of the League to Enforce Peace, Abbott located the conflict between America and Germany as the fulfillment of the promise Christians had long identified with Christ in Genesis 3. In that passage, immediately after the serpent has inspired the fall of Adam and Eve into sin, God promises Eve that one of her offspring will one day crush the head of the serpent, traditionally viewed as Satan incarnate. Abbott applied the prophecy to America and the Great War: "'The serpent shall bruise man's heel; man's heel shall bruise the head of the serpent.' Now the head of the serpent is erect, it is running out its forked tongue, its eyes are red with wrath; its very breath is poison. We have a difficult task to get our heel on its head, but when we do, we will grind it to powder."[30]

This Christian nationalism—this ideology forged in the war with Spain— proved unable to survive intact the untold carnage of the First World War. Even conservative estimates place military deaths near the ten million mark, with several million civilians also killed. Add to this more than twenty million individuals wounded, many of them left amputees or severely scarred.[31] During the brief war with Spain, losses on all sides barely reached into the thousands, with the vast majority caused by disease rather than the battlefield.[32] This had been a war easily explained for Americans within a progressive view of history, a war in the interests of peace that in its result promised the hope of a new world. Many had heralded American entrance into the Great War on these very terms. But the scale of the conflict, the brutality with which it was waged, the mass destruction made possible by new technologies produced in the so-called progress of civilization—these set the stage for an ideological crisis.

The level of self-inflicted human suffering displayed in World War I dealt a severe blow to the Progressive Era confidence that social progress was linear and inevitable, that universal brotherhood was just within reach, and that scientific advances would heal and build up, not wound and destroy. Religious understandings of America's redemptive significance fostered in that hopeful environment suffered the effects as well. It would be inaccurate to credit this war with the demise of the progressive optimism associated with liberal Protestants. Critiques of the scale of this confidence in the inevitable progress of social improvement had emerged before the war, not only from fundamentalist adversaries like J. Gresham Machen but also from within liberal ranks. And many Protestants would sustain a progressive vision for forming a Christian society indefinitely after the war, though in modified forms.[33] But unambiguous confidence in the centrality of America to the progress of God's earthly kingdom and in the possibility of the imminent establishment of that kingdom would never again enjoy the hegemony of the prewar years.

One of the principal critics of Progressive Era Protestantism in subsequent decades was the theologian Reinhold Niebuhr, to whom fell a lion's share of the responsibility for building an alternative social and theological vision. Niebuhr, notable for reasserting the radical effects of sin within individuals and societies, was himself groomed during the optimistic climate of the 1910s, and he greeted American intervention in Europe with typical hopes for its potential for furthering the cause of world renovation. His experience of the Great War as a moment of ideological transformation offers an especially poignant example of the importance of that event in reshaping perspectives on the world and America's significance within it. "The war," Niebuhr wrote for the *Christian Century* in 1928, ". . . created my whole world-view. It made me a child of the age of disillusionment. When the war started I was a young man trying to be an optimist without falling into sentimentality. When it ended and the full tragedy of its fratricides had been revealed, I had become a realist trying to save myself from cynicism."[34] This article, titled "What the War Did to My Mind," reads like a coming-of-age story relating the numerous ways the war changed Niebuhr's perspective. His perspective had been rooted in the nineteenth-century hope that freedom would continue its march and that "virtue needed only time and the aid of electricity to win its victories." In short, Niebuhr recalled, "I identified civilization with the kingdom of God." But the war changed this conviction forever. He came to believe that civilization represented more than the "victory of the human spirit over nature. . . . It was also the arming of the brute in man. Vanished were all the hopes of automatic process. Whatever might be accomplished by education and religious suasion the moral problem of man had been aggravated and not solved by civilization. The war convinced me that religion can be effective only if it resists the embraces of civilization."[35] This new perspective on civilization understandably held drastic implications for Niebuhr's views on patriotism and national identity. When the war began, he had "taken patriotism for granted," convinced that nations were at least progressing toward greater social harmony, but this was precisely the sort of absolute loyalty he would come to regard as most dangerous when misdirected: "I saw that the war was made inevitable not by bad people who plotted against the peace of the world, but by good people who had given their conscience into the keeping of their various political groups."[36] Here, Niebuhr argued, was the chief failure of the churches, American and otherwise, which had supported the war with an "undue vehemence." They had failed to evaluate their commitment to the nation in the light of transcendent values, of higher loyalties. Their "excessive fervor was in part simply unreflective emotion; but in part it was the church playing up to the nation, an ancient religion maintaining its waning life by skilfully [*sic*] compounding itself with the newer religion of nationalism."[37]

❖

This "compounding" that Niebuhr lamented—this Christian nationalism— had seemed perfectly plausible, even inevitable, in 1898, and little had changed in 1917. But ten years later American Christians inhabited a new mental world, a world indelibly marked by unimaginable suffering. The mental world of the 1920s and 1930s proved a far less conducive environment for the full-orbed religious ideology of American identity fostered during the war with Spain. Gone, too, was the striking level of unanimity noted during that earlier era.

Responses to future wars offer a case in point. World War II came on the heels of the isolationist backlash against the First World War and followed an unprecedented economic depression that had brought America to its knees. In this climate and given both the cause of the earlier war and its results, World War II invited the sorts of Manichean analysis familiar from previous periods of conflict. And, granted, some did interpret the war's meaning in such terms, and it enjoyed wide support among the American public. Yet, following men like Niebuhr and Harry Emerson Fosdick, American church leaders responded to the war and America's possible role in it with what the historian Gerald Sittser has described as a "cautious patriotism."[38] There remained a general level of support for America and its interests among many church leaders, but there was also a marked hesitancy to profess unqualified devotion to the nation and its cause. And even where there was qualified support for America's role in the war and hope for God's purposes for the nation, there were significant divisions over how to define the nation in Christian terms. These divisions not only separated Catholics from Protestants but emerged within Protestantism as well, with the divergence between evangelicals and liberals as only the most prominent example.[39] This contest for meaning was merely a foretaste of what would arise in far greater force during America's wars in Vietnam and in Iraq.[40]

Since World War I no definition of American identity and purpose has proven able to command the level of widespread assent that pervaded the public rhetoric of Christian leaders during the Spanish-American War. However, this is not to suggest that the ideology fostered there perished in the trenches of eastern France. Rather, the conviction that America holds a unique role in providential designs for the good of the world has proven resilient. Many diverse forces drove America to war against Spain in 1898 and shaped the response to its results, but at least in part—and at least in public—a sizable and vocal portion of the nation's religious leaders insisted that Christian principles required America to act unselfishly on behalf of a weak and oppressed neighbor. They insisted God had prepared them for and now presented them with this task. And they believed—as few had before them—that this intervention marked a new phase of national life, a new sense of purpose, which would see America play the role of Christ in the world, actively using its power for the good of others. In his now classic study of the redeemer-nation myth, Ernest Tuveson aptly referred to this conviction as "active messianism." Writing in the midst of the Cold War, facing the early days of Vietnam, and looking back to both World Wars, Tuveson perceptively labeled this "active messianism" a "recessive gene": "in the right situation," he argued, "it could become dominant."[41] Here Tuveson captured the lasting relevance of the conception of American identity articulated with such devotion in 1898, as it has survived in chastened forms. Wherever this ideology has surfaced—wherever the religious have called on America to fulfill its God-given duties abroad—it has never been far removed from the belief that America, with its distinctive moral character and providential favor, could act in ways not constrained by self-interest. For some, this conviction may stem from the hope that the tragic developments following the war with Spain can be avoided. For most, perhaps, those mistakes have simply been forgotten.

Notes

Introduction

1. Abraham Lincoln, "Address at Gettysburg, Pennsylvania," in *Selected Speeches and Writings: Abraham Lincoln*, introduction by Gore Vidal (New York: Vintage, 1992), 405.

2. Abraham Lincoln, "Annual Message to Congress," in *Selected Speeches*, 364.

3. Woodrow Wilson, "For Declaration of War against Germany: Address Delivered at a Joint Session of the Two Houses of Congress," in *The Public Papers of Woodrow Wilson: War and Peace*, vol. 1, ed. Ray Stannard Baker and William Edward Dodd (New York: Harper and Brothers, 1927), 14.

4. Liah Greenfeld, *Nationalism: Five Roads to Modernity* (Cambridge, MA: Harvard University Press, 1992), 3.

5. I am most indebted here to Clifford Geertz, "Ideology as a Cultural System," in *The Interpretation of Cultures: Selected Essays* (New York: Basic Books, 1973), 193–233.

6. Greenfeld's illuminating comparative study highlights this distinct feature of the American experience. She observes that "in America, at the outset, ideology, the firm conviction that the American society (every objective attribute of which—territory, resources, institutions, and character—was as yet uncertain) was a *nation*, was the only thing that was certain" (*Nationalism*, 402; emphasis original). For a helpful overview see pp. 15–25; for a detailed discussion see pp. 399–484.

7. I am using Christian nationalism to define phenomena often described by the term "civil religion." Robert Bellah first drew the term from Rousseau and applied it to what he argued was a distinct system of belief and practice centered on the political state, possessing its own theology, moral code, holy days, holy figures, and ritual practices. For Bellah's original essay, along with several others that capture the essence of the early discussion of civil religion, see Russell Richey and Donald Jones, eds., *American Civil Religion* (New York: Harper and Row, 1974). Despite some overlap in subject matter, I have chosen to use Christian nationalism rather than civil religion for two reasons. First, my primary interest is how American Christians have adopted the nation as an object of religious significance within the Christian worldview. I am interested in nationalism as a feature of American Christianity. But civil religion more typically refers to the religious

143

dimension of the political sphere or to the use of religion by the powers-that-be for political purposes. Ronald Beiner's 2011 study defines civil religion as "the appropriation of religion by politics for its own purposes" (*Civil Religion: A Dialogue in the History of Political Philosophy* [Cambridge: Cambridge University Press, 2011], 1). Second, in my judgment the primary concerns driving contemporary usage of civil religion are theoretical and normative, rather than the narrowly descriptive goals of my study. Historians have used the term for descriptive studies similar to my own (see, for example, Harry Stout, *Upon the Altar of the Nation: A Moral History of the Civil War* [New York: Viking, 2006], xx–xxii). But the term seems best suited for discussions among political scientists and sociologists about what should be the role of religion in American public life. See, for example, Philip Gorski's essay "Barack Obama and Civil Religion," along with the several scholarly responses in *Political Power and Social Theory* 22 (2011): 179–256. For an earlier example, see Leroy Rouner, ed., *Civil Religion and Political Theology* (Notre Dame, IN: University of Notre Dame Press, 1986).

8. See Harry Stout, "Review Essay: Religion, War, and the Meaning of America," *Religion and American Culture* (Summer 2009): 275–79.

9. See Jill Lepore, *The Name of War: King Philip's War and the Origins of American Identity* (New York: Knopf, 1998), x.

10. Harry Stout, in *Upon the Altar of the Nation* (xx–xxii), offers a compelling account of the importance of the Civil War for forming a fully national version of what he calls civil religion. Liah Greenfeld, too, identifies the Civil War as a decisive moment for establishing the nation-state as the geopolitical center for American nationalism (see *Nationalism*, 480).

11. See Ernest Tuveson, *Redeemer Nation: The Idea of America's Millennial Role* (Chicago: University of Chicago Press, 1968).

12. H. W. Brands offers an excellent account of what he calls the struggle for the "soul" of American foreign policy, a struggle between those he terms "exemplarists" and "vindicationists." See H. W. Brands, *What America Owes the World: The Struggle for the Soul of Foreign Policy* (Cambridge: Cambridge University Press, 1998). See also Winthrop Hudson, *Nationalism and Religion in America: Concepts of American Identity and Mission* (New York: Harper, 1970), 109–11.

13. Conrad Cherry, ed., *God's New Israel: Religious Interpretations of American Destiny*, rev. and updated ed. (Chapel Hill: University of North Carolina Press, 1998), 20. See also Tuveson, *Redeemer Nation*, 213.

14. In this version of Christian nationalism, American ministers dove headlong into a debate that has continued to shape the historiography of the war ever since, a debate about whether or not America acted in its own interests when intervening in Cuba. Three perspectives, each of them represented in commentary contemporary to the war, have dominated historians' attempts to explain American policy in 1898 and the motives that drove that policy. The most pervasive account, common especially in the earliest histories of the war, celebrates American action as an unprecedented example of national altruism. The American character, according to this view, was too sensitive to

allow unbridled oppression to continue at the nation's doorstep; Americans intervened in Cuba, then, only in the interests of humanity. A second account, associated most with realist historians of the mid-twentieth century, concedes the basic shape of the humanitarian view but condemns the American intervention on those grounds. America, on this view, had no business interfering—and at great cost—where there were no substantial national interests at stake. A final perspective challenges the central assumption of the first two, namely that America acted without regard to its own interests. Most pervasive since the late twentieth century and best represented in the work of Louis A. Pérez, this view insists that behind the cloak of humanitarian outrage was a long-standing interest in American acquisition of Spain's Caribbean colonies and especially Cuba, the so-called pearl of the Antilles. My study has little to do with whether or not the United States did in fact act in a disinterested manner toward Cuba. Rather, I am interested in the roots of this debate in the rhetoric of the period. I am interested in the perception of national policy as a feature of American public culture. Many Americans remained resilient in their conviction that their nation acted altruistically, even in the face of mounting counterexamples. And this resilience, I argue, was at least in part a product of the full-scale efforts of Christian leadership to frame the significance of America's action, using an ideology wherein disinterestedness was just shy of inevitable. Pérez offers an excellent, concise overview of the debate and the major voices on each side. See Pérez, *The War of 1898: The United States and Cuba in History and Historiography* (Chapel Hill: University of North Carolina Press, 1998).

15. Geertz, "Ideology as a Cultural System," 193–233. For a similar view of nationalistic ideology as the product of public intellectuals with sociopolitical power, see Greenfeld, *Nationalism*, 22.

16. In places, I have supplemented my treatment of these sources with complementary themes from political rhetoric in Congress and in the wartime speeches of President William McKinley, which are laced with appeals to American religious identity. But here, for the most part, I rely on fine studies like Paul T. McCartney's *Power and Progress: American National Identity, the War of 1898, and the Rise of American Imperialism* (Baton Rouge: Louisiana State University Press, 2006), focusing instead on sources produced within the religious communities themselves.

17. For general information on periodicals in this period, including circulation size, influence, and a brief description of key themes, see Frank Luther Mott, *A History of American Magazines,* vol. 4, *1885–1905* (Cambridge, MA: Harvard University Press, 1957). Mott's volume includes an extended treatment of denominational papers.

18. Edwin Gaustad and Leigh Schmidt, *The Religious History of America: The Heart of the American Story from Colonial Times to Today* (San Francisco: HarperSanFrancisco, 2002), 277–79. See also Mark Noll, *A History of Christianity in the United States and Canada* (Grand Rapids, MI: Eerdmans, 1992), 360–62; Edwin Gaustad, *Historical Atlas of Religion in America* (New York: Harper and Row, 1962), 37–55.

19. For example, I do not often consider the perspectives of those typically critical of nationalism or opposed to war in general, like the Mennonites, the Quakers, the

Unitarians, or the Universalists. It is, however, a noteworthy indicator of the public climate that even stalwart pacifists recognized that this was not their moment. Pacifist groups like the Quakers and the Mennonites did argue against joining the war in the days leading up to the American intervention. But their arguments focused on the ills of war in general, rarely attacking American policy itself, and once America entered the war most of these groups kept quiet (see Julius Pratt, *Expansionists of 1898* [1936; repr., Chicago: Quadrangle, 1964], 288–89; Peter Marchand, *The American Peace Movement and Social Reform, 1898–1918* [Princeton: Princeton University Press, 1973], 24–29). Some even found ways to support the war effort without entering the fighting (see James Juhnke, "Kansas Mennonites during the Spanish-American War," *Mennonite Life* 26, no. 2 [April 1971]: 70–72).

20. Catherine Albanese, writing of civil religion, rightly notes it has been imbibed, at best, by "some Americans some of the time" (*America: Religions and Religion*, 3rd ed. [Belmont, CA: Wadsworth, 1999], 434).

21. Stout, "Religion, War, and the Meaning of America," 283ff.

22. See, for example, Hudson, *Nationalism and Religion*, 86ff; Conor Cruise O'Brien, *God Land: Reflections on Religion and Nationalism* (Cambridge, MA: Harvard University Press, 1988), 33ff.

23. Most helpful is Paul T. McCartney's 2006 monograph *Power and Progress*, a study of the influence of national identity on the pursuit of national interests in the Spanish-American War. But for McCartney civil religion is never an object of study in its own right; it is useful to him as one of several ideological streams that informed the policy decisions of America's political leaders. His interest, in other words, is in how civil religion helps explain political developments of the period, not in what effect the developments of the period had upon civil religion itself. For all its emphasis on religion, McCartney's study rarely shifts focus from the public officials in Congress and the White House to the clergy and religious communities among whom many of their ideas received the most thorough development. His sources include fewer than fifteen sermons, and no examples from the widely circulated religious periodical literature. Given the purposes of McCartney's volume, this omission is understandable; its important contribution remains its careful description of the national identity that gave shape to the decisions of political leaders. But his study invites further analysis of the perspective on American identity among Christian groups, especially as they responded to the events of 1898.

24. See, for example, Robert Handy, *Undermined Establishment: Church-State Relations in America, 1880–1920* (Princeton: Princeton University Press, 1991), 7–29.

25. See Michael Zoller, *Washington and Rome: Catholicism in American Culture* (Notre Dame, IN: University of Notre Dame Press, 1999). For a specific account of the role of Catholicism in shaping American policy during and after the Spanish-American War, see Frank Reuter, *Catholic Influence on American Colonial Policies, 1898–1904* (Austin: University of Texas Press, 1967).

26. Hudson, *Nationalism and Religion*, xii.

27. Pratt, *Expansionists of 1898*, 279–316; Richard Welch, *Response to Imperialism: The United States and the Philippine-American War, 1899–1902* (Chapel Hill: University of North Carolina Press, 1979), 89–100.

28. Kenneth MacKenzie, *The Robe and the Sword: The Methodist Church and the Rise of American Imperialism* (Washington, DC: Public Affairs Press, 1961); Reuter, *Catholic Influence on American Colonial Policies*. Beyond their exclusive focus on Methodism and Catholicism, these studies by MacKenzie and Reuter focus less on the war itself and its implications for American identity than on missions interests in the aftermath of the war, as groups wrangled for influence in the islands under U.S. control.

29. This limitation holds true for the two most extensive studies to date of religious commentary on the Spanish-American War: William Karraker, "The American Churches and the Spanish-American War" (unpublished PhD dissertation, University of Chicago, 1940); and John Edwin Smylie, "Protestant Clergymen and America's World Role, 1865–1900: A Study of Christianity, Nationality and International Relations" (unpublished ThD dissertation, Princeton Theological Seminary, 1959). Karraker's dissertation draws from an impressive number of periodicals published mostly in the Northeast and offers an extensive catalog of nearly everything said in these periodicals by church leaders about the war with Spain. But his goal is consistently encyclopedic breadth, not analysis; chapter titles include "Attitudes during the Initial Period of the War," "Attitudes during the Concluding Period of the War," and "Attitudes and Interests Superextensive to Both Periods of the War." An unpublished ThD dissertation by John Edwin Smylie offers a more robust analysis of this data, with conclusions that often mirror my own. A study of Protestant views of history and of America's role in the world, Smylie's six-hundred-page work provides a thorough intellectual lineage for the ideas represented in commentary on the war with Spain. But for Smylie, the rhetoric surrounding the events of 1898–99 serves only as a case study illustrating the analytical points made in the bulk of the dissertation, and he openly admits using merely a subset of Karraker's evidence. These two works offer an important guide for my own research and interpretation, but they also invite further analysis of perspectives from other areas of the United States. Without considering voices from the South and the West, not to mention the perspectives of American Catholics, one cannot appreciate the full power of Christian nationalism in this period.

Chapter 1
"My Brother's Keeper"

1. For historical details here and throughout, I rely heavily on David Trask, *The War with Spain in 1898* (1981; repr., Lincoln: University of Nebraska Press, 1996). Other useful histories include David Traxel, *1898: The Birth of the American Century* (New York: Knopf, 1998); Philip Sheldon Foner, *The Spanish-American War and the Birth of American Imperialism*, 2 vols. (New York: Monthly Review Press, 1972); Kenneth E. Hendrickson

Jr., *The Spanish-American War* (Westport, CT: Greenwood, 2003). As a study of American religious nationalism, this chapter necessarily focuses on the American perspective on the events in Cuba. For an excellent treatment of the Cuban perspective on this war as part of the ongoing struggle of Cuban insurgents against Spain, see Ada Ferrer, *Insurgent Cuba: Race, Nation, and Revolution, 1868–1898* (Chapel Hill: University of North Carolina Press, 1999).

2. See John Oldfield, "Remembering the *Maine*: The United States, 1898 and Sectional Reconciliation," in *The Crisis of 1898: Colonial Redistribution and Nationalist Mobilization*, ed. Angel Smith and Emma Dávila-Cox (New York: St. Martin's Press, 1999), 49–56.

3. William Hutchison, *Errand to the World: American Protestant Thought and Foreign Missions* (Chicago: University of Chicago Press, 1987), 91 and 1, respectively. Hutchison's study offers the longest view of Protestant missions, describing the constant interaction of missionary ideologies with the prominent themes of American identity, themes like an American mission and its relationship to Christian evangelism. Other studies routinely confirm the importance of these decades as a time of awakening to the wider world through missionary activism. See, for example, these surveys of American religious history: Mark Noll, *A History of Christianity in the United States and Canada* (Grand Rapids, MI: Eerdmans, 1992), 291–94; Sydney Ahlstrom, *A Religious History of the American People* (New Haven: Yale University Press, 1975), 862–67; Catherine Albanese, *America: Religions and Religion*, 3rd ed. (Belmont, CA: Wadsworth, 1999), 180–87.

4. For a useful narrative of these events and an overview of the American public outcry, including the perspective of religious groups, see Arman Kirakossian, ed., *The Armenian Massacres 1894–1896: U.S. Media Testimony* (Detroit: Wayne State University Press, 2004), 23–45. This volume includes examples of numerous columns by missionaries and editors in the religious press, with excerpts from the *Outlook* and the *Catholic World*, among other periodicals. For an additional example of the burgeoning culture of humanitarianism during this period as a precursor to American imperialism, see Heather Curtis, "Depicting Distant Suffering: Evangelicals and the Politics of Pictorial Humanitarianism in the Age of American Empire," *Material Religion* 8, no. 2 (June 2012): 154–83.

5. See Robert Handy, *Undermined Establishment: Church-State Relations in America, 1880–1920* (Princeton: Princeton University Press, 1991), 92–93; Arthur Schlesinger, "The Missionary Enterprise and Imperialism," in *The Missionary Enterprise in China and America*, ed. John Fairbank (Cambridge, MA: Harvard University Press, 1974), 353–56. Similarly, the Evangelical Alliance, of which Strong was president, actively lobbied the American government on behalf of persecuted Christians abroad. See Philip Jordan, *The Evangelical Alliance for the United States of America, 1847–1900: Ecumenism, Identity, and the Religion of the Republic* (New York: Edwin Mellon Press, 1982), 100ff.

6. For details, see Ferrer, *Insurgent Cuba*, 15–69; Alistair Hennessy, "The Origins of the Cuban Revolt," in *The Crisis of 1898: Colonial Redistribution and Nationalist Mobilization*, ed. Angel Smith and Emma Dávila-Cox (New York: St. Martin's Press, 1999), 76–79.

7. John Offner, *An Unwanted War: The Diplomacy of the United States and Spain over Cuba, 1895–1898* (Chapel Hill: University of North Carolina Press, 1992), 13.

8. Trask, *War with Spain*, 9.

9. See William Karraker, "The American Churches and the Spanish-American War" (PhD dissertation, University of Chicago, 1940), 23.

10. For specific examples of such rhetoric, see ibid., 22–29.

11. For a popular overview of these challenges in the 1890s, see H. W. Brands, *The Reckless Decade: America in the 1890s* (New York: St. Martin's Press, 1995). For more detail and a longer view, see, for example, Robert Wiebe, *The Search for Order, 1877–1920* (New York: Hill and Wang, 1967); Nell Irvin Painter, *Standing at Armageddon: The United States, 1877–1919* (New York: Norton, 1987).

12. Handy, *A Christian America: Protestant Hopes and Historical Realities*, 2nd ed. (New York: Oxford University Press, 1984), 127. Handy here echoes the language of the prominent minister and activist Josiah Strong, whose wildly popular *Our Country* is a perfect example of the conviction that America's resistance to the evils confronting its society was the key to its positive influence on the world (Josiah Strong, *Our Country: Its Possible Future and Present Crisis* [New York: Baker and Taylor, 1891; repr., Cambridge, MA: Harvard University Press, 1963]). For more detail on the Christian preoccupation with problems of urbanization, immigration, and industrialization at the end of the nineteenth century, see Edwin Gaustad and Leigh Schmidt, *The Religious History of America: The Heart of the American Story from Colonial Times to Today* (San Francisco: HarperSanFrancisco, 2002), 209–54; Winthrop Hudson and John Corrigan, *Religion in America: An Historical Account of the Development of American Religious Life*, 5th ed. (Upper Saddle River, NJ: Prentice Hall, 1992), 233–54, 282–304.

13. These dailies earned their "yellow press" label for what many considered to be their jaundiced coverage of events. Locked in a circulation war, they featured extravagant headlines unashamedly built to sell more papers. Their coverage of events following the *Maine* disaster was perhaps the most decisive influence leading to war with Spain, and this was certainly their intent. See Charles Brown, *The Correspondents' War: Journalists in the Spanish-American War* (New York: Scribner's, 1967), 123, see 122ff; see also Gerald Linderman, *The Mirror of War: American Society and the Spanish-American War* (Ann Arbor: University of Michigan Press, 1974), 148–73. For more on the "yellow press," see for example David Spencer, *The Yellow Journalism: The Press and America's Emergence as a World Power* (Evanston, IL: Northwestern University Press, 2007).

14. Julius Pratt, in one of the earliest studies to take account of religious commentary on the war, argued that the religious press welcomed the prospect of war with Spain wholeheartedly (*Expansionists of 1898: The Acquisition of Hawaii and the Spanish Islands* [1936; repr., Chicago: Quadrangle, 1964], 279–316). However, in a 1973 article, the historian Arthur Shankman challenged Pratt's assessment in a study of the Southern Methodist press that showed strong disapproval of possible war among that group ("Southern Methodist Newspapers and the Coming of the Spanish-American War: A Research Note," *Journal of Southern History* 39, no. 1 [February 1973]: 93–96). In their hesitancy,

especially regarding the issue of the *Maine* disaster and their disdain for the yellow press, the Southern Methodists were hardly alone. Examples from other groups and regions are plentiful, but see *Christian Recorder*, 24 February 1898; *Standard*, 10 March 1898; *Independent*, 10 March and 17 March 1898; *Florida Baptist Witness*, 16 March 1898; *United Presbyterian*, 10 March 1898; *Friends' Intelligencer*, 5 March 1898. For sermons reflecting this perspective see Richard Boynton, "Lead Us Not into Temptation," sermon preached April 3 (Richard Boynton Papers, bMS 625 no. 139, Andover-Harvard Theological Library); and Minot Savage, "Civilization and War," preached April 8, and published in *Messiah Pulpit, New York: Sermons of M.J. Savage* 2, no. 27 (1898): 3–16. The perspectives of the religious press also mirrored those of the more conservative secular news magazines. See for example *Harper's Weekly*, 12 March 1898; *Nation*, 24 February 1898.

15. See John Dobson, *Reticent Expansionism: The Foreign Policy of William McKinley* (Pittsburgh, PA: Duquesne University Press, 1988), 46; Offner, *Unwanted War*, 127ff.

16. A summary of Johnston's sermon was printed in the *New York Times*, as was customary for the paper during this period. Each Monday issue would include numerous excerpts from various sermons, mostly from New York pulpits. Sometimes these were summarized by the editor, and at other times they quoted at length from the sermon recorded by a stenographer (as in this case). See *New York Times*, 28 February 1898. For summaries of additional services expressing these themes, as well as a record of patriotic services held in both Protestant and Catholic churches, see "Sermons on the Maine," *New York Times*, 21 February and 28 February 1898.

17. Charles Parkhurst, "The State of the Country," printed in the Presbyterian *Evangelist*, 10 March 1898, pp. 11–12.

18. *Nation*, 3 March 1898.

19. *Christian Standard*, 5 March 1898.

20. *Outlook*, 12 March 1898.

21. Broadly conceived, the notion that America would help to spread liberty around the world was not a new one in 1898. Examples abound in the rhetoric of Protestant missionaries. See Hutchison, *Errand to the World*, especially 43–61. And there was even some precedent for acknowledging the useful effects of war on efforts to extend Christian civilization. For example, see Jennifer Graber's account of the way in which missionaries with the American Board of Commissioners for Foreign Missions capitalized on decisive military victories against the Dakotas in their work among that population: "Mighty Upheaval on the Minnesota Frontier: Violence, War, and Death in Dakota and Missionary Christianity," *Church History* 80, no. 1 (March 2011): 76–108. What was new in 1898 was the strong and widespread belief that America should forcibly intervene in the affairs of those acknowledged to be other nations, not for American self-interest but only for the liberation of a subject people. This justification for war with Spain built upon missions' interests and some Northern interpretations of the Civil War but dramatically extended these themes into the realm of American foreign policy.

22. Linderman offers the most comprehensive treatment of Proctor's address, which he places in the context of the senator's wider career. See Linderman, *Mirror of War*, 37–59.

23. For commentary on Proctor's history of skepticism regarding conditions in Cuba and on the compelling calm of his report, see for example *Congregationalist,* 31 March 1898; *Christian Evangelist,* 24 March 1898; *Evangelist,* 24 March 1898; *Western Christian Advocate,* 23 March 1898. These features of Proctor's testimony also had an important effect on the business community, which, like the religious leaders, had remained cool toward the prospect of war to that point. See Linderman, *Mirror of War,* 40ff. But Linderman admits that the reason for the speech's amazing and undisputed scope of influence in moving America toward war remains unclear. And according to Linderman the widespread interpretations of the implications of the speech, which came to mean several things to several groups of people, went beyond anything Proctor had intended (see 49–54).

24. *The Advance,* 28 April 1898. Washington Gladden offered a similar assessment of the speech and its effects in his *Recollections* (Boston: Houghton Mifflin, 1909), 386.

25. Acknowledgment of the significance of Proctor's speech was so widespread as to almost be universal. For examples from a diverse group of periodicals, see *Baptist Courier,* 31 March 1898; *Independent,* 31 March 1898; *United Presbyterian,* 24 March and 31 March 1898; *Evangelist,* 24 March 1898; *Advance,* 24 March and 31 March 1898; *Congregationalist,* 17 March and 24 March 1898. Several studies addressing religious responses to the war have noted both the importance of the Proctor report and the disavowal of the *Maine* incident in favor of humanitarian justifications. See, e.g., Karraker, "The American Churches and the Spanish-American War," 44–48; Paul T. McCartney, *Power and Progress: American National Identity, the War of 1898, and the Rise of American Imperialism* (Baton Rouge: Louisiana State University Press, 2006), 100–103; Hudson, "Protestant Clergy," 110–118; Walter Millis, *The Martial Spirit: A Study of Our War with Spain* (Cambridge, MA: Literary Guild of America, 1931), 124.

26. For examples of sermons for and against military action in early April, see respectively B. H. Carroll, "Sermon on John 15:13," preached April 3 and printed in the *Baptist Standard,* 21 April 1898, pp. 6–7; and Savage, *Civilization and War,* 11–16. Carroll's sermon argued that the United States had both a "right and duty" to interfere in Cuba, criticizing business interests for opposing that action and even McKinley for allowing himself to be held back by Wall Street selfishness. Carroll, especially in his criticism of McKinley and his invocation of the *Maine* as a legitimate factor, is not fully representative of the broader religious commentary, but he does express a common perspective on the necessity of intervention in light of full information on the state of affairs in Cuba. For examples of each extreme in the religious press, both for and against war, see respectively *Western Christian Advocate,* 23 March and 30 March 1898; and *Christian Advocate* (New York), 7 April, 14 April, and 21 April 1898; *Advance,* 7 April, 14 April, and 21 April 1898.

27. *Congregationalist,* 7 April 1898.

28. See Trask, *War with Spain,* 35–37.

29. *Christian Advocate,* 31 March 1898. See also "The Cuban Question" (*Independent,* 31 March 1898, pp. 13–15), which makes similar distinctions before giving excerpts from many other religious publications reflecting the same perspective.

30. *Herald of Gospel Liberty*, 24 March 1898; *Outlook*, 31 March 1898. The Cubans "struggling to be free" evoked for many a clear analogy to the American fight for independence just a century past, a personal connection that only intensified sympathy for Cuba. See for example the article by Eric Gambrell, *Baptist Standard*, 10 March 1898, p. 1; *Pacific*, 30 March 1898; *Independent*, 14 April 1898; and a sermon by Erwin Dennett preached March 20 and printed in the *New York Times*, 21 March 1898.

31. Trask, *War with Spain*, 44. For details on the breakdown of diplomacy in the weeks leading to war, see 30–59.

32. To this point, many had favored Spain's desire to establish autonomy in Cuba on the model of Canada's relationship to Great Britain. But after events like Proctor's speech this option had lost its viability in the minds of most Americans. See ibid.

33. "Message of the President of the United States Communicated to the Two Houses of Congress on the Relations of the United States to Spain by Reason of the Warfare on the Island of Cuba, 11 April 1898," *Papers of William McKinley*, Library of Congress microfilm. Cited in McCartney, *Power and Progress*, 128–29.

34. *Papers Relating to the Foreign Relations of the United States, with the Annual Message of the President: Transmitted to Congress December 5, 1898* (Washington, DC: U.S. State Department, 1901). Cited in Trask, *War with Spain*, 56.

35. Examples of this early support for war, beyond what has been cited already, include the *Standard*, 9 April 1898; *Western Christian Advocate*, 6 April 1898; *Star of Zion*, 7 April 1898.

36. *Watchman*, 21 April 1898. For a similar argument, see *Watchman*, 28 April 1898.

37. *Congregationalist*, 28 April 1898.

38. The *Florida Baptist Witness* offered a typical assessment along these lines on 27 April 1898.

39. MacArthur's sermon of May 1 was printed in the *New York Times*, 2 May 1898. For an explicit connection of the war with Spain to the crusades of the Middle Ages, so identified because of America's holy and disinterested motives, see *Baptist and Reflector*, 28 April 1898.

40. *Western Christian Advocate*, 20 April 1898.

41. *Christian Standard*, 30 April 1898.

42. *New York Times*, 25 April 1898. This central argument for the war as disinterested, a case of national self-sacrifice, was not limited to church leaders or religious publications. It had its place in political rhetoric and in secular publications as well. See for example Carl Schurz, "A Case of Self-Sacrifice," *Harper's Weekly*, 23 April 1898, p. 387.

43. Charles Albertson, "Sermon on Eccl. 3:8," preached 1 May 1898 in the Delaware Avenue Methodist Episcopal Church, Buffalo, NY. It is printed in the *Western Christian Advocate*, 25 May 1898, p. 652.

44. See, e.g., *United Presbyterian*, 5 May, 12 May, and 19 May 1898; *Baptist Standard*, 12 May 1898; *Religious Herald*, 21 April 1898.

45. See *Annual*, Southern Baptist Convention, 1898, p. 43; *Minutes of the General Assembly of the Presbyterian Church in the United States of America, with an Appendix. New Series,*

Vol. XXI, A.D. 1898. 110th General Assembly (Philadelphia: MacCalla and Co., 1898), 65–66; *Minutes of the General Assembly of the United Presbyterian Church of North America, 1896–1899*, vol. 9 (Pittsburgh: United Presbyterian Board of Publication, 1899), 541; *Journal of the Thirteenth General Conference of the Methodist Episcopal Church, South, Held in Baltimore, MD., May 5–23, 1898* (Nashville, TN: Publishing House of the Methodist Episcopal Church, South, 1898), 52. These minutes of the MEC South General Conference also record a letter of thanks from the president, to whom they had sent a copy of their resolution of support. See ibid., 92. An almost identical resolution of support for the president and prayer for the success of American arms appeared in the African Methodist Episcopal *Christian Recorder*, 26 May 1898. For an example of the rhetoric and displays of patriotism attending these denominational meetings, see the extensive report on the American Baptist meetings held at Rochester May 17–23, recorded in the *Watchman*, 26 May 1898, pp. 15–24.

46. "The Church in the War," *Nation*, 19 May 1898, pp. 377–78. This unity of perspective among ministers was also noted by Lyman Abbott in the *Outlook*, 21 May 1898, p. 157. See also Karakker's extensive list of examples of support from each denomination in "The American Churches and the Spanish-American War," 49–55.

47. A very useful collection of opinion on the war within the black press is George Marks, *The Black Press Views Imperialism, 1898–1900* (New York: Arno Press, 1973). According to Marks, "the position of most black newspapers on the Spanish-American War was a cautious and prudent patriotism" (xvii), with a general acceptance of the dominant humanitarian justification for the war but a mixed response to the events of the war as they unfolded, especially in the Philippines. Willard Gatewood's extensive study of black responses to issues of imperialism during the years surrounding the war with Spain confirms this pattern. See Gatewood, *Black Americans and the White Man's Burden, 1898–1903* (Urbana: University of Illinois Press, 1975). This mixed response and the consistent emphasis on the impact of these international events on the interests of the domestic black community remained features of religious commentary as well. But statements of strong support for American humanitarianism appear in the religious press in ways not found by the authors above in the secular press.

48. H. H. Proctor, *A Sermon on the War: "The duty of colored citizens to their country," Delivered before the Colored Military Companies of Atlanta, Sunday Evening, May 1st, 1898, at the First Congregational Church, Atlanta, Ga., by Rev. H.H. Proctor.* Held by the Library of Congress, Washington, DC, Daniel A. P. Murray Collection, 1818–1907.

49. For examples in the religious press, see *Star of Zion*, 26 May, 9 June, and 14 July 1898; *Christian Recorder*, 9 June 1898; *National Baptist Magazine* (June 1898): 100. In a column contributed to the *Star of Zion* titled "This Present War; Should Charity Begin at Home," L. S. Slaughter wrote, "Our patriotism is being chilled because our willingness to help to defend the flag is not appreciated. Let us wait on the Lord who will see that justice is done" (14 July 1898, p. 6).

50. *Star of Zion*, 7 April 1898.

51. Reverdy Ransom, *The Pilgrimage of Harriet Ransom's Son* (Nashville, TN: Sunday School Union, 1949), 321.

52. J. M. Henderson, "The Position of the Negro towards the Spanish-American War," *National Baptist Magazine* (July 1898): 123.

53. Willard Gatewood has argued that blacks' perspective on the war with Spain was united in its primary emphasis on what would most advance the interests of their race at home. Henderson, along with others in the religious leadership, do not contradict this pattern. Rather, they believed that embracing this definition of American identity and purpose was the best course toward black advancement. In addition to Gatewood, *Black Americans and the White Man's Burden*, see Lawrence Little, *Disciples of Liberty: The African Methodist Episcopal Church in the Age of Imperialism, 1884–1916* (Knoxville: University of Tennessee Press, 2000). Little's study of AME commentary further confirms this emphasis on the supremacy of American civilization and support for its extension, even in spite of the inconsistent application of American values at home.

54. *Churchman*, 30 April 1898.

55. *Baptist and Reflector*, 28 April 1898.

56. *Outlook*, 7 May 1898.

57. According to Gerald Linderman, on the perceived sincerity of the humanitarian sentiment, "there was no significant dissent from this view of American motives" (*Mirror of War*, 7).

58. *Harper's Weekly*, 7 May 1898.

59. Carroll, "Sermon on John 15:13."

60. "The Christianity of It," *Independent*, 28 April 1898, p. 12.

61. "A Word to Ministers," *Independent*, 19 May 1898, p. 12.

62. *Christian Evangelist*, 28 April 1898.

63. Matthew Parkhurst, cited in Kenneth MacKenzie, *The Robe and the Sword: The Methodist Church and the Rise of American Imperialism* (Washington, DC: Public Affairs Press, 1961), 72. See also *New Orleans Christian Advocate*, 12 May 1898.

64. William Rainsford, *Our Duty to Civilization, or Who Is My Neighbor?*, 6–14. This sermon was preached May 1, but the page numbers refer to the edition published later as a pamphlet. There is no publisher information or publication date, but the sermon is available through the Pamphlets in American History microfiche collection.

65. Ibid., 17–19. In these closing pages of the sermon, Rainsford especially insisted on the need to condemn both vengeance for the *Maine* and any desire for conquest as motives for the war.

66. John Donaldson, *What Shall We Do with Our Colonies?* (Davenport, IA: n.p., 1898), 3. The foregoing examples were selected only for their proximity to the actual decision to go to war, but the Good Samaritan image would remain a feature of religious commentary through the following months. For later examples, see *Christian Observer*, 18 May 1898; *Independent*, 28 July 1898; *Religious Herald*, 21 July 1898.

67. The connection between messianic sacrifice and national policy was made even before the war with Spain. George Herron, of Iowa College, gave an extensive treatment of the theme in his 1895 book, *The Christian State: A Political Vision of Christ* (New York: Thomas Crowell, 1895). For an excellent analysis of this book, see John Edwin Smylie, "Protestant Clergymen and America's World Role, 1865–1900: A Study of Christianity,

Nationality and International Relations" (unpublished ThD dissertation, Princeton Theological Seminary, 1959), 77–79.

68. See Harry Stout, *Upon the Altar of the Nation: A Moral History of the American Civil War* (New York: Viking, 2006).

69. Those who supported the Civil War as a war for the emancipation of slaves offer some precedent for war on behalf of "another people," given that entrenched racism in the North defined the slaves as something less than American citizens. But the abolition of slavery as a dangerous presence in American society was believed to be very much in the national interest. Lincoln's 1862 State of the Union address offers a fine example: "In giving freedom to the slave, we assure freedom to the free—honorable alike in what we give, and what we preserve. We shall nobly save, or meanly lose, the last best hope of earth" ("Annual Message to Congress," in *Selected Speeches and Writings: Abraham Lincoln*, introduction by Gore Vidal [New York: Vintage, 1992], 364).

70. *Outlook*, 16 April 1898. The editor claimed to have drawn this analogy from a Palm Sunday sermon of George Gordon, minister of Boston's Old South Church, but insisted that this framing of the issue and the sentiment behind it captured not just that sermon "but the Christian thought of the Christian Church."

71. *Congregationalist*, 28 April 1898.

72. *Standard*, 7 May 1898.

73. "Mother Bunch's Letter," *Word and Way*, 26 May 1898, p. 6.

74. Sermons that reference this verse of the hymn include Carroll, "Sermon on John 15:13"; Albertson, "Sermon on Eccl. 3:8."

75. Edward Packard, "Sermon on Genesis 3," preached April 17 and printed in the *Homiletic Review* (June 1898): 233–37.

76. David Gregg, *The National Crisis, or God's Purposes Worked Out through International Relations: Sermon Delivered by Rev. David Gregg, L.L.D. at Lafayette Ave. Presbyterian Church, Sunday, April 24th, 1898*, pamphlet (New York: n.p., 1898), 5–6, 12. Part of the Pamphlet Collection of the Presbyterian Historical Society, Philadelphia, PA. The *New York Times* reported on the original delivery of this sermon, noting that it was interrupted by antiwar protests from a member of the congregation. In a show of solidarity with the minister and his support for the war, the congregation responded with three cheers for the flag, placed behind the pulpit. *New York Times*, 25 April 1898.

77. See Ahlstrom, *Religious History of the American People*, 777.

78. Henry van Dyke, *The Cross of War: A Sermon Preached by the Rev. Dr. Henry van Dyke, Pastor of the Brick Presbyterian Church, New York, on May First, 1898* (New York: n.p., 1898), 3–8.

79. Thomas Dixon, "The Battle Cry of Freedom," *Dixon's Sermons: A Monthly Magazine* (June 1898): 4–6.

80. *New Orleans Christian Advocate*, 12 May 1898. Many others remarked on what they believed to be the unprecedented nature of this conflict. See, for example, *Western Christian Advocate*, 20 April 1898; *Christian Standard*, 30 April 1898; *Christian Evangelist*, 28 April 1898; *Pacific*, 27 April 1898; *Advance*, 28 April 189.

81. *Congregationalist*, 5 May 1898.

Chapter 2
Clash of Civilizations

1. On MacArthur, see also, e.g., Robert Handy, *A Christian America: Protestant Hopes and Historical Realities*, 2nd ed. (New York: Oxford University Press, 1984), 78.

2. For detailed descriptions of the American Baptists' meeting, its consistent patriotic tone, and MacArthur's address in that context, see especially *Watchman*, 26 May 1898; *Standard*, 28 May 1898. The *Standard* also noted a rendition of the sermon before the Boston Baptist Social Union (25 June 1898), and several periodicals reported on the Christian Endeavor Convention address, e.g., *Christian Standard*, 16 July 1898; *Christian Evangelist*, 14 July 1898; *Baptist Argus*, 28 July 1898; *Baptist and Reflector*, 14 July 1898.

3. This and all subsequent quotations are taken from the address as printed in full in the *Baptist and Reflector*, 28 July 1898 (pp. 2–4) and 4 August 1898 (pp. 3–4), following the Christian Endeavor Convention.

4. The brutality of American military tactics in the recent Indian Wars, not to mention the harsh experience of freedpeople in America during this period, was not a prominent feature of Christian commentary on American character in the war with Spain. But it is not difficult to imagine these realities gave special urgency to this question of national fitness, and made the opportunity for self-definition against the Spanish all the more welcome. Though the counterevidence of the Indian Wars went largely unacknowledged in these wartime celebrations of American character, it became a strong them of the anti-imperialists in the months after the war. For an example among Christian leaders, see Henry van Dyke, *The American Birthright and the Philippine Pottage: A Sermon Preached on Thanksgiving Day, 1898* (New York: Charles Scribner's Sons, 1898). For an account of American national character that highlights the shaping influence of the Indian Wars, see Richard Slotkin, *The Fatal Environment: The Myth of the Frontier in the Age of Industrialization, 1800–1890* (New York: Harper, 1985).

5. Frank Ninkovich, *The United States and Imperialism* (Malden, MA: Blackwell, 2001), 21.

6. Bartolome Las Casas, *The Tears of the Indians: Being an Historical and True Account of the Cruel Massacres and Slaughters of above Twenty Millions of Innocent People Committed by the Spaniards in the Islands of Hispaniola, Cuba, Jamaica, &tc. As also, in the Continent of Mexico, Peru, & other Place of the West-Indies, to the Total Destruction of Those Countries*, trans. J. Phillips (London: Printed by J. C. for Nath. Brook, at the Angel in Cornhil., 1656). See especially the introductory comments, written first to Oliver Cromwell and then to all English people.

7. Bartolome Las Casas, *Horrible Atrocities of Spaniards in Cuba* (repr., New York: J. Boller, 1898), 12.

8. Gerald Linderman shows that Americans had been taught from popular periodicals and even from grammar school textbooks to consider "Spain stuck in its own history, frozen in her primitive stage, a people that had been and would be cruel" (*The Mirror of War: American Society and the Spanish-American War* [Ann Arbor: University of Michigan Press, 1974], 122). Linderman's discussion well illustrates the common tendency to view

national character through the lens of history and to view that character as fixed, practically immutable (114–27).

9. For a good discussion of the ways the French and then the British served to reinforce American identity as the home of the free, see Nathan Hatch, *The Sacred Cause of Liberty: Republican Thought and the Millennium in Revolutionary New England* (New Haven: Yale University Press, 1977).

10. Jennifer Graber offers an excellent discussion of how Protestant missionaries framed war with the Dakotas as a clash of religions and the war's results as a referendum on their respective quality and power. See "Mighty Upheaval on the Minnesota Frontier: Violence, War, and Death in Dakota and Missionary Christianity," *Church History* 80, no. 1 (March 2011): 76–108.

11. See Paul T. McCartney, *Power and Progress: American National Identity, the War of 1898, and the Rise of American Imperialism* (Baton Rouge: Louisiana State University Press, 2006), 109–12. For examples in the religious press, see *Pacific*, 20 April 1898; *Outlook*, 16 April 1898.

12. *Baptist Standard*, 12 May 1898.

13. *Churchman*, 14 May 1898.

14. *Christian Standard*, 4 June 1898.

15. Ibid.

16. Here and later, this overview relies on the most comprehensive of the many treatments of Spain's history, an article by the Methodist minister E. O. Dunton: "Devolution of Spain: or the Hand of God in History," *Western Christian Advocate*, 11 May 1898, p. 7. Another useful extended treatment appeared on the front page of the *New Orleans Christian Advocate*, 9 June 1898.

17. Dunton, "Devolution of Spain."

18. Ibid.

19. Eliphalet Nott Potter, in the *New York Times*, 7 May 1898. Spain's unwillingness to change, for many, was an underlying feature explaining the difference between American and Spanish civilizations. This was the argument of R. R. Meredith, pastor of Tompkins Avenue Congregational Church in Brooklyn, to whom was granted the honor of delivering the annual sermon to Boston's Ancient and Honorable Artillery Company. See R. R. Meredith, *A Sermon Preached at the Old South Church on the 260th Anniversary of the Ancient and Honorable Artillery Company, June 6, 1898* (Boston: n.p., 1898), 148–50. Overall, Meredith's sermon is an excellent representative of the common historical comparison between Spain and America as sketched here.

20. References to illiteracy and bullfighting abounded as anecdotal evidence for the deleterious effects of the Spanish character. See, e.g., *New Orleans Christian Advocate*, 9 June 1898; *Christian Standard*, 4 June 1898; MacArthur, "Hand of God," *Baptist and Reflector*, 28 July 1898.

21. For similar examples beyond New York, see, e.g., F. B. Cherington, "Ours a Righteous Cause," a sermon delivered 19 June 1898 and printed in the *Pacific*, 24 June 1898. See also Meredith, *Sermon Preached at the Old South Church.*

22. This sermon, like most of those discussed later, was printed in an excerpted, transcript form in the *New York Times*. See *New York Times*, 9 May 1898.

23. *New York Times*, 9 May 1898.

24. King's sermon was printed in excerpt in the *New York Times*, 16 May 1898, but was also discussed in various periodicals (see New York's *Christian Advocate*, 19 May 1898). Like other notable sermons of the period, King's was published separately as a pamphlet, from which the quotation was drawn: James M. King, *Situation and Justification of the Nation at War with Spain: An Address before the Empire State Society Sons of the American Revolution* (New York: printed by order of the Society, 1898), 9.

25. Ibid., 13.

26. *Outlook*, 7 May 1898.

27. *New York Times*, 9 May 1898.

28. Ibid.

29. Ibid. The argument that, in Manila specifically and in the war generally, God was judging Spain for its crimes appeared in additional sermons and in the religious press. For sermons echoing those quoted, see excerpts of May 8 sermons by John Shaw in *New York Times*, 9 May 1898, and C. E. Jefferson in *The Treasury* (June 1898): 109–12. For editorial examples, see *Pacific*, 12 May 1898; *Evangelist*, 12 May 1898.

30. MacArthur, "Hand of God," *Baptist and Reflector*, 28 July 1898, p. 4.

31. Ibid.

32. For a full account of these negotiations, with an emphasis on Ireland's role in the process, see Marvin O'Connell, *John Ireland and the American Catholic Church* (Saint Paul: Minnesota Historical Society Press, 1988), 443–54.

33. *Independent*, 14 April 1898; *Congregationalist*, 14 April 1898.

34. See, e.g., *Word and Way*, 14 April 1898; *Baptist Standard*, 14 April 1898; *Christian Standard*, 30 April 1898; *Christian Advocate* (New York), 7 April 1898; *Advance*, 21 April 1898.

35. This excerpt by the editor of the *Central Baptist* appeared in Georgia's *Christian Index*, 14 April 1898. For similar examples, see *Lutheran Church Review* (July 1898); *Advance*, 21 April 1898; *Christian Index*, 2 June 1898; *Christian Advocate* (New York), 7 April 1898.

36. Hatch, *The Sacred Cause of Liberty*, 1–50.

37. See Lyman Beecher, "A Plea for the West," in *God's New Israel: Religious Interpretations of American Destiny*, ed. Conrad Cherry, revised and updated ed. (Chapel Hill: University of North Carolina Press, 1998), 122–30.

38. See Josiah Strong, *Our Country: Its Possible Future and Present Crisis* (New York: Baker and Taylor, 1891; repr., Cambridge, MA: Harvard University Press, 1963). For a classic description of Protestant concerns in this period, including the prevalence of anti-Catholicism, see Handy, *Christian America*.

39. J. G. McCall, "The Spanish-American War," *Christian Index*, 5 May 1898.

40. From the *Western Recorder*, as excerpted in the *Christian Index*, 9 June 1898. See also *Biblical Recorder*, 23 June 1898; *Religious Herald*, 16 June 1898.

41. All quotations are drawn from the *Christian Evangelist*, 30 June 1898.

42. *Christian Standard*, 4 June 1898. For an example of a similar argument from a Disciples' pulpit, see the Oakland minister Thomas Butler's "Why Spain Is a Dying Nation," a sermon delivered 10 July 1898. Held by the Disciples of Christ Historical Society, Thomas Davemal Butler Papers, Box 3, folder 45.

43. *Christian Recorder*, 4 August 1898. For an excellent description of the anti-Catholicism inspired by the war in many white Methodist periodicals, see Kenneth MacKenzie, *The Robe and the Sword: The Methodist Church and the Rise of American Imperialism* (Washington: Public Affairs Press, 1961), 30–75.

44. S. J. Humphrey, "Spain and the Spanish People," *Advance*, 21 April 1898, p. 532. Interestingly, Protestants were not alone in condemning Spain's Catholicism. See, for example, the address to New York's Society for Ethical Culture by the prominent religious skeptic M. M. Mangasarian, printed in the *New York Times*, 4 April 1898.

45. *Baptist and Reflector*, 7 July 1898.

46. *Alabama Baptist*, 16 June 1898.

47. J. C. Williams, "Catholic Reverses in War," *Christian Observer*, 20 July 1898, p. 9.

48. See, for example, *Biblical Recorder*, 27 April 1898; *Florida Baptist Witness*, 11 May 1898; *Baptist Standard*, 23 June 1898; *Baptist Courier*, 4 August 1898; *Baptist Argus*, 11 August 1898.

49. This parallel with the biblical story of Elijah was featured in an editorial titled "God's Hand or Baal's," *Christian Observer*, 10 August 1898.

50. Patrick Carey, *The Roman Catholics in America* (Westport, CT: Praeger, 1996), 59.

51. This description of the issues and much of what follows relies upon Michael Zoller's fine study, *Washington and Rome: Catholicism in American Culture* (Notre Dame, IN: University of Notre Dame Press, 1999), 87–138. For further general information on the controversy see Jay Dolan, *The American Catholic Experience: A History from Colonial Times to the Present* (Notre Dame, IN: University of Notre Dame Press, 1992), 294–320.

52. Zoller, *Washington and Rome*, 131.

53. See Thomas Wangler, "The Birth of Americanism: 'Westward the Apocalyptic Candlestick,'" *Harvard Theological Review* 65, no. 3 (July 1972): 415–36. See especially 419, 435–36.

54. See Neil Storch, "John Ireland's Americanism after 1899: The Argument from History," *Church History* 51, no. 4 (December, 1982): 434.

55. *Pilot*, 19 March 1898. The discussion to follow traces Catholic opinion primarily through this weekly paper. The *Pilot* is useful for this purpose for several reasons. It was perhaps the most prominent periodical among those Catholics with the most to say about public issues, namely the second- and third-generation Irish Americans. And, though located in Boston, the geographic heart of Irish American Catholicism, it was more than a state or regional paper. It was national not only in circulation but in subject matter and routinely ran articles, letters, and sermon excerpts from Catholic leaders across the country. For a broader treatment of the Catholic response to the war, which corresponds to the trajectory outlined here through the *Pilot*, see Frank Reuter, *Catholic Influence on American Colonial Policies, 1898–1904* (Austin: University of Texas Press, 1967),

3–19. Of the *Pilot*, Reuter himself claimed it was "the most Irish and perhaps the most Catholic newspaper in the country" (13). See also Julius Pratt, *Expansionists of 1898: The Acquisition of Hawaii and the Spanish Islands* (1936; repr., Chicago: Quadrangle, 1964), 279–316. Pratt's brief treatment of Catholic patriotism considers prominent journals, including the *Catholic World*, the *Catholic Herald*, and the *Ave Maria*.

56. *Pilot*, 2 April 1898.

57. *Pilot*, 30 April 1898.

58. *Pilot*, 7 May 1898.

59. Ibid.

60. See Reuter, *Catholic Influence*, 11–12. The letter received some public notoriety, with a mixed response from Protestant quarters. See, e.g., *Independent*, 19 May 1898; *Word and Way*, 26 May 1898; *Outlook*, 21 May 1898.

61. For examples of these arguments, see *Pilot*, 4 June 1898; *New York Times*, 2 May 1898; *Catholic World* (August 1898): 715.

62. Cited in O'Connell, *John Ireland*, 455.

63. *Pilot*, 21 May 1898.

64. *Pilot*, 4 June 1898.

65. *Pilot*, 21 May 1898.

66. For a description of this event, see Zoller, *Washington and Rome*, 123.

67. *New York Times*, 20 February 1898.

68. See Malone's sermon excerpts, printed in the *New York Times*, 20 February and 28 February 1898.

69. *New York Times*, 18 April 1898.

70. *New York Times*, 2 May 1898.

71. *Pilot*, 28 May 1898.

72. Ibid.

73. See, e.g., *Congregationalist*, 12 May 1898; *Outlook*, 21 May 1898; *Independent*, 19 May 1898.

74. See especially *Baptist Standard*, 29 July 1898; but see also *Biblical Recorder*, 23 June and 30 June 1898; *Word and Way*, 26 May 1898.

75. *Outlook*, 28 May 1898.

Chapter 3
"The Hand of God in the Nation's Victory"

1. George Herring, *From Colony to Superpower: U.S. Foreign Relations since 1776* (Oxford: Oxford University Press, 2008), 314. For more detail on the attempts to mobilize the American military and the numerous problems this entailed, see David Trask, *The War with Spain in 1898* (1981; repr., Lincoln: University of Nebraska Press, 1996), 145–77.

2. Nicholas Guyatt, *Providence and the Invention of the United States, 1620–1876* (Cambridge: Cambridge University Press, 2007). Though unique in its transatlantic focus, its useful categorization of the forms of providential reasoning, and the breadth of years

covered, Guyatt's study is hardly the first to describe the importance of providence as a theme in American self-conceptions. For other prominent examples, see Ernest Tuveson, *Redeemer Nation: The Idea of America's Millennial Role* (Chicago: University of Chicago Press, 1968); Harry Stout, *The New England Soul: Preaching and Religious Culture in Colonial New England* (Oxford: Oxford University Press, 1988); Conrad Cherry, *God's New Israel: Religious Interpretations of American Destiny*, rev. and updated ed. (Chapel Hill: University of North Carolina Press, 1998).

3. Guyatt, *Providence*, 6.

4. Though in the Civil War era many Americans abandoned a common faith in the providential destiny of the Union, historical providentialism as an ideological and rhetorical device remained strong in the competing visions proposed by the North and the South. See Harry Stout, *Upon the Altar of the Nation: A Moral History of the American Civil War* (New York: Viking, 2006); Mark Noll, *The Civil War as a Theological Crisis* (Chapel Hill: University of North Carolina Press, 2006).

5. Though described variously in numerous historical studies of Protestantism, the definitive account of this "modernist impulse" remains William Hutchison's *The Modernist Impulse in American Protestantism* (Cambridge, MA: Harvard University Press, 1976). My discussion closely follows Hutchison. Another useful study of Protestantism that treats the significance of modernism in less depth includes Robert Handy, *A Christian America: Protestant Hopes and Historical Realities*, 2nd ed. (New York: Oxford University Press, 1984).

6. For a succinct summary of these key traits, within Hutchison's brief definition of modernism, see *Modernist Impulse*, 2. For best development, see chapter 3.

7. John Smylie, "Protestant Clergymen and American Destiny: II. Prelude to Imperialism, 1865–1900," *Harvard Theological Review* 56, no. 4 (October 1963): 299. In this article, which abbreviates a much more substantial treatment in his dissertation, Smylie places Protestant reflection on providence, history, and American destiny in the context of the nineteenth century's major philosophical interpretations of history. See also John Edwin Smylie, "Protestant Clergymen and America's World Role, 1865–1900" (unpublished ThD dissertation, Princeton Theological Seminary, 1959).

8. Smylie, "Protestant Clergymen and American Destiny," 301. The most important differences among Protestant thinkers, which Smylie traces in great detail, had to do with their views on the relationship between the nation and the church as institutional locales for God's kingdom work. Some of Smylie's most important examples of this perspective on nations and especially America in providential history include Elisha Mulford, *The Nation: The Foundations of Civil Order and Political Life in the United States* (New York: Hurd and Houghton, 1870), and the works of Josiah Strong, especially *Our Country: Its Possible Future and Its Present Crisis* (New York: Baker and Taylor, 1891; repr., Cambridge, MA: Harvard University Press, 1963) and *The New Era; or, The Coming Kingdom* (New York: Baker and Taylor, 1893).

9. Thomas Dixon, "The Nation's Call the Voice of God," *Dixon's Sermons: A Monthly Magazine* (July 1898): 32–33.

10. These differences are well described in Grant Wacker, "The Holy Spirit and the Spirit of the Age in American Protestantism, 1880–1910," *Journal of American History* 72, no. 1 (June 1985): 45–62. Wacker describes three major categories of American Protestants in this period: mainstream conservatives, who represented the status quo, Protestant establishment; new theologians, made up of the progressives, those interested in scientific norms and divine immanence in culture; and "higher life" evangelicals, who emphasized urban revivalism, missions, and individual conversion as the beginning of social transformation.

11. Ibid., 54–58.

12. Trask, *War with Spain*, 101.

13. This ignorance is evident from the articles written for many periodicals in the weeks after the battle offering historical and demographic information. See, for example, *Watchman*, 12 May 1898; *The Missionary* (June 1898): 254–56; *Outlook*, 11 June 1898.

14. See James McPherson, *Battle Cry of Freedom: The Civil War Era* (New York: Oxford University Press, 1988), 854.

15. *Religious Herald*, 21 April 1898.

16. See, for example, the comments of John Williamson Nevin on the Civil War in Noll, *The Civil War as a Theological Crisis*, 76–77. See also Stout, *New England Soul*, 235–38.

17. Sermon printed in the *New York Times*, 16 May 1898.

18. Robert MacArthur, "The Hand of God in the Nation's Conflict," printed in the *Baptist and Reflector*, 28 July 1898, pp. 2–3. For a similar sermonic example, see Thomas Dixon, "The Victory at Manila," *Dixon's Sermons: A Monthly Magazine* (June 1898): 14–16. For reflection on the providential significance of the battle in the religious press, see, for example, *Evangelist*, 12 May 1898; *Baptist and Reflector*, 19 May 1898. The victory at Manila would remain a central feature in religious commentary on the significance of the war even after the fighting had ended. For later sermonic examples, see Arthur Metcalf, *The Reign of God: A Sermon Preached at the Congregational Church, Bancroft, Mich.* (n.p.: n.p., 1898); A. C. Dixon, *Our Greater Country* (New York: n.p., 1898). From the latter, note Dixon's invocation of providence and the Armada parallel: "The God that led the British fleet quietly past the Spanish vessels out in the open sea, guided Dewey that May morning. . . . The bravery of our navy and army deserves high praise, but the victory at Manila and Santiago is due, I believe, more directly to the superintending and directing Providence of God" (4).

19. For examples of such cautionary advice, see *Western Christian Advocate*, 11 May 1898; *Watchman*, 19 May 1898.

20. For details on the battles, see Trask, *War with Spain*, 257–69. See also David Traxel, *1898: The Birth of the American Century* (New York: Knopf, 1998), 204–6; Joseph Smith, *The Spanish-American War: Conflict in the Caribbean and the Pacific, 1895–1902* (London: Longman, 1994), 86–159.

21. *Alabama Baptist*, 14 July 1898.

22. *United Presbyterian*, 7 July 1898.

23. The identification of God's providence in the events of battle extended beyond America's religious leaders. Former Secretary of War Russell Alger, in his 1901 account of the war with Spain, reflected on the importance of an unplanned delay in taking El Caney that helped the American cause, concluding, "I shall always regard the unexpected delay experienced in taking Caney as one of the many incidents connected with the Santiago campaign in which the guiding hand of Providence seems to have interposed for America" (*The Spanish-American War* [New York: Harper and Brothers, 1901], 150).

24. *Zion's Herald*, 27 July 1898.

25. *Outlook*, 16 July 1898.

26. *Christian Observer*, 13 July 1898. For similar commentary, see *Living Church*, 23 July 1898.

27. *Outlook*, 9 July 1898.

28. *Baptist Standard*, 7 July 1898.

29. Printed in *Zion's Herald*, 13 July 1898.

30. *United Presbyterian*, 14 July 1898. See also *Christian Evangelist*, 14 July 1898; *Christian Index*, 14 July 1898; *Western Christian Advocate*, 13 July 1898; *Star of Zion*, 14 July 1898; *Independent*, 14 July 1898; *Outlook*, 16 July 1898.

31. Denominational periodicals provide helpful lists of churches that complied with the president's call for thanksgiving, along with some descriptions of the services and sermons delivered. See *Congregationalist*, 14 July and 21 July 1898; *Living Church*, 23 July 1898; see also *New York Times*, 11 July 1898.

32. See, for example, the sermon by a Disciples of Christ minister, Thomas Butler, "Why Spain Is a Dying Nation," preached July 10. Held by the Disciples of Christ Historical Society, Thomas Davemal Butler Papers, Box 3, folder 45.

33. See, for example, sermons printed in the *Evangelist* and the *Living Church*, one by an unnamed Stockbridge minister (*Evangelist*, 14 July 1898) and another by Long Island's William Gardam (*Living Church*, 20 August 1898).

34. Randall Roswell Hoes, *God's Hand at Santiago: A Sermon Preached on Board U.S. Battle-ship "Iowa" in Guantanamo Bay, Cuba, July 10, 1898, The Sunday Following the Naval Battle of Santiago*, pamphlet published "by request of the crew of the Battle-ship 'Iowa'" (New York: privately printed, 1898), 7–13. Pamphlet held at the Congregational Library, Boston. See chapter 2 for further discussion of similar comparisons of America and Spain.

35. All quotations are taken from the full text of Ireland's sermon, as printed two weeks later in the *Pilot*, 23 July 1898. Excerpts from the sermon also appeared in the *New York Times*, 11 July 1898. For another excellent example of this form of providentialism among American Catholics, see the July 4 oration by Father Denis O'Callahan at Boston's Faneuil Hall, printed by the *Pilot* on 9 July 1898. O'Callahan's sermon, though not specifically about the events of the war with Spain, offers excellent confirmation for the providential view of American history, just one week before Ireland's sermon. He claimed, for example, "As regards history, these United States are providential in origin, in history and in preservation. In us the cause of human liberty and progress is bound up."

36. For an excellent description of the past-oriented outlook of the Puritans, often dubbed primitivism, see especially T. Dwight Bozeman, *To Live Ancient Lives: The Primitivist Dimension in Puritanism* (Chapel Hill: Published for the Institute of Early American History and Culture, Williamsburg, Virginia, by the University of North Carolina Press, 1988). For additional works on the nature of the Puritan jeremiad specifically, see Stout, *New England Soul*; Perry Miller, *The New England Mind: From Colony to Province* (Cambridge, MA: Belknap Press of Harvard University Press, 1953), 28–39; Sacvan Bercovitch, *The American Jeremiad* (Madison: University of Wisconsin Press, 1980).

37. In their association of manhood with a code of civilization marked by disciplined self-restraint and willing self-sacrifice for the weak, these interpreters echoed the dominant understanding of the masculine ideal in the Victorian era. Gail Bederman, in *Manliness and Civilization*, offers a compelling account of this definition of manhood and of the transformed understanding of masculinity already taking hold at the turn of the century (*Manliness and Civilization: A Cultural History of Gender and Race in the United States, 1880–1917* [Chicago: University of Chicago Press, 1996]). The new masculinity, represented by figures as divergent as the educator Stanley Hall and the Rough Rider Theodore Roosevelt, emphasized the virtues of strenuous activity, aggression, and even violence as a corrective for overcivilization.

38. All quotations are from the sermon as published in pamphlet form: Stephen Dana, *Our New Place Among the Nations: A Sermon Preached by the Rev. Stephen Dana, D.D. Pastor of the Walnut Street Presbyterian Church Philadelphia* (Philadelphia: George Cole and Bro., 1898). This pamphlet is held at the Presbyterian Historical Society, Philadelphia, PA.

39. For examples of such services and brief descriptions, see *Florida Baptist Witness*, 1 June 1898; *Congregationalist*, 16 June 1898.

40. A record of the entire service was published in pamphlet form; a copy is held by the Presbyterian Historical Society, Philadelphia, PA. See *Memorial Day, May 30, 1898. Special Union Service of Prayer for Our Country; Our Rulers; and for Our Army and Navy*, 6–9.

41. Carroll's sermon of May 29 was printed in the *Baptist Standard*, 11 August 1898, pp. 6–7. For additional sermons on America's emergence from isolation to world power, see *New York Times*, 13 June and 27 June 1898.

42. For an early example in this vein, see the contributed article by Methodist bishop J. M. Thoburn written May 7 and printed on May 25: "The New Era," *Western Christian Advocate*, 25 May 1898, p. 11. More than just a case for expanded world influence, Thoburn's argument is a strong and very early endorsement of a new colonial policy in the Philippines. For similar early reflections on the nation's new era, see *Western Christian Advocate*, 4 May 1898; *Christian Standard*, 14 May 1898; *Independent*, 12 May 1898; *Baptist Argus*, 19 May 1898.

43. *Christian Advocate*, 26 May 1898.

44. *Zion's Herald*, 1 June 1898. See also *Baptist and Reflector*, 16 June 1898; *Outlook*, 18 June 1898; *Missionary* (June 1898): 251.

45. *Pacific,* 1 June 1898.

46. *United Presbyterian,* 23 June 1898.

47. See the principles listed in the front matter for the church's monthly publication of Dixon's sermons, e.g., "Some Principles for Which We Stand," *Dixon's Sermons: A Monthly Magazine* (June 1898).

48. Dixon, "The Nation's Call the Voice of God," 32.

49. Thomas Dixon, "The Fourth of July," *Dixon's Sermons: A Monthly Magazine* (August 1898): 37–41.

50. Thomas Dixon, "The New Thanksgiving Day," *Dixon's Sermons: A Monthly Magazine* (August 1898): 48–51.

51. Some appealed to the earlier wars as evidence that war is not always wrong and can have good results; others found precedent for war awakening a new sense of national purpose or securing a worthy, humanitarian cause. See, for example, *Evangelist,* 19 May 1898; *Western Christian Advocate,* 25 May 1898; *American Missionary* (June 1898). For another sermonic example, see the Artillery Sermon delivered by R. R. Meredith to the Ancient and Honorable Artillery Company of Massachusetts in June 1898. Meredith's sermon ran the gamut of popular themes, especially emphasizing the war as a definitive, irreversible step for America into world affairs, led by providence. Like Dixon and others, he drew the trajectory from the Revolution, a fight for national life, through the Civil War, a fight to be rid of slavery, to the Spanish-American War as the first to be declared solely on a humanitarian basis. See R. R. Meredith, *A Sermon Preached at the Old South Church on the 260th Anniversary of the Ancient and Honorable Artillery Company, June 6, 1898* (Boston: n.p., 1898).

52. Other wars were rarely mentioned. The War of 1812 was presumably viewed as insignificant to this trajectory. The Mexican War and the more recent Indian Wars did not contribute to the liberty gained–liberty purified–liberty given narrative. Some admitted as much of the Mexican War, now several decades distant, acknowledging that war as an embarrassment (see, e.g., *Living Church,* 4 June 1898). The relevance of the Indian Wars to the narrative of American preparation was largely unaddressed until the anti-imperialists began their polemics after the war.

53. This sermon, preached May 22, was printed in the *Herald of Gospel Liberty,* 9 June 1898, p. 9.

54. *Congregationalist,* 26 May 1898.

55. See, for example, an editorial titled "To the Front," *Outlook,* 7 May 1898. See also a summary of Abbott's sermon from May 15 printed in the *New York Times,* 16 May 1898.

56. "The New Duties of the New Hour," *Outlook,* 28 May 1898, pp. 211–12.

57. John Mayhew Fulton, sermon on Jeremiah 47:6–7, p. 16. Held by the Presbyterian Historical Society, John Mayhew Fulton Papers, Box 1, folder 3.

58. John Mayhew Fulton, sermon on Proverbs 14:34. Held by the Presbyterian Historical Society, John Mayhew Fulton Papers, Box 1, folder 13.

59. *Christian Advocate* (New York), 30 June 1898.

60. *Independent*, 7 July 1898.

61. Cf. *Christian Standard*, 16 July 1898; *Christian Evangelist*, 14 July 1898.

62. In "The Present Crisis: God's Voice," for example, the *Christian Evangelist* offered a summary of the divine faithfulness that had established and guided the republic from its infancy as it had for ancient Israel. The war was to be viewed in light of that past, the article argued, seeing here a warning not to go the way of Spain, that God punishes national sin even as he opens possibilities for good through war (*Christian Evangelist*, 21 July 1898). See also *Congregationalist*, 21 July 1898; *Independent*, 21 July 1898.

63. *United Presbyterian*, 28 July 1898.

64. Examples from the religious press are too numerous to list. Nearly every editor commented on the significance of Philip's actions. Even more telling, however, is the fact that secular accounts of the war published in the following years routinely discussed the episode. For example, see Henry Watterson, *History of the Spanish-American War: Embracing a Complete Review of Our Relations with Spain* (New York: Werner Co., 1898), 301; Harry Keenan, *The Conflict with Spain: A History of the War Based on Official Reports and Descriptions of Eye-Witnesses* (Philadelphia: P. W. Ziegler, 1898), 208, 231–34; Marshall Everett, ed., *Exciting Experiences in Our Wars with Spain and the Filipinos* (Chicago: Educational Co., 1900), 224–25; Andrew Draper, *The Rescue of Cuba: An Episode in the Growth of Free Government* (Boston: Silver, Burdett and Co., 1899), 123.

65. Philip's statements were quoted widely with some insignificant variations, but most accounts depended heavily on the testimony of the ship's chaplain, Harry Jones, in a letter written for the *New York Herald* and reprinted in some religious periodicals. See, for example, *Evangelist*, 21 July 1898; *United Presbyterian*, 28 July 1898; *Biblical Recorder*, 27 July 1898.

66. "Captain Philip of the Texas: The Devout Christian Sailor, a Loyal Congregationalist," *Congregationalist*, 21 July 1898. This column, like several others, also celebrated Philip's unwillingness to initiate a battle on the sabbath. See *Christian Advocate* (New York), 28 July 1898; *Zion's Herald*, 27 July 1898.

67. *Churchman*, 30 July 1898.

68. For examples of this celebration of America's treatment of the defeated enemy, see *Congregationalist*, 14 July 1898; *Pacific*, 1 July and 29 July 1898; *Evangelist*, 21 July 1898; *Watchman*, 28 July 1898. For typical negative assessments of the Cuban insurgents, see *Baptist Courier*, 28 July 1898; *Pacific*, 15 July 1898; *Christian Advocate* (New York), 28 July 1898. And for a good description of these events from the perspective of the Cuban insurgents, as well as the devolving American opinion of their character, see Ada Ferrer, *Insurgent Cuba: Race, Nation, and Revolution, 1868–1898* (Chapel Hill: University of North Carolina Press, 1999), 170–94.

69. George Winton, "Was the War Providential?," *Methodist Review* (November–December 1898): 660–61. Though the article was published in November, the editor's notes indicate that it was written before the end of the war.

Chapter 4
To Anglo-Saxonize the World

1. George Winton, "Was the War Providential?," *Methodist Review* (November–December 1898): 666–67.

2. For an excellent description of the influence of this racial ideology on conceptions of America's redemptive mission, see Ernst Tuveson, *Redeemer Nation: The Idea of America's Millennial Role* (Chicago: University of Chicago Press, 1980), ch. 5. For further description of the prevalence of Anglo-Saxonism within American Protestantism of the period, see Robert Handy, *A Christian America: Protestant Hopes and Historical Realities*, 2nd ed. (Oxford: Oxford University Press, 1984), ch. 4.

3. Richard Hofstadter, *Social Darwinism in American Thought*, rev. ed. (Boston: Beacon Press, 1955), 172.

4. For more on this process, and an excellent description of race theory at work during this period, see Matthew Frye Jacobson, *Whiteness of a Different Color: European Immigrants and the Alchemy of Race* (Cambridge, MA: Harvard University Press, 2001).

5. See Philip Jordan, *The Evangelical Alliance for the United States of America, 1847–1900: Ecumenism, Identity, and the Religion of the Republic* (New York: Edwin Mellon Press, 1982).

6. See James Eldin Reed, "American Foreign Policy, the Politics of Missions and Josiah Strong, 1890–1900," *Church History* 41, no. 2 (June 1972): 230–45.

7. Paul Meyer, "The Fear of Cultural Decline: Josiah Strong's Thought about Reform and Expansion," *Church History* 42, no. 3 (September 1973): 396.

8. Josiah Strong, *Our Country: Its Possible Future and Present Crisis* (New York: Baker and Taylor, 1891; repr., Cambridge, MA: Harvard University Press, 1963). The following page citations refer to the Harvard University Press reprint edition. Strong's two additional works from this period that make significant use of his Anglo-Saxonism are *The New Era; or, The Coming Kingdom* (New York: Baker and Taylor, 1893) and *Expansion under New World-Conditions* (New York: Baker and Taylor, 1900).

9. For a similar comparative list, see Strong, *New Era*, 16.

10. Strong, *Our Country*, 200–202, 209–11. To further establish the centrality of America to the quality of the Anglo-Saxon race, Strong cited Darwin's claim that America would be supreme because the best stock had left Europe and congregated there, which fact corroborated Strong's belief that the overall superiority of the race was a result of its "highly mixed origin" (210). Theodore Roosevelt also shared Strong's conviction that the strength of America's racial stock was a consequence of the admixture of Europe's greatest specimens. See Gary Gerstle, *American Crucible: Race and Nation in the Twentieth Century* (Princeton: Princeton University Press, 2002), 14–25.

11. Strong, *Our Country*, 203–8.

12. Ibid., 213.

13. Ibid., 214–17.

14. See Strong, *Our Country*, 217–18; Strong, *New Era*, 80. These qualifications to Strong's racism have influenced a measured attempt to recuperate some of his image. See, e.g., Dorothea Muller, "The Social Philosophy of Josiah Strong: Social Christianity and American Progressivism," *Church History* 28, no. 2 (June 1959): 183–201; Muller, "Josiah Strong and American Nationalism: A Reevaluation," *Journal of American History* 53, no. 3 (December 1966): 487–503. Handy, similarly, emphasizes that Strong clearly wrote against Anglo-Saxon mistreatment of other races and emphasized the universal appeal of the gospel that could incorporate all races into God's kingdom (*Christian America*, 155–58).

15. C. Vann Woodward, *The Strange Career of Jim Crow*, new and rev. ed. (New York: Oxford University Press, 1965), 9; cited in Handy, *Christian America*, 155.

16. Strong, *Our Country*, 215.

17. An excellent resource that places Anglo-American relations during the Spanish-American War in this larger context is Charles Soutter Campbell, *Anglo-American Understanding: 1898–1903* (Baltimore: Johns Hopkins University Press, 1957). My discussion here relies heavily on Campbell's analysis.

18. Ibid., 19–24.

19. The *New York Times*, for example, noted on 4 June 1898 that an Anglo-American banquet was held in London on the subject of a common purpose, with flags of both nations on display alongside one blended flag.

20. Cited in Campbell, *Anglo-American Understanding*, 47. Chamberlain's speech was famous in both Britain and America, and Campbell notes that it was especially well received in the House of Commons, where it was discussed and widely affirmed the following month. For a useful description of many examples of this Anglo-American good will in practice, see especially pp. 42–55.

21. *Western Christian Advocate*, 4 May 1898. This same editor was even more explicit about the racial implications of such an alliance, writing in a later column: "the instincts of race compel us . . . to link our destiny again with that of Mother England in an alliance, for the glory of God, the preservation of the Anglo-Saxon race, and the integrity of its dominion" (*Western Christian Advocate*, 18 May 1898).

22. *Congregationalist*, 5 May 1898. Cf. *Congregationalist*, 2 June 1898.

23. See *New York Times*, 30 May 1898.

24. These quotations are taken from the full reproduction of MacArthur's "Hand of God" rendition at the Christian Endeavor Convention printed in the *Baptist and Reflector*, 28 July 1898, pp. 2–4. For a similar reference to MacArthur's views on the issue, see *Baptist Argus*, 8 September 1898. And for examples of similar rhetoric among other ministers, see Ruen Thomas's address on an Anglo-American alliance, printed in *Zion's Herald*, 13 June 1898; and James King, *Situation and Justification of the Nation at War with Spain: An Address before the Empire State Society, Sons of the American Revolution, in Union Methodist Episcopal Church, New York City, May 15th, 1898* (New York: printed by order of the Society, 1898).

25. *Baptist Standard*, 9 June 1898. For similar examples of this argument, see Nashville's *Christian Advocate*, 16 June 1898; and Chicago's *Standard*, 28 May 1898.

26. Examples abound of commentary on the Anglo-American friendliness inspired by the war, with varying degrees of support for official alliance. The following, in addition to those noted earlier, are representative: *Congregationalist,* 5 May and 26 May, 2 June and 9 June, 29 September 1898; *Baptist Courier,* 5 May 1898; *Independent,* 12 May and 19 May 1898; *Christian Standard,* 14 May, 2 July 1898; *Florida Baptist Witness,* 25 May 1898; *Churchman,* 21 May 1898; *Advance,* 2 June 1898; *Christian Evangelist,* 26 May 1898; *United Presbyterian,* 30 June 1898; *Evangelist,* 7 July 1898. See also William Karraker, "The American Churches and the Spanish-American War" (unpublished PhD thesis, University of Chicago, 1940), 89–95. Many Catholics, especially the prominent Irish American community, opposed this perspective on the meaning of the war they supported. Commentary in the Boston periodical the *Pilot* through the fall is the best example.

27. Many excellent studies describe the details of white reunion during these years, some specifically noting the importance of this war in that process. David Blight's *Race and Reunion: The Civil War in American Memory* (Cambridge, MA: Belknap Press of Harvard University Press, 2001) is the most comprehensive, but see also Edward Blum, *Reforging the White Republic: Race, Religion, and American Nationalism, 1865–1898* (Baton Rouge: Louisiana State University Press, 2007), 209–242; Charles Reagan Wilson, *Baptized in Blood: The Religion of the Lost Cause, 1865–1920* (Athens: University of Georgia Press, 1980); Patricia O'Leary, *To Die For: The Paradox of American Patriotism* (Princeton: Princeton University Press, 1999), ch. 11; Gaines Foster, "Coming to Terms with Defeat: Post–Vietnam War America and the Post–Civil War South," *Virginia Quarterly Review* 66 (Winter 1990): 27, cited in George Herring, *From Colony to Superpower: U.S. Foreign Relations since 1776* (Oxford: Oxford University Press, 2008), 335.

28. *Christian Index,* 9 June 1898, citing an anecdote from the *Standard.*

29. *Western Christian Advocate,* 18 May 1898.

30. This piece, written for the *Standard* of Chicago, is quoted here as printed in excerpt in Georgia's *Christian Index,* 9 June 1898. The same piece also appeared in excerpt in the *Alabama Baptist,* 16 June 1898. Examples of this strain of commentary are abundant in periodicals published in both the North and the South, especially in articles summarizing important results of the war. See, for example, *Outlook,* 25 June 1898; *American Missionary* (June 1898); *Baptist Courier,* 9 June 1898; *Baptist Argus,* 25 August 1898; *Congregationalist,* 17 November 1898.

31. The speech, widely reported through the religious press, was published separately in pamphlet form: J. B. Hawthorne, *The Present Feeling in the South Towards the Federal Union and the People of the North* (n.p.: n.p., 1898). Hawthorne's speech struck precisely the bargain described so well by David Blight and Nicholas Guyatt, among others. Cf. Blight, *Race and Reunion;* Nicholas Guyatt, *Providence and the Invention of the United States, 1607–1876* (Cambridge: Cambridge University Press, 2007), 302–9.

32. Hawthorne, *Present Feeling,* 8–9.

33. Ibid., 11.

34. For examples, see *Speeches and Addresses of William McKinley: From March 1, 1897 to May 30, 1900* (New York: Doubleday and McClure, 1900), 83–153.

35. Ibid., 85.

36. For an excellent description of excruciating task of managing the Civil War dead, especially in the South, and an account of the context in which McKinley's gesture would have resonated so powerfully, see Drew Gilpin Faust, *This Republic of Suffering: Death and the American Civil War* (New York: Knopf, 2008), ch. 7.

37. McKinley, *Speeches and Addresses*, 159.

38. The best example of this antipathy toward the notion of an Anglo-American alliance is Boston's Irish Catholic periodical the *Pilot*, which commented on the development of that sentiment throughout 1898. For the larger Catholic context, see Frank Reuter, *Catholic Influence on American Colonial Policies, 1898–1904* (Austin: University of Texas Press, 1967), ch. 1. For examples of a positive assessment of Britain's empire in the context of Anglo-American friendship, see *Advance*, 5 May 1898; *Independent*, 16 June 1898; W. O. Carver, *Missions and the Kingdom of Heaven*, an address given at the Southern Baptist Theological Seminary, 1 October 1898 (n.p.: n.p., 1898).

39. See, for example, *Baptist Standard*, 1 December 1898; *Congregationalist*, 17 November 1898; Robert Bachman, Thanksgiving sermon printed in the *Evangelist*, 29 December 1898, pp. 11–12; Edward Noyes, "The Nation's Thanksgiving," a sermon preached for Thanksgiving, 20 November 1898, pp. 10–12. Held by the Congregational Library, Boston, MA. Newton, MA, First Church (Congregational)-Records, 1773–1972, Box 36, folder "Edward M. Noyes." See also Thomas Butler, Sermon on Neh. 7:70–8:12, delivered 20 November 1898. Held by Disciples of Christ Historical Society, Box 2, folder 42.

40. *Biblical Recorder*, 20 July 1898.

41. For additional examples, see Carver, *Missions and the Kingdom of God*; Miles Saunders, "The Outlook," *Christian Observer*, 14 December 1898; B. J. Hoadley, "The Bright Side of War," *Western Christian Advocate*, 7 September 1898; *Baptist Argus*, 8 September and 20 October 1898. See especially Winton, "Was the War Providential?," 665–67.

42. William Gardam, "America's Mission," a sermon preached July 10 and printed in the *Living Church*, 20 August 1898, p. 459.

43. Ibid., 460. For another excellent, even more explicit example of this rhetoric later in the fall, see George Pentecost, *The Coming of Age of America. A Retrospect and a Forecast* (New York: n.p., 1898), 23–25. Held by the Presbyterian Historical Society.

44. John Clifford, "The Anglo-American Alliance," printed in the *Watchman*, 29 September 1898, pp. 12–13, 28. For reports of this address elsewhere, see *Zion's Herald*, 21 September 1898; *Baptist Argus*, 20 October 1898. The sermon of Clifford's counterpart in the exchange, delivered by George Lorimer in Nottingham, is less important for understanding the nature of Anglo-Saxon identity, focusing instead on the role of the race in missions. See *Watchman*, 6 October 1898.

45. Clifford, "The Anglo-American Alliance," 13.

46. Fascination with images of foreign peoples—and defining the national identity in contrast to those peoples—had been a long-standing American pastime on all levels of society, as evidenced in popular travel writing, romantic novels, and academic

disciplines like anthropology and eugenics. Matthew Frye Jacobson's excellent study of racism in this period describes a powerful cycle of self-fulfilling prophecy, where degrading perspectives on non-Europeans provided the lens for viewing foreign peoples in this literature, and the image of such peoples provided by the literature then helped reinforce the lens. If the war with Spain did not create the impression of other peoples as inferior, it still helped solidify those perspectives with further evidence of inferiority, offering Americans in particular more intimate contact with foreign, non-European populations on an unprecedented scale. Matthew Frye Jacobson, *Barbarian Virtues: The United States Encounters Foreign Peoples at Home and Abroad, 1876–1917* (New York: Hill and Wang, 2000), esp. chs. 3–4. Jacobson may overplay the influence of economic motivation as an explanation of America's turn to imperialism; he argues that Americans came to view "inferior" races as merely pawns or stepping stones towards dominance of the global marketplace. Here Jacobson is in good company, but his emphasis tends to flatten a complex case for expansion that also included powerful humanitarian and religious notions of racial identity and destiny. However, as a description of the complex layers in the process of race construction in this period, Jacobson's study—especially part two—is unmatched.

47. See David Trask, *The War with Spain in 1898* (1981; repr., Lincoln: University of Nebraska Press, 1996), 54.

48. *Baptist Courier*, 28 July 1898. Though the discussion to follow interacts mostly with sources in the religious press, religious editors reflected much more broad editorial trends. See, for example, *Harper's Weekly*, 27 August 1898; *Nation*, 11 August 1898.

49. For commentary on these events that reflected this perspective on the insurgents, see, e.g., *Independent*, 28 July 1898; *Pacific*, 15 July 1898; *Watchman*, 14 July and 28 July 1898, 4 August and 25 August 1898; *New Orleans Christian Advocate*, 11 August 1898.

50. *Christian Advocate*, 28 July 1898.

51. *Watchman* as cited by Georgia's *Christian Index*, 21 July 1898.

52. *Outlook*, 28 January 1899. For earlier examples of this perspective, see *Congregationalist*, 4 August and 18 August 1898; *Herald of Gospel Liberty*, 4 August 1898; *Churchman*, 2 July 1898.

53. *Christian Evangelist*, 4 August 1898.

54. Some in the black press objected to condescending descriptions of the Cubans and Filipinos, doubtless seeing in them a reflection of the dominant white perspective on their communities. See, e.g., *AME Church Review* (January 1899). But even within African American communities there was some significant support for the notion that America, for all its problems at home, still possessed a civilization that would benefit the people of these territories. So, some editors and ministers in the months following the war focused less on the expansion debate than on praising the record of black soldiers during the war as proof that they were themselves ready and able to participate fully in American society. See, e.g., *Star of Zion* through October and November; *Christian Recorder*, 27 October 1898. For more detail on this spectrum of perspectives in the black press, see Lawrence Little, *Disciples of Liberty: The African Methodist Episcopal Church in the Age of Imperialism,*

1884–1916 (Knoxville: University of Tennessee Press, 2000), 64–108; Willard Gatewood, *Black Americans and the White Man's Burden, 1898–1903* (Urbana: University of Illinois Press, 1975).

55. This was a theme in the two most famous anti-imperialist sermons. See Henry van Dyke, *The American Birthright and the Philippine Pottage* (New York: Charles Scribner's Sons, 1898), 12ff. See also the sermon by Charles Parkhurst ("Our Duties after the War," a sermon preached Thanksgiving Day 1898 at Madison Square Church, printed in the *Evangelist*, 1 December 1898, pp. 9–11), who argued that the American propensity for governing the "semi civilized" or "savages is not just what you would call reassuring. I would rather be a Malay, subject to Spain, than be an American Indian, subject to the Indian Bureau" (11).

Chapter 5
Duty and Destiny

1. Frank Ninkovich offers a helpful description of the difference between "imperialism" as it is used in the twenty-first century and "colonialism." Imperialism has a broader range of meaning that can include limited political control or influence, as well as various cultural imperialisms, none of which requires the imposition of official colonial status. See *The United States and Imperialism* (Oxford: Blackwell, 2001), 5–7. In 1898, imperialism carried all the connotations of outright colonialism, whereas expansion evoked a larger field of political and cultural involvement.

2. A fine example of this use of the term is a sermon by Charles Eaton of New York's Church of the Divine Paternity, printed in excerpt in the *New York Times*, 25 November 1898. Eaton argued strongly for a protectorate rather than permanent, militaristic colonialism but then praised the idea of "expansion" in no uncertain terms: we "should rejoice in the idea of expansion. We have held too narrow and selfish views of the destiny and responsibility of the American Republic. There need be no limit to our expansion as a civilizing agency and educating force, as a moral and religious power."

3. See especially Julius Pratt, *Expansionists of 1898: The Acquisition of Hawaii and the Spanish Islands* (1936; repr., Chicago: Quadrangle, 1964), 279–316. See also Ernest May, *American Imperialism: A Speculative Essay* (New York: Atheneum, 1968), 17–43.

4. See Winthrop Hudson, "Protestant Clergy Debate the Nation's Vocation, 1898–1899," *Church History* 42, no. 1 (March 1973): 110–118. Hudson, like his interlocutors, remains dependent on prominent ministers in New York, Boston, and Chicago, even though his attention to chronology is a valuable improvement.

5. This general consensus was noted by some contemporary observers. See, for example, *Baptist Argus*, 9 September 1898. The majority opinion seems to have been in favor of some form of protectorate or provisional government and against permanent retention of the Philippines.

6. *Baptist Standard*, 3 November 1898. A similar fatalistic providentialism also featured prominently in the rhetoric on both sides of the Civil War, as observers attempted to

justify mounting losses. See Harry Stout, *Upon the Altar of the Nation: A Moral History of the Civil War* (New York: Viking, 2006). See also Mark Noll, *The Civil War as a Theological Crisis* (Chapel Hill: University of North Carolina Press, 2006), 75–86.

7. For an excellent description of the influence and perspective of American Catholics, both on the war and on the subsequent policy debates, see Frank Reuter, *Catholic Influence in American Colonial Policies, 1898–1904* (Austin: University of Texas Press, 1967). Reuter shows that most vocal American Catholics supported the war against Spain, eager to prove their loyalty to America in its war against a Catholic nation and to distinguish Catholicism from Spanish abuses. After the war, in the debate over expansion, the landscape was more diverse, as some favored expansion and others did not, most notably the Irish Catholic communities that saw traces of their own experiences with British imperialism. What all Catholics agreed upon in the days following the war was that the former Spanish colonies did not require Protestant missionaries, and they worked tirelessly to ensure the American government would treat their interests fairly.

8. See, for example, Kenton Clymer, "Religion and American Imperialism: Methodist Missionaries in the Philippine Islands, 1899–1913," *Pacific Historical Review* 49, no. 1 (February 1980): 29–50; Kenneth MacKenzie, *The Robe and the Sword: The Methodist Church and the Rise of American Imperialism* (Washington: Public Affairs Press, 1961); Arthur Schlesinger, "The Missionary Enterprise and Imperialism," in *The Missionary Enterprise in China and America*, ed. John Fairbank (Cambridge, MA: Harvard University Press, 1974), 336–73.

9. See, for example, Louis A. Pérez, *The War of 1898: The United States and Cuba in History and Historiography* (Chapel Hill: University of North Carolina Press, 1998).

10. For a similar argument that applies to American leaders more broadly, see Paul T. McCartney, *Power and Progress: American National Identity, the War of 1898, and the Rise of American Imperialism* (Baton Rouge: Louisiana State University Press, 2006), 182–98. McCartney's larger argument presumes the sincerity of the prominent faith in American exceptionalism and that this identity, with its deep commitment to the idea of an American mission, helps explain why Americans chose the policies they did. My argument supports his larger claim by more fully examining the underpinnings of American identity supplied by religious leaders and distinctly religious arguments.

11. Hudson, "Protestant Clergy," 114.

12. Examples of early support for, or at least openness to, the idea of ongoing control of the Philippines include New York's *Independent*, South Carolina's *Baptist Courier*, the *Alabama Baptist*, the Disciples' *Christian Evangelist*, the Congregationalist *Pacific* in San Francisco, the Presbyterian *New York Observer*, and Boston Methodists' *Zion's Herald*, among others. Though nearly all of the examples to follow come from Protestant sources, a similar level of support and rationale for expansion was present in Catholic public opinion as well. See Reuter, *Catholic Influence*; Richard Welch, *Response to Imperialism: The United States and the Philippine-American War, 1899–1902* (Chapel Hill: University of North Carolina Press, 1979), 10–16. And some African American religious leaders, at least within the African Methodist Episcopal Church, were early supporters of some

form of expansion, believing in the civilizing power of American institutions and seeking opportunities for missions that would accompany American control. Their support waned more quickly than that of their Euro-American counterparts, particularly in response to the American suppression of the Filipino insurgency. See Lawrence Little, *Disciples of Liberty: The African Methodist Episcopal Church in the Age of Imperialism, 1884–1916* (Knoxville: University of Tennessee Press, 2000), chs. 2–3. For a larger view of African American responses to U.S. expansion, see Willard Gatewood, *Black Americans and the White Man's Burden, 1898–1903* (Urbana: University of Illinois Press, 1975).

13. *Watchman*, 26 May 1898. Other critics of early expansionism include New York's *Christian Advocate*, the Congregationalist *Herald of Gospel Liberty*, the Nashville *Christian Advocate*, the *Congregationalist*, the *Biblical Recorder*, the *Standard*, and the *Living Church*. Except for the two *Christian Advocates* and perhaps the *Standard*, these periodicals eventually came to support expansion in some form.

14. See, for example, *Congregationalist*, 12 May 1898.

15. *Standard*, 14 May and 21 May 1898. As was typical for other early critics of expansion, the *Standard* never identified exactly who these crazed imperialists were. Though some certainly did favor permanent retention of the territories and active expansionism, including a few religious leaders, most were far less specific in their optimistic musings on what they considered an open future of increased American world responsibility.

16. *Baptist Courier*, 19 May 1898.

17. *Independent*, 9 June 1898.

18. *Independent*, 16 June 1898.

19. *Independent*, 30 June 1898.

20. *New York Observer*, 4 August 1898.

21. *New York Observer*, 18 August 1898.

22. *Christian Evangelist*, 1 September 1898. For a similar framing of Philippine policy as a question of selflessness over against selfishness, see Washington Gladden, "The Issues of the War," *Outlook*, 16 July 1898, pp. 673ff.

23. See, for example, John Dobson, *Reticent Expansionism: The Foreign Policy of William McKinley* (Pittsburgh, PA: Duquesne University Press, 1988), 103–5.

24. See chapter 4 for more on this argument and the prevalent Anglo-Saxonism from which it emerged. One additional line of argument on this front appealed to the American experience with "Negro rule" during the Reconstruction era, a cautionary tale for editors North and South. See, e.g., *Christian Evangelist*, 4 August 1898; *Baptist Standard*, 18 August 1898; *Christian Index*, 3 November 1898; *Churchman*, 3 December 1898; Nashville *Christian Advocate*, 1 December 1898.

25. *Christian Index*, 21 July 1898.

26. *New York Observer*, 16 June 1898.

27. This argument is well represented throughout the religious press. For examples spanning region and denomination, see *Independent*, 12 May 1898; *Christian Evangelist*, 26 May 1898; *Christian Observer*, 7 September 1898; *Zion's Herald*, 1 June 1898.

28. *Zion's Herald*, 8 June 1898. For another early example with similarly stark language of providential imposition, see the column written by the Methodist bishop J. M. Thoburn in *Western Christian Advocate*, 25 May 1898, pp. 650–51.

29. *Advance*, 16 June 1898.

30. *Pacific*, 19 August 1898.

31. *Baptist Standard*, 9 June 1898; cf. 30 June 1898.

32. *Baptist Standard*, 7 July 1898. See also *Christian Index*, 25 August 1898; *Zion's Herald*, 13 July 1898; *Outlook*, 21 May 1898.

33. *Baptist Standard*, 28 July 1898.

34. "Our Future Policy," *Outlook*, 21 May 1898, p. 158.

35. Gladden, "The Issues of the War," 674. Here Gladden was echoing themes from a popular pamphlet he published in support of America's cause in the war, *Our Nation and Her Neighbors* (Columbus, OH: Quinius and Ridenous, 1898).

36. For another early usage of this argument, see Joseph Cook, "Ultimate Imperialism," *Independent*, 28 July 1898.

37. *Outlook*, 16 July 1898. For other examples of Abbott's important perspective, see *Outlook*, 2 July and 23 July 1898. For other periodicals reflecting the same views, see *Churchman*, 2 July, 9 July, 16 July, and 23 July 1898; *Evangelist*, 11 August 1898.

38. *Christian Index*, 18 August 1898.

39. *Independent*, 7 July 1898.

40. *Zion's Herald*, 13 July 1898. For several later examples of this line of argument, see *Baptist Courier*, 1 September 1898; *Baptist and Reflector*, 17 November 1898; *Outlook*, 17 December 1898; *Baptist Argus*, 11 August 1898.

41. For good descriptions of Christian social activism during this period, see Robert Handy, *A Christian America: Protestant Hopes and Historical Realities*, 2nd ed. (New York: Oxford University Press, 1984); Edwin Gaustad and Leigh Schmidt, *The Religious History of America: The Heart of the American Story from Colonial Times to Today* (San Francisco: HarperSanFrancisco, 2002).

42. *Christian Standard*, 30 July 1898. For further development of this idea, see *Christian Standard*, 10 September and 24 September 1898.

43. *Homiletic Review* (August 1898): 192–93.

44. *Baptist Argus*, 7 July 1898.

45. *Baptist Argus*, 8 September 1898.

46. *United Presbyterian*, 4 August 1898.

47. *United Presbyterian*, 11 August 1898.

48. *United Presbyterian*, 1 September 1898. For further examples of this perspective as developed through the fall, see *United Presbyterian*, 22 September, 10 November, and especially 8 December 1898, which includes the following from a column called "Not for Territorial Aggrandizement": "We believe that our President and the peace commission desire to follow, as they have been following, the leadings of divine providence in their negotiations with Spain. And we also believe that the great Jehovah, who has so manifestly 'gone forth with our hosts' and 'covered their heads in the day of battle,'

will lead on until 'His way shall be known upon the earth, his saving health among all nations.'"

49. *Congregationalist*, 18 August 1898. Cf. *Congregationalist*, 1 September 1898.

50. *Congregationalist*, 13 October 1898. See also 6 October, 20 October, 27 October, and 10 November 1898.

51. *Congregationalist*, 27 October 1898. See also *Evangelist*, 18 August and 25 August 1898; *Christian Observer*, 24 August 1898; *Baptist Courier*, 4 August 1898; *Baptist Standard*, 18 August 1898; *Christian Evangelist*, 21 July and 25 August 1898.

52. Henry van Dyke, *The American Birthright and the Philippine Pottage. A Sermon Preached on Thanksgiving Day, 1898* (New York: Charles Scribner's Sons, 1898), 7–8.

53. George Winton, "Was the War Providential?," *Methodist Review* (November–December 1898): 660–66.

54. Ibid., 660.

55. Ibid., 661. Italics mine.

56. Ibid., 665.

57. Ibid., 665–66.

58. Featherston's comments were printed from a letter to the editor in Nashville's Methodist *Christian Advocate*, 8 September 1898. Italics mine.

59. On July 10, the day McKinley had set aside for national thanksgiving and with the president in attendance, Bristol preached a celebrated sermon on the theme of providence in history and in America's war. The sermon was printed the following month in *The Treasury* (August 1898): 265–71.

60. For a useful overview of the literature on McKinley, see Ephraim Smith, "William McKinley's Enduring Legacy: The Historiographical Debate on the Taking of the Philippine Islands," in *Crucible of Empire: The Spanish-American War and Its Aftermath*, ed. James Bradford (Annapolis: Naval Institute Press, 1993), 205–49; McCartney, *Power and Progress*, 199ff; Dobson, *Reticent Expansionism*, 1–5.

61. Dobson, *Reticent Expansionism*, 4–5.

62. Ibid., 104. See 100–105 for full discussion of this point, including Dobson's summary of McKinley's dismissal of common alternatives such as self-government or the return of the islands to Spain.

63. The first and most cited secondary account of this conversation is Charles Olcott, *The Life of William McKinley* (New York: Houghton Mifflin, 1916), 2:109–111. Olcott cites as his source an account by General James Rusling, one of the persons present, and published first in the *Christian Advocate* (New York), 22 January 1903.

64. See Robert Ferrell, *American Diplomacy: A History*, 3rd ed. (New York: Norton, 1975), 367–69. Cited in Welch, *Response to Imperialism*, 162n13.

65. See *Christian Advocate* (New York), 22 January 1903. Dobson's account appears on 115ff of *Reticent Expansionism*.

66. See Welch, *Response to Imperialism*, 10.

67. Dobson has a brief description of the midwestern tour on 112–13 of *Reticent Expansionism*. But the best account, one that shapes the following discussion, is McCartney, *Power and Progress*, 211–18.

68. The authoritative collection of William McKinley's speeches is the *Papers of William McKinley*, held by the Library of Congress. A more convenient collection of his wartime rhetoric, however, and what will be used for this discussion is *Speeches and Addresses of William McKinley: From March 1, 1897, to May 30, 1900* (New York: Doubleday and McClure, 1900). The quotation here appears on 85.

69. Ibid., 87.

70. Ibid., 100.

71. Ibid., 102.

72. Ibid., 105.

73. Ibid., 105–6.

74. Ibid., 114.

75. Ibid., 116.

76. Ibid., 118.

77. Ibid., 133–34.

78. Ibid., 134–35.

79. See, for example, McKinley's speeches in Clinton, IL (129), and Chicago (135).

80. See David Trask, *The War with Spain in 1898* (1981; repr., Lincoln: University of Nebraska Press, 1996), 452–56; Dobson, *Reticent Expansionism*, 113–14.

81. The *Baptist Standard*, for example, criticized McKinley for what it called a "fatalistic optimism," even as it remained consistently in favor of some form of national expansion (3 November 1898). See also *Churchman*, 5 November 1898.

82. For examples of the endorsement of McKinley's rhetoric, see *Evangelist*, 27 October 1898; *United Presbyterian*, 27 October 1898; *Congregationalist*, 20 October 1898.

83. *Congregationalist*, 10 November 1898.

84. The *Evangelist* printed Bachman's sermon in its 29 December 1898 issue, pp. 10–12.

85. Edward Noyes, "The Nation's Thanksgiving," a sermon preached for Thanksgiving, 20 November 1898, p. 9. Held by the Congregational Library, Boston, MA. Newton, MA, First Church (Congregational) Records, 1773–1972, Box 36, folder "Edward M. Noyes."

86. *New York Times*, 25 November 1898.

87. Ibid.

88. George Pentecost, *The Coming of Age of America. A Retrospect and a Forecast* (New York: n.p., 1898), 12. Held by the Presbyterian Historical Society.

89. George Whitefield Stone, "Thanksgiving 1898: National Problems," 7. George Whitefield Stone Sermons and Lectures: bMS 495/1 (2) "National Problems." (Spanish War) Thanksgiving. No. 18. November 27, 1898. Held by Andover-Harvard Theological Library Manuscripts and Archives Department, Cambridge, MA. Stone's thanksgiving sermon as preserved in this collection is built around the manuscript of an earlier sermon preached during the course of the war, further reinforcing the stability of the interpretations of national development articulated then.

90. George Pentecost, and perhaps John Donaldson (*What Shall We Do with Our Colonies?* [Davenport, IA: n.p., 1898]), were two of the only Thanksgiving preachers to

favor permanent annexation, but they justified their position in precisely the terms others used to defend provisional control. So what is most significant here, and what has been the focus of this chapter, is the underlying shared conviction about the nature of the American nation as the basis for any number of policy proposals, or for not caring much about specific policy at all.

91. See Pentecost, *Coming of Age*; Marcus Brownson, *The National Thanksgiving, November the Twenty-fourth, 1898. American Expansion, a Discourse Delivered in the Tenth Presbyterian Church, Philadelphia* (Philadelphia: Published under the Direction of the Men's League of the Church, 1898); Donaldson, *What Shall We Do*; Stone, "National Problems"; Noyes, "Nation's Thanksgiving."

92. See, for example, Pentecost, *Coming of Age*; MacArthur from *New York Times*, 25 November 1898.

93. Brownson, *American Expansion*, 12. See also Pentecost, *Coming of Age*; Stone, "Thanksgiving."

94. See, for example, Donaldson, *What Shall We Do*; Brownson, *American Expansion*; Pentecost, *Coming of Age*.

95. *New York Times*, 25 November 1898. See also Bachman from the *Evangelist*, 29 December 1898, p. 11; Stone, "National Problems," 8–9.

96. Donaldson, *What Shall We Do*, 8.

97. Stone, "National Problems," 15.

98. Noyes, "Nation's Thanksgiving."

99. Donaldson, *What Shall We Do*, 3. See also Arthur Metcalf, *The Reign of God: A Sermon Preached at the Congregational Church, Bancroft, Mich.* (n.p.: n.p., 1898), 8–9.

100. Pentecost, *Coming of Age*, 13.

101. Brownson, *American Expansion*, 19–20.

102. Bachman from the *Evangelist*, 29 December 1898, p. 12. See also Metcalf, *Reign of God*. Metcalf's sermon is perhaps the most useful compendium of the themes traced earlier. It is an extended treatment of God's providential reign in the world, beginning with a survey of the biblical era, then proceeding to argue that God remains no less active and reigns no less supremely today than in ancient Israel.

103. Charles Parkhurst, "Our Duties after the War," a sermon preached Thanksgiving Day 1898 at Madison Square Church, printed in the *Evangelist*, 1 December 1898, p. 9.

104. Van Dyke, *American Birthright*, 7–8. The two sermons by Van Dyke and Parkhurst are excellent representative examples of the opposition to imperialism among religious groups, such as it was. New York City was home to a larger than typical group of anti-imperialist ministers; see Hudson, "Protestant Clergy." Among the religious periodicals, besides the those of the Quakers, Unitarians, and Universalists, the Methodist *Christian Advocate* of New York and the *Christian Advocate* of Nashville remained two of the most consistent—and only—critics of the administration's policy; see Pratt, *Expansionists of 1898*, 294–95, 312–14. For a helpful discussion of the anti-imperialism among religious communities and how it was overwhelmed by a dominant optimism, see Welch, *Response*

to Imperialism, 93–100. Less helpful is his claim that support for and opposition to expansion can be traced along lines of Calvinist influence.

105. See John Edwin Smylie, "Protestant Clergymen and America's World Role, 1865–1900" (unpublished ThD dissertation, Princeton Theological Seminary, 1959), 532–37.

106. Van Dyke, *American Birthright*, 1. For a similar concession from Parkhurst, see "Our Duties," 11. Parkhurst argued for treating the Philippines as the nation would treat Cuba. America should "help them to help themselves and teach them to govern themselves. There may be opportunity to do some vast civilizing work there if it is undertaken with the spirit in which Paul proceeded when he said 'I seek not yours but you'" (11). Also noteworthy is the fact that Van Dyke never questioned the propriety of permanent possession of Puerto Rico. See *American Birthright*, 6.

107. An excerpt of Abbott's sermon "New Duties of the New Hour" was printed in the *New York Times*, 25 November 1898. Undoubtedly Abbott and Van Dyke would have differed over the details of American governance in the Philippines, not least its length and its extent. But they agreed that it should be provisional, not permanent. For examples of accounts treating Abbott and Van Dyke as archetypal opponents in the expansion debate, see Hudson, "Protestant Clergy," 114–18.

108. For celebrations of the treaty, see, for example, *United Presbyterian*, 8 December 1898; *Herald of Gospel Liberty*, 8 December 1898; *Christian Index*, 29 December 1898; *Outlook*, 3 December 1898.

109. See Welch, *Response to Imperialism*, 10–16.

110. *Pacific*, 29 December 1898.

111. *United Presbyterian*, 8 December 1898.

112. *Outlook*, 17 December 1898.

Conclusion

1. *Evangelist*, 1 December 1898. The motive of the editor in leading with this psalm is not clear, certainly not so clear as the provocative content of the psalm might suggest. There was no editorial comment on the psalm, but the paper was not a univocal supporter of the taking of the Philippines. In fact, this same issue included a full-text version of Charles Parkhurst's sermon criticizing imperial ambitions. But whatever the purpose of the quotation, the appearance of the psalm in this context raises the issue of kingly rule as a component of the biblical portrait of the messiah.

2. I am grateful to Kathleen Flake for first raising the issue of kingship in the biblical portrait of the messiah.

3. Rudyard Kipling, "The White Man's Burden," *McClure's Magazine* (February 1899): 290.

4. See, for example, *Christian Recorder*, 2 March 1899. For more detail on the response to this poem, see Lawrence Little, *Disciples of Liberty: The African Methodist Episcopal Church in the Age of Imperialism, 1884–1916* (Knoxville: University of Tennessee Press, 2000), ch. 2.

5. *Christian Evangelist*, 9 February 1898. Other editors similarly commented on the poem and its significance, and the title, "The White Man's Burden," emerged as something of a slogan. See, e.g., *Pacific Christian*, 30 March 1899; *American Missionary* (July 1899): 49–51; A. E. Dunning, "The White Man's Burden," *Homiletic Review* (June 1899): 522–24; Edward Wright, *"The White Man's Burden"; or "The Debt of the Christian to the Barbarian," a Sermon Preached at the First Presbyterian Church, Austin, Texas, February 12, 1899* (published by the Session of the Church, 1899). Held by the Presbyterian Historical Society, Pamphlets Collection.

6. Kipling, "White Man's Burden," 291.

7. Josiah Strong, *Expansion under New World-Conditions* (New York: Baker and Taylor, 1900), 212. For this citation and more on its context, see Robert Handy, *Undermined Establishment: Church-State Relations in America, 1880–1920* (Princeton: Princeton University Press, 1991), 81–83.

8. Strong, *Expansion*, 204.

9. See Richard Welch, *Response to Imperialism: The United States and the Philippine-American War, 1899–1902* (Chapel Hill: University of North Carolina Press, 1979), 14–25.

10. William C. Doane, "Imperialism," *Churchman*, 4 February 1899, p. 171.

11. *Churchman*, 25 February 1899.

12. *Christian Evangelist*, 13 April 1899.

13. These similarities in part explain the surge of historiographical interest in imperialism and the Philippine-American War in the 1960s and 1970s among historians interested in the roots of American policy in Vietnam. See Richard Welch, *Response to Imperialism*, xiii–xvi, for examples of the trend and his corrective response. Welch's interests are far more useful to the themes of my study. He finds the primary significance of the war not in its relationship to later American policy but in what the response to these events suggests about American society at this period. In a 1974 article and even more in his 1979 monograph, Welch traces the atrocities committed by American troops as their frustration escalated over the years. Further, he describes the response to reports of abuse among several prominent interest groups in American society, including press, business, academic, and religious leaders. What he found was a mixture of confusion, optimism, and outright unwillingness to believe things were as horrible as reported.

14. For details on this phase of the war as summarized later, see, for example, Welch, *Response to Imperialism*, ch. 2; Leon Wolff, *Little Brown Brother: How the United States Purchased and Pacified the Philippine Islands at the Century's Turn* (Garden City, NY: Doubleday, 1961), ch. 11.

15. Richard Welch, "American Atrocities in the Philippines: The Indictment and the Response," *Pacific Historical Review* 43, no. 2 (May 1974): 234–38. Drawing from official government records and some anti-imperialist literature, Welch notes six murders of soldiers, eighteen murders of civilians, fifteen instances of rape, fourteen of the "water cure," and four "other" forms of torture.

16. See Wolff, *Little Brown Brother*, 306.

17. See especially Welch, *Response to Imperialism*, 43–57.

18. See Welch, "American Atrocities," 244–47. For further discussion of the response to the war among religious groups, see Welch, *Response to Imperialism*, 89–100.

19. Welch, "American Atrocities," 251. See also Welch's similar conclusion in *Response to Imperialism*: "In America at the turn of the twentieth century, the dominant mood was one of optimism and romantic nationalism. Optimism was generated not by a belief that all was right, but rather a belief that all could be righted. At home the search for order, efficiency, and social harmony would succeed. Abroad the nation's mission to do its duty, strengthen its diplomatic power, and expand its trade would be accomplished. And as the nation's promise was redeemed at home and abroad, so the individual participant was assured a sense of purpose and self-fulfillment" (148).

20. For a general description of this and a variety of factors that undermined support for active territorial expansion, see Ernest May, *American Imperialism: A Speculative Essay* (New York: Atheneum, 1968), 210ff.

21. Wilson's "faith-based foreign policy" is the subject of a 2008 monograph by Malcolm Magee, which includes a detailed description of Wilson's providentialist world-view. See Magee, *What the World Should Be: Woodrow Wilson and the Crafting of a Faith-Based Foreign Policy* (Waco, TX: Baylor University Press, 2008).

22. A speech given to the Railway Business Association, New York, 27 January 1916, in *The Papers of Woodrow Wilson* (Princeton: Princeton University Press, 1966–1993), 36:10. Cited by Richard Gamble, *The War for Righteousness: Progressive Christianity, the Great War, and the Rise of the Messianic Nation* (Wilmington: ISI Books, 2003), 277n580. For further discussion of these themes in Wilson's speeches on American duty abroad, see Gamble, *War for Righteousness*, 86–87. And for more on the Mexico intervention and Wilson's justification, see Magee, *What the World Should Be*, 47–64.

23. David Kennedy, *Over Here: The First World War and American Society* (New York: Oxford University Press, 1980), 51.

24. Woodrow Wilson, "For Declaration of War against Germany: Address Delivered at a Joint Session of the Two Houses of Congress," in *The Public Papers of Woodrow Wilson: War and Peace*, ed. Ray Stannard Baker and William Edward Dodd (New York: Harper and Brothers, 1927), 1:14.

25. Ray Abrams, *Preachers Present Arms: A Study of the War-Time Attitudes and Activities of the Churches and the Clergy in the United States, 1914–1918* (New York: Round Table, 1933), 51. Abrams's account offers many good examples illustrating the early division over appropriate national policy (ch. 2) and the near-universal support for the war effort once begun (ch. 3). For a general but more nuanced descriptive account of church perspectives on the war, see John Piper, *The American Churches in World War I* (Athens: Ohio University Press, 1985). Piper confirms the high levels of support described by Abrams but also highlights a greater diversity in the response of a wider variety of religious groups, not all of which provided the sorts of vocal support Abrams emphasizes.

26. Gamble, *War for Righteousness*, 182.

27. Gamble's focus on the more theologically liberal, progressive clergy is indicative of the fact that by this point American Protestantism was more clearly divided along

liberal and conservative lines than was the case in 1898. Gamble's progressives, some of whom were active and vocal during the war with Spain, were the primary heirs to the Christian nationalism formed and reinforced during that conflict, for they more than others sustained the optimistic, progressive view of history so important to that identity. However, conservative Christians, now known as fundamentalists, supported American intervention in Europe as well, albeit for somewhat different reasons, as described well in George Marsden, *Fundamentalism and American Culture: The Shaping of Twentieth-Century Evangelicalism, 1870–1925* (New York: Oxford University Press, 1980), 141–52. Most significant, both progressives and fundamentalists agreed about the redemptive significance of America in history and in this war specifically. Also, though Gamble and Marsden share my focus on interpretations of the war's meaning among church leaders, Jonathan Ebel has shown that similar religious conceptions of America's purpose in the war existed among the soldiers as well. See Ebel, *Faith in the Fight: Religion and the American Soldier in the Great War* (Princeton: Princeton University Press, 2010), especially ch. 1.

28. See especially Gamble, *War for Righteousness*, ch. 5, but the application of the Christ motif to American action remains a central feature throughout Gamble's study. By his reckoning, the progressive clergy "identified the war as the collective reenactment of Christ's crucifixion on Calvary" (159).

29. Lyman Abbott, "The Duty of Christ's Church To-Day," *Outlook*, 2 May 1917, pp. 13–14. Cited in Gamble, *War for Righteousness*, 155.

30. Lyman Abbott, "Democracy or Autocracy—Which?," in League to Enforce Peace, *Win the War for Permanent Peace: Addresses Made at the National Convention of the League to Enforce Peace, in the City of Philadelphia, May 16th and 17th, 1918* (New York: League to Enforce Peace, 1918), 104. Cited in Gamble, *War for Righteousness*, 160.

31. See Peter Hart, *The Great War: A Combat History of the First World War* (New York: Oxford University Press, 2013), 468.

32. See Jerry Keenan, *Encyclopedia of the Spanish-American and Philippine-American Wars* (Santa Barbara, CA: ABC-CLIO, 2001), 68–69. These figures would be considerably greater, of course, if expanded to include losses by the Spanish and Cubans in their extended insurgent war or if casualties from the Philippine-American War were also counted.

33. For information on the nature and extent of the prewar critique of liberalism, see William Hutchison, *The Modernist Impulse in American Protestantism* (Cambridge, MA: Harvard University Press, 1976), 185–225. Hutchison also provides the standard account of the Great War as a crisis point for the optimism he describes as definitive of Progressive Era religious liberalism. But in thus adapting their outlook to accommodate the datum of secular culture, in this case the tragic results of the war, these Protestants proved consummate modernists after all. See especially 226–56. Gamble also notes the persistence of progressive hopes at least through the 1920s and into the 1930s (*War for Righteousness*, 233–52). Finally, the 1920s and 1930s have been somewhat controversially described by Robert Handy as a period of "spiritual depression" within Protestantism in part because of the aftermath of the war but also because of a group of complex factors. So, for the

larger religious context in which hopes for the Christianization of the world declined, see Robert Handy, *A Christian America: Protestant Hopes and Historical Realities*, 2nd ed. (New York: Oxford University Press, 1984), 159–84.

34. Reinhold Niebuhr, "What the War Did to My Mind," *Christian Century*, 27 September 1928, p. 1161.

35. Ibid., 1162.

36. Ibid., 1161.

37. Ibid., 1162. Niebuhr's articulate perspective holds an understandably important place in the common narrative of disillusionment among American intellectuals after the war. But Jonathan Ebel's *Faith in the Fight* offers an important counterbalance to this narrative. Ebel charts what he calls a process of "reillusionment" among veterans in particular. Through organizations like the American Legion, those who had celebrated the redemptive significance of the war continued to fight for freedom and civilization on the home front, targeting a wide variety of "un-American" activities. See especially *Faith in the Fight*, 168–90.

38. Gerald Sittser, *A Cautious Patriotism: The American Churches and the Second World War* (Chapel Hill: University of North Carolina Press, 1997).

39. For detail on the unity and diversity described here, see ibid., chs. 4–6.

40. David Settje's study of Christian commentary on the events of the Cold War confirms division among Christian groups along the same basic lines reflected throughout American society. See *Faith and War: How Christians Debated the Cold and Vietnam Wars* (New York: New York University Press, 2011). Settje's examples show that Christian leaders remained willing to express their opinions on American foreign policy, but the terms they used were more often those of the various political factions than anything overtly Christian in content.

41. Ernest Tuveson, *Redeemer Nation: The Idea of America's Millennial Role* (Chicago: University of Chicago Press, 1968), 213.

Bibliography

Manuscript Collections

Andover-Harvard Theological Library Manuscripts and Archives Department, Cambridge, MA

        Richard Boynton Papers

        George Whitefield Stone Sermons and Lectures

Congregational Library, Boston, MA

        Newton, MA, First Church (Congregational) Records, 1773–1972

Disciples of Christ Historical Society, Nashville, TN

        Thomas Davemal Butler Papers

Library of Congress, Washington, DC

        Daniel A. P. Murray Collection, 1818–1907

Presbyterian Historical Society, Philadelphia, PA

        John Mayhew Fulton Papers

        Pamphlets Collection

Newspapers and Periodicals

Advance (Chicago)

Alabama Baptist (Montgomery, AL)

American Missionary (New York)

Baptist and Reflector (Nashville, TN)

Baptist Argus (Louisville, KY)

Baptist Courier (Greenville, SC)

Baptist Standard (Dallas)

Biblical Recorder (Raleigh, NC)

Christian Advocate (Nashville, TN)

Christian Advocate (New York)

Christian Century (Chicago)

Christian Evangelist (St. Louis)

Christian Index (Atlanta)
Christian Observer (Louisville, KY)
Christian Recorder (Philadelphia)
Christian Standard (Cincinnati)
Churchman (New York)
Congregationalist (Boston)
Evangelist (New York)
Florida Baptist Witness (Ocala, FL)
Friends' Intelligencer (Philadelphia)
Harper's Weekly (New York)
Herald of Gospel Liberty (Portsmouth, NH)
Homiletic Review (New York)
Independent (New York)
Living Church (Chicago)
Lutheran Church Review (Philadelphia)
McClure's Magazine (New York)
Methodist Review (Nashville, TN)
Methodist Review (New York)
Missionary (Nashville, TN)
Nation (New York)
National Baptist Magazine (Washington, DC)
New Orleans Christian Advocate (New Orleans)
New York Observer (New York)
New York Times (New York)
Outlook (New York)
Pacific (San Francisco)
Pacific Christian (San Francisco)
Pilot (Boston)
Religious Herald (Richmond, VA)
Standard (Chicago)
Star of Zion (Charlotte, NC)
Treasury (New York)
United Presbyterian (Pittsburgh)
Watchman (Boston)
Western Christian Advocate (Cincinnati)
Word and Way (Kansas City, MO)
Zion's Herald (Boston)

Denominational Records

General Assembly of the Presbyterian Church in the United States of America. *Minutes.*
    1898.

General Assembly of the United Presbyterian Church of North America. *Minutes*. 1898.

General Conference of the Methodist Episcopal Church, South. *Journal*. 1898.

Southern Baptist Convention. *Annual*. 1898.

Published Primary Sources

Brownson, Marcus. *The National Thanksgiving, November the Twenty-fourth, 1898. American Expansion, a Discourse delivered in the Tenth Presbyterian Church, Philadelphia*. Philadelphia: Published under the Direction of the Men's League of the Church, 1898.

Carver, W. O. *Missions and the Kingdom of Heaven*. N.P.: n.p., 1898.

Dana, Stephen. *Our New Place among the Nations: A Sermon Preached by the Rev. Stephen Dana, D.D. Pastor of the Walnut Street Presbyterian Church Philadelphia*. Philadelphia: George Cole and Bro., 1898.

Dixon, A. C. *Our Greater Country*. New York: n.p., 1898.

Dixon, Thomas. "The Battle Cry of Freedom." *Dixon's Sermons: A Monthly Magazine* (June 1898): 4–6.

———. "The Fourth of July." *Dixon's Sermons: A Monthly Magazine* (August 1898): 37–41.

———. "The Nation's Call the Voice of God." *Dixon's Sermons: A Monthly Magazine* (July 1898): 32–33.

———. "The New Thanksgiving Day." *Dixon's Sermons: A Monthly Magazine* (August 1898): 48–51.

———. "The Victory at Manila." *Dixon's Sermons: A Monthly Magazine* (June 1898): 14–16.

Donaldson, John. *What Shall We Do with Our Colonies*. Davenport, IA: n.p., 1898.

Draper, Andrew. *The Rescue of Cuba: An Episode in the Growth of Free Government*. Boston: Silver, Burdett and Co., 1899.

Dunning, A. E. "The White Man's Burden." *Homiletic Review* (June 1899): 522–24.

Everett, Marshall, ed. *Exciting Experiences in Our Wars with Spain and the Filipinos*. Chicago: Educational Co., 1900.

Gladden, Washington. *Our Nation and Her Neighbors*. Columbus, OH: Quinius and Ridenous, 1898.

Gregg, David. *The National Crisis, or God's Purposes Worked Out through International Relations: Sermon Delivered by Rev. David Gregg, L.L.D., at Lafayette Ave. Presbyterian Church, Sunday, April 24th, 1898*. New York: n.p., 1898.

Hawthorne, J. B. *The Present Feeling in the South Towards the Federal Union and the People of the North*. N.P.: n.p., 1898.

Herron, George. *The Christian State: A Political Vision of Christ*. New York: Thomas Crowell, 1895.

Hoes, Randall Roswell. *God's Hand at Santiago: A Sermon Preached on Board U.S. Battle-ship "Iowa" in Guantanamo Bay, Cuba, July 10, 1898, the Sunday Following the Naval Battle of Santiago*. New York: n.p., 1898.

Keenan, Harry. *The Conflict with Spain: A History of the War Based on Official Reports and Descriptions of Eye-Witnesses*. Philadelphia: P. W. Ziegler, 1898.

King, James. M. *Situation and Justification of the Nation at War with Spain: An Address before the Empire State Society Sons of the American Revolution*. New York: printed by order of the Society, 1898.

Las Casas, Bartolome. *Horrible Atrocities of Spaniards in Cuba*. New York: J. Boller, 1898.

McKinley, William. *Speeches and Addresses of William McKinley: From March 1, 1897, to May 30, 1900*. New York: Doubleday and McClure, 1900.

Meredith, R. R. *A Sermon Preached at the Old South Church on the 260th Anniversary of the Ancient and Honorable Artillery Company, June 6, 1898*. Boston: n.p., 1898.

Metcalf, Arthur. *The Reign of God. A Sermon Preached at the Congregational Church, Bancroft, Mich.* N.P.: n.p., 1898.

Mulford, Elisha. *The Nation: The Foundations of Civil Order and Political Life in the United States*. New York: Hurd and Houghton, 1870.

Packard, Edward. "Sermon on Genesis 3." *Homiletic Review* (June 1898): 233–37.

Pentecost, George. *The Coming of Age of America: A Retrospect and a Forecast*. New York: n.p., 1898.

Rainsford, William. *Our Duty to Civilization, or Who Is My Neighbor?* N.P.: n.p., 1898.

Ransom, Reverdy. *The Pilgrimage of Harriet Ransom's Son*. Nashville, TN: Sunday School Union, 1949).

Savage, Minot. "Civilization and War." In *Messiah Pulpit, New York: Sermons of M. J. Savage* 2, no. 27 (1898): 3–16.

Strong, Josiah. *Expansion under New World-Conditions*. New York: Baker and Taylor, 1900.

———. *The New Era; or, The Coming Kingdom*. New York: Baker and Taylor, 1893.

———. *Our Country: Its Possible Future and Present Crisis*. New York: Baker and Taylor, 1891; repr., Cambridge, MA: Harvard University Press, 1963.

Van Dyke, Henry. *The American Birthright and the Philippine Pottage: A Sermon Preached on Thanksgiving Day, 1898*. New York: Charles Scribner's Sons, 1898.

———. *The Cross of War: A Sermon Preached by the Rev. Dr. Henry van Dyke, Pastor of the Brick Presbyterian Church, New York, on May First, 1898*. New York: n.p., 1898.

Watterson, Henry. *History of the Spanish-American War: Embracing a Complete Review of Our Relations with Spain*. New York: Werner Co., 1898.

Winton, George. "Was the War Providential?" *Methodist Review* (November–December 1898): 658–68.

Wright, Edward. *"The White Man's Burden"; or "The Debt of the Christian to the Barbarian", A Sermon Preached at the First Presbyterian Church, Austin, Texas, February 12, 1899*. Published by the Session of the Church, 1899.

Secondary Sources

Abrams, Ray Hamilton. *Preachers Present Arms: A Study of the War-Time Attitudes and Activities of the Churches and the Clergy in the United States, 1914–1918*. New York: Round Table, 1933.

Ahlstrom, Sydney. *A Religious History of the American People*. New Haven: Yale University Press, 1975.

Albanese, Catherine. *America: Religions and Religion*. 3rd ed. Belmont, CA: Wadsworth, 1999.

Angell, Stephen Ward. *Bishop Henry McNeal Turner and African-American Religion in the South*. Knoxville: University of Tennessee Press, 1992.

Bederman, Gail. *Manliness and Civilization: A Cultural History of Gender and Race in the United States, 1880–1917*. Chicago: University of Chicago Press, 1996.

Beiner, Ronald. *Civil Religion: A Dialogue in the History of Political Philosophy*. Cambridge: Cambridge University Press, 2011.

Bellah, Robert Neelly. *The Broken Covenant: American Civil Religion in Time of Trial*. 2nd ed. Chicago: University of Chicago Press, 1992.

———. "Civil Religion in America." *Daedalus* 96, no. 1 (1967): 1–21.

Bercovitch, Sacvan. *The American Jeremiad*. Madison: University of Wisconsin Press, 1978.

———. *The Puritan Origins of the American Self*. New Haven: Yale University Press, 1975.

Blaisdell, Charles R. "The Attitude of the Christian-Evangelist Towards the Spanish-American War." *Encounter* 50, no. 3 (1989): 233–45.

Blight, David W. *Race and Reunion: The Civil War in American Memory*. Cambridge, MA: Belknap Press of Harvard University Press, 2001.

Bloch, Ruth H. *Visionary Republic: Millennial Themes in American Thought, 1756–1800*. New York: Cambridge University Press, 1985.

Blum, Edward J. *Reforging the White Republic: Race, Religion, and American Nationalism, 1865–1898*. Baton Rouge: Louisiana State University Press, 2005.

Bozeman, Theodore Dwight. *To Live Ancient Lives: The Primitivist Dimension in Puritanism*. Chapel Hill: Published for the Institute of Early American History and Culture, Williamsburg, Virginia, by the University of North Carolina Press, 1988.

Brands, H. W. *The Reckless Decade: America in the 1890s*. New York: St. Martin's Press, 1995.

———. *What America Owes the World: The Struggle for the Soul of Foreign Policy*. New York: Cambridge University Press, 1998.

Brock, Peter. *Pacifism in the United States, from the Colonial Era to the First World War*. Princeton: Princeton University Press, 1968.

———. *Pacifism to 1914: An Overview*. 3rd ed. Toronto: P. Brock, 1994.

Brown, Charles Henry. *The Correspondents' War: Journalists in the Spanish-American War*. New York: Scribner, 1967.

Campbell, Charles Soutter. *Anglo-American Understanding, 1898–1903*. Baltimore: Johns Hopkins University Press, 1957.

Carey, Patrick. *The Roman Catholics in America*. Westport, CT: Praeger, 1996.

Casey, Michael. "From Religious Outsiders to Insiders: The Rise and Fall of Pacifism in the Churches of Christ." *Journal of Church and State* 44, no. 3 (2002): 455–75.

Cherry, Conrad. *God's New Israel: Religious Interpretations of American Destiny*. Rev. and updated ed. Chapel Hill: University of North Carolina Press, 1998.

Clymer, Kenton. "Religion and American Imperialism: Methodist Missionaries in the Philippine Islands, 1899–1913." *Pacific Historical Review* 49, no. 1 (1980): 29–50.

Cook, Barak. "The Greatest Crusade: Mission, Religion, and Conflict in American Foreign Relations, 1898–1945." PhD dissertation, University of Missouri–Columbia, 2005.

Curtis, Heather. "Depicting Distant Suffering: Evangelicals and the Politics of Pictorial Humanitarianism in the Age of American Empire." *Material Religion* 8, no. 2 (June 2012): 154–83.

Dobson, John M. *Reticent Expansionism: The Foreign Policy of William McKinley*. Pittsburgh, PA: Duquesne University Press, 1988.

Dolan, Jay P. *The American Catholic Experience: A History from Colonial Times to the Present*. Notre Dame, IN: University of Notre Dame Press, 1992.

Ebel, Jonathan. *Faith in the Fight: Religion and the American Soldier in the Great War*. Princeton: Princeton University Press, 2010.

Faust, Drew Gilpin. *This Republic of Suffering: Death and the American Civil War*. New York: Knopf, 2008.

Ferrell, Robert H. *American Diplomacy: A History*. 3rd ed. New York: Norton, 1975.

Ferrer, Ada. *Insurgent Cuba: Race, Nation, and Revolution, 1868–1898*. Chapel Hill: University of North Carolina Press, 1999.

Foner, Philip Sheldon. *The Spanish-Cuban-American War and the Birth of American Imperialism, 1895–1902*. New York: Monthly Review Press, 1972.

Foster, Gaines. "Coming to Terms with Defeat: Post–Vietnam War America and the Post–Civil War South." *Virginia Quarterly Review* 66 (1990): 17–35.

Gamble, Richard M. *The War for Righteousness: Progressive Christianity, the Great War, and the Rise of the Messianic Nation*. Wilmington, DE: ISI Books, 2003.

Gatewood, Willard B. *Black Americans and the White Man's Burden, 1898–1903*. Urbana: University of Illinois Press, 1975.

———. *"Smoked Yankees" and the Struggle for Empire: Letters from Negro Soldiers, 1898–1902*. Urbana: University of Illinois Press, 1971.

Gaustad, Edwin. *Historical Atlas of Religion in America*. New York: Harper and Row, 1962.

Gaustad, Edwin S., and Leigh Eric Schmidt. *The Religious History of America*. Rev. ed. San Francisco: HarperSanFrancisco, 2002.

Geertz, Clifford. "Ideology as a Cultural System." In *The Interpretation of Cultures: Selected Essays*, 193–233. New York: Basic Books, 1973.

Gerstle, Gary. *American Crucible: Race and Nation in the Twentieth Century*. Princeton: Princeton University Press, 2001.

Gorski, Philip. "Barack Obama and Civil Religion." *Political Power and Social Theory* 22 (2011): 179–256.

Graber, Jennifer. "Mighty Upheaval on the Minnesota Frontier: Violence, War, and Death in Dakota and Missionary Christianity." *Church History* 80, no. 1 (March 2011): 76–108.

Greenfeld, Liah. *Nationalism: Five Roads to Modernity*. Cambridge, MA: Harvard University Press, 1992.

Guyatt, Nicholas. *Providence and the Invention of the United States, 1607–1876*. New York: Cambridge University Press, 2007.

Handy, Robert T. *A Christian America: Protestant Hopes and Historical Realities*. 2nd ed. New York: Oxford University Press, 1984.

———. *Undermined Establishment: Church-State Relations in America, 1880–1920*. Princeton: Princeton University Press, 1991.

Hart, Peter. *The Great War: A Combat History of the First World War*. New York: Oxford University Press, 2013.

Hatch, Nathan O. *The Sacred Cause of Liberty: Republican Thought and the Millennium in Revolutionary New England*. New Haven: Yale University Press, 1977.

Hendrickson, Kenneth E., Jr. *The Spanish-American War*. Westport, CT: Greenwood Press, 2003.

Hennessy, Alistair. "The Origins of the Cuban Revolt." In *The Crisis of 1898: Colonial Redistribution and Nationalist Mobilization*, edited by Angel Smith and Emma Dávila-Cox, 65–95. New York: St. Martin's Press, 1999.

Herring, George C. *From Colony to Superpower: U.S. Foreign Relations since 1776*. New York: Oxford University Press, 2008.

Hofstadter, Richard. "Cuba, the Philippines, and Manifest Destiny." In *The Paranoid Style in American Politics: And Other Essays*, 145–87. New York: Vintage, 1967.

———. *Social Darwinism in American Thought*. Rev. ed. Boston: Beacon Press, 1955.

Hoganson, Kristin L. *Fighting for American Manhood: How Gender Politics Provoked the Spanish-American and Philippine-American Wars*. New Haven: Yale University Press, 1998.

Hudson, Winthrop. *Nationalism and Religion in America: Concepts of American Identity and Mission*. New York: Harper, 1970.

———. "Protestant Clergy Debate the Nation's Vocation, 1898–1899." *Church History* 42, no. 1 (1973): 110–18.

Hudson, Winthrop, and John Corrigan. *Religion in America: An Historical Account of the Development of American Religious Life*. 5th ed. Upper Saddle River, NJ: Prentice Hall, 1992.

Hutchison, William R. *Errand to the World: American Protestant Thought and Foreign Missions*. Chicago: University of Chicago Press, 1987.

———. *The Modernist Impulse in American Protestantism*. Cambridge, MA: Harvard University Press, 1976.

Jacobson, Matthew Frye. *Barbarian Virtues: The United States Encounters Foreign Peoples at Home and Abroad, 1876–1917*. New York: Hill and Wang, 2000.

———. *Whiteness of a Different Color: European Immigrants and the Alchemy of Race*. Cambridge, MA: Harvard University Press, 1998.

Jordan, Philip D. *The Evangelical Alliance for the United States of America, 1847–1900: Ecumenism, Identity, and the Religion of the Republic*. New York: Edwin Mellen Press, 1982.

Juhnke, James. "Kansas Mennonites during the Spanish-American War." *Mennonite Life* 26, no. 2 (April 1971): 79–72.

Karraker, William Archibald. "The American Churches and the Spanish-American War." PhD dissertation, University of Chicago, 1940.

Keenan, Jerry. *Encyclopedia of the Spanish-American and Philippine-American Wars*. Santa Barbara, CA: ABC-CLIO, 2001.

Kennedy, David M. *Over Here: The First World War and American Society*. New York: Oxford University Press, 1980.

Kirakossian, Arman, ed. *The Armenian Massacres 1894–1896: U.S. Media Testimony*. Detroit: Wayne State University Press, 2004.

Lepore, Jill. *The Name of War: King Philip's War and the Origins of American Identity*. New York: Knopf, 1998.

Linderman, Gerald. *The Mirror of War: American Society and the Spanish-American War*. Ann Arbor: University of Michigan Press, 1974.

Little, Lawrence S. *Disciples of Liberty: The African Methodist Episcopal Church in the Age of Imperialism, 1884–1916*. Knoxville: University of Tennessee Press, 2000.

MacKenzie, Kenneth M. *The Robe and the Sword: The Methodist Church and the Rise of American Imperialism*. Washington, DC: Public Affairs Press, 1961.

Magee, Malcolm D. *What the World Should Be: Woodrow Wilson and the Crafting of a Faith-Based Foreign Policy*. Waco, TX: Baylor University Press, 2008.

Marchand, Peter. *The American Peace Movement and Social Reform, 1898–1918*. Princeton: Princeton University Press, 1973.

Marks, George P. *The Black Press Views American Imperialism (1898–1900)*. New York: Arno Press, 1971.

Marsden, George M. *Fundamentalism and American Culture: The Shaping of Twentieth Century Evangelicalism, 1870–1925*. New York: Oxford University Press, 1980.

Marty, Martin. "Two Kinds of Two Kinds of Civil Religion." In *American Civil Religion*, edited by Russell Richey and Donald Jones, 139–57. New York: Harper, 1974.

May, Ernest R. *American Imperialism: A Speculative Essay*. New York: Atheneum, 1968.

May, Henry F. *Protestant Churches and Industrial America*. New York: Harper, 1949.

McCartney, Paul T. *Power and Progress: American National Identity, the War of 1898, and the Rise of American Imperialism*. Baton Rouge: Louisiana State University Press, 2006.

McPherson, James M. *Battle Cry of Freedom: The Civil War Era*. New York: Oxford University Press, 1988.

Mead, Sidney. "The 'Nation with the Soul of a Church.'" In *American Civil Religion*, edited by Russell Richey and Donald Jones, 45–75. New York: Harper and Row, 1974.

Meyer, Paul. "The Fear of Cultural Decline: Josiah Strong's Thought about Reform and Expansion." *Church History* 42, no. 3 (1973): 396–405.

Miller, Perry. *The New England Mind: From Colony to Province*. Cambridge, MA: Belknap Press of Harvard University Press, 1983.

Miller, Stuart Creighton. *"Benevolent Assimilation": The American Conquest of the Philippines, 1899–1903*. New Haven: Yale University Press, 1982.

Millis, Walter. *The Martial Spirit: A Study of Our War with Spain*. Cambridge, MA: Literary Guild of America, 1931.

Mott, Frank Luther. *A History of American Magazines.* Vol. 4, *1885–1905.* Cambridge, MA: Harvard University Press, 1957.

Muller, Dorothea. "Josiah Strong and American Nationalism: A Reevaluation." *Journal of American History* 53, no. 3 (1966): 487–503.

———. "The Social Philosophy of Josiah Strong: Social Christianity and American Progressivism." *Church History* 28, no. 2 (1959): 183–201.

Ninkovich, Frank A. *The United States and Imperialism.* Malden, MA: Blackwell, 2001.

Noll, Mark A. *The Civil War as a Theological Crisis.* Chapel Hill: University of North Carolina Press, 2006.

———. *A History of Christianity in the United States and Canada.* Grand Rapids, MI: Eerdmans, 1992.

O'Brien, Conor Cruise. *God Land: Reflections on Religion and Nationalism.* Cambridge, MA: Harvard University Press, 1988.

O'Connell, Marvin Richard. *John Ireland and the American Catholic Church.* Saint Paul: Minnesota Historical Society Press, 1988.

Offner, John L. *An Unwanted War: The Diplomacy of the United States and Spain over Cuba, 1895–1898.* Chapel Hill: University of North Carolina Press, 1992.

———. "European Perceptions of the Spanish-American War of 1898." *Journal of American History* 88, no. 1 (2001): 229.

Olcott, Charles Sumner. *The Life of William McKinley.* New York: Houghton Mifflin, 1916.

Oldfield, John. "Remembering the *Maine*: The United States, 1898 and Sectional Reconciliation." In *The Crisis of 1898: Colonial Redistribution and Nationalist Mobilization,* edited by Angel Smith and Emma Dávila-Cox, 45–64. New York: St. Martin's Press, 1999.

O'Leary, Cecilia Elizabeth. *To Die For: The Paradox of American Patriotism.* Princeton: Princeton University Press, 1999.

Painter, Nell Irvin. *Standing at Armageddon: The United States, 1877–1919.* New York: Norton, 1987.

Pérez, Louis A. *The War of 1898: The United States and Cuba in History and Historiography.* Chapel Hill: University of North Carolina Press, 1998.

Piper, John F. *The American Churches in World War I.* Athens: Ohio University Press, 1985.

Pratt, Julius William. *Expansionists of 1898: The Acquisition of Hawaii and the Spanish Islands.* 1936; repr., Chicago: Quadrangle, 1964.

Reed, James Eldin. "American Foreign Policy, the Politics and Missions and Josiah Strong, 1890–1900." *Church History* 41, no. 2 (1972): 230–45.

Reuter, Frank T. *Catholic Influence on American Colonial Policies, 1898–1904.* Austin: University of Texas Press, 1967.

Richey, Russell E., and Donald G. Jones. *American Civil Religion.* New York: Harper and Row, 1974.

Rouner, Leroy, ed. *Civil Religion and Political Theology.* Notre Dame, IN: University of Notre Dame Press, 1986.

Schlesinger, Arthur. "The Missionary Enterprise and Imperialism." In *The Missionary Enterprise in China and America*, edited by John Fairbank, 336–73. Cambridge, MA: Harvard University Press, 1974.

Settje, David. *Faith and War: How Christians Debated the Cold and Vietnam Wars*. New York: New York University Press, 2011.

Shankman, Arthur. "Southern Methodist Newspapers and the Coming of the Spanish-American War: A Research Note." *Journal of Southern History* 39, no. 1 (1973): 93–96.

Sittser, Gerald Lawson. *A Cautious Patriotism: The American Churches and the Second World War*. Chapel Hill: University of North Carolina Press, 1997.

Slotkin, Richard. *The Fatal Environment: The Myth of the Frontier in the Age of Industrialization, 1800–1890*. New York: Harper, 1985.

Smith, Angel, and Emma Dávila Cox, eds. *The Crisis of 1898: Colonial Redistribution and Nationalist Mobilization*. New York: St. Martin's Press, 1999.

Smith, Ephraim. "William McKinley's Enduring Legacy: The Historiographical Debate on the Taking of the Philippine Islands." In *Crucible of Empire: The Spanish-American War and Its Aftermath*, edited by James Bradford, 205–49. Annapolis: Naval Institute Press, 1993.

Smith, Joseph. *The Spanish-American War: Conflict in the Caribbean and the Pacific, 1895–1902*. New York: Longman, 1994.

Smylie, John . "Protestant Clergymen and American Destiny: II. Prelude to Imperialism, 1865–1900." *Harvard Theological Review* 56, no. 4 (1963): 297–311.

———. "Protestant Clergymen and America's World Role, 1865–1900: A Study of Christianity, Nationality and International Relations." ThD dissertation, Princeton Theological Seminary, 1959.

Spencer, David Ralph. *The Yellow Journalism: The Press and America's Emergence as a World Power*. Evanston, IL: Northwestern University Press, 2007.

Storch, Neil. "John Ireland's Americanism after 1899: The Argument from History." *Church History* 51, no. 4 (1982): 434–44.

Stout, Harry S. *The New England Soul: Preaching and Religious Culture in Colonial New England*. New York: Oxford University Press, 1986.

———. "Review Essay: Religion, War, and the Meaning of America." *Religion and American Culture* 19, no. 2 (Summer 2009): 275–289.

———. *Upon the Altar of the Nation: A Moral History of the American Civil War*. New York: Viking, 2006.

Trask, David F. *The War with Spain in 1898*. 1981; repr., Lincoln: University of Nebraska Press, 1996.

Traxel, David. *1898: The Birth of the American Century*. New York: Knopf, 1998.

Tuveson, Ernest Lee. *Redeemer Nation: The Idea of America's Millennial Role*. Chicago: University of Chicago Press, 1968.

Wacker, Grant. "The Holy Spirit and the Spirit of the Age in American Protestantism, 1880–1910." *Journal of American History* 72, no. 1 (1985): 45–62.

Wangler, Thomas. "The Birth of Americanism: 'Westward the Apocalyptic Candlestick.'" *Harvard Theological Review* 65, no. 3 (1972): 415–36.

Warner, W. Lloyd. "An American Sacred Ceremony." In *American Civil Religion*, edited by Russell Richey and Donald Jones, 89–111. New York: Harper and Row, 1974.

Welch, Richard E. "American Atrocities in the Philippines: The Indictment and the Response." *Pacific Historical Review* 43, no. 2 (1974): 233–53.

———. *Response to Imperialism: The United States and the Philippine-American War, 1899–1902.* Chapel Hill: University of North Carolina Press, 1979.

Wiebe, Robert H. *The Search for Order, 1877–1920.* New York: Hill and Wang, 1967.

Wilson, Charles Reagan. *Baptized in Blood: The Religion of the Lost Cause, 1865–1920.* Athens: University of Georgia Press, 1980.

Wilson, John. "A Historian's Approach to Civil Religion." In *American Civil Religion*, edited by Russell Richey and Donald Jones, 115–38. New York: Harper and Row, 1974.

Wolff, Leon. *Little Brown Brother: How the United States Purchased and Pacified the Philippine Islands at the Century's Turn.* Garden City, NY: Doubleday, 1961.

Woodward, C. Vann. *The Strange Career of Jim Crow.* New and rev. ed. New York: Oxford University Press, 1965.

Young, Marilyn Blatt. *American Expansionism: The Critical Issues.* Boston: Little, Brown, 1973.

Zoller, Michael. *Washington and Rome: Catholicism in American Culture.* Notre Dame, IN: University of Notre Dame Press, 1999.

Index